BASIC for MICROCOMPUTERS:
Apple, TRS-80, PET

ROGER W. HAIGH
West Virginia Northern Community College

LOREN E. RADFORD
Baptist College at Charleston

VNR VAN NOSTRAND REINHOLD COMPANY
NEW YORK CINCINNATI TORONTO LONDON MELBOURNE

001.6424
H149

Hardbound edition by Van Nostrand Reinhold Company Inc.
135 West 50th Street, New York, N.Y. 10020
by arrangement with PWS Publishers, a division of Wadsworth, Inc.
20 Providence Street, Boston, Massachusetts 02116

Copyright © 1983 by PWS Publishers

Library of Congress Catalog Card Number: 82-21860
ISBN: 0-442-27843-8

All rights reserved. No part of this work covered by the copyright hereon may be reproduced or used in any form or by any means — graphic, electronic, or mechanical, including photocopying, recording, taping, or information storage and retrieval systems — without permission of the publisher.

Manufactured in the United States of America

Published by Van Nostrand Reinhold Company Inc.
135 West 50th Street, New York, N.Y. 10020

Van Nostrand Reinhold Publishing
1410 Birchmount Road
Scarborough, Ontario M1P 2E7, Canada

Van Nostrand Reinhold
480 Latrobe Street
Melbourne, Victoria 3000, Australia

Van Nostrand Reinhold Company Limited
Molly Millars Lane
Wokingham, Berkshire, England

15 14 13 12 11 10 9 8 7 6 5 4 3 2 1

Library of Congress Cataloging in Publication Data

Haigh, Roger W.
    BASIC for microcomputers.

    Includes index.
    1. Basic (Computer program language) 2. Microcomputers — Programming. I. Radford, Loren E. II. Title.
III. Title: B.A.S.I.C. for microcomputers.
QA76.73.B3H33   1983   001.64′24   82-21860
ISBN 0-442-27843-8

Cover design and art by Julia Gecha. Text design by Sara Waller.

CONTENTS

1 COMPUTERS—COMPONENTS AND TERMINOLOGY — 1
- **1.1** Introduction to Computers — 1
- **1.2** Components of a Computer — 2
- **1.3** Interaction with the Computer — 5
- **1.4** The Communication Process — 6
- **1.5** Hardware and Software — 8
- **1.6** Screen Characteristics — 8
- Review — 16

2 ELEMENTARY PROGRAMMING TECHNIQUES — 19
- **2.1** Introduction to Elementary Programming Techniques — 19
- **2.2** Program Entry — 20
- **2.3** The Nature of a Variable — 20
- **2.4** Storing Values in Memory — 22
- **2.5** Arithmetic Operations — 24
- **2.6** Obtaining Output from the Program — 26
- **2.7** Editing the Program — 31
- Review — 36

3 PREPARING A COMPLETE PROGRAM — 37
- **3.1** Introduction to Preparing a Complete Program — 37
- **3.2** A Problem-Solving Model — 38

3.3	The Nature of an Algorithm	39
3.4	Pseudocode Illustrated	41
3.5	Coding the Algorithm	45
3.6	Completing the Job—Documentation	48
	Review	50

4 SIMPLE LOOPS AND DECISIONS 53

4.1	Introduction to Loops and Decisions	53
4.2	The Simple Loop	53
4.3	The IF-THEN Statement	56
4.4	Relational Operators	57
4.5	Variations on Loops—Counters	59
4.6	Variations on Loops—Accumulators	60
4.7	Decision Structures—Single Alternative	65
4.8	Decision Structures—Double Alternatives	69
	Review	72

5 INDEXED LOOPS 73

5.1	Introduction to Indexed Loops	73
5.2	The Indexed Loop in BASIC	74
5.3	Using the Loop Index	76
5.4	Summation Notation	78
5.5	Loops with Conditional Transfers	81
5.6	Loops to Calculate Area	82
	Review	86

6 FUNCTIONS 89

| 6.1 | Introduction to Functions | 89 |
| 6.2 | Functions that Modify Output Values | 90 |

6.3	Random Numbers	93
6.4	User-Defined Functions	97
6.5	Coding Mathematical Functions	101
6.6	Rules for Coding	103
6.7	Numeric Input and Output	104
6.8	A Caution about Functions	107
	Review	107

7 SUBSCRIPTS AND ARRAYS — 109

7.1	Introduction to Subscripts and Arrays	109
7.2	Subscripts	110
7.3	Using Arrays	110
7.4	Declaring Arrays	114
7.5	Using an Array as an Accumulator	117
7.6	Sorting with an Array	118
7.7	The Median	121
7.8	Reading a Data Set more than Once	123
7.9	Two-Dimensional Arrays	124
7.10	Matrix Operations	127
7.11	Order Exploding Using Arrays	130
	Review	133

8 STRINGS AND STRING FUNCTIONS — 135

8.1	Introduction to Strings and String Functions	135
8.2	Character Data and the ASCII Coding System	135
8.3	String Variables	136
8.4	Translating from ASCII Code to Character and Back	137
8.5	Basic String Operations	139
8.6	String Comparison	140

8.7	String Concatenation	141
8.8	String Length Determination	141
8.9	Substring Selection	143
8.10	Substring Indexing	145
8.11	String Applications: Decimal Point Alignment	149
8.12	String Applications: Random Words	151
8.13	String Applications: Sorting Strings	154
8.14	String Applications: Input Validation	155
8.15	String Applications: Lower Case	157
	Review	160

9 PROGRAM STRUCTURE AND DEBUGGING 161

9.1	Introduction to Program Structure and Debugging	161
9.2	Preventing Errors	162
9.3	Program Structure	162
9.4	Structured Programming	166
9.5	Program Blocks	167
9.6	Subroutines	170
9.7	The Case Structure	174
9.8	Debugging Techniques	179
	Review	188

10 FORMATTING AND GRAPHICS 191

10.1	Introduction to Formatting and Graphics	191
10.2	The Tab Function	192
10.3	Using a Print Image	195
10.4	Teletype Graphics	197
10.5	Teletype Graphics—X-Y Plots	200

10.6	Up with the Bar Graph	**202**
10.7	Low Resolution Graphics	**204**
10.8	High Resolution Graphics—for Apples only	**211**
10.9	Control of Data Format	**216**
10.10	Forcing Scientific Notation	**217**
10.11	Significant Digits	**219**
10.12	Real Time Displays—for PETs only	**220**
	Review	**222**

11 FILES **225**

11.1	Introduction to Files	**225**
11.2	Files Generally	**225**
11.3	Sequential Disk Files	**227**
11.4	Direct Access Files	**234**
11.5	PET Files	**240**
11.6	What to do if the PET Crashes	**244**
11.7	PET File Applications	**248**
11.8	TRS-80 Tape File Applications	**249**
	Review	**250**

12 MODELS AND SIMULATIONS **253**

12.1	Introduction to Models and Simulations	**253**
12.2	Leontief Model of an Economy	**254**
12.3	Model of a Pasture Ecosystem	**257**
12.4	Okun's Law Simulation	**261**
12.5	A Genetics Simulation	**266**
12.6	Monte Carlo Inventory Simulation	**268**
	Review	**272**

13 ADVANCED GRAPHICS TECHNIQUES   273
- 13.1 Computer Mapping   273
- 13.2 Creating a Map Coordinates File   276
- 13.3 Finding the Midrange of the Coordinates   278
- 13.4 Drawing a Map   279
- 13.5 Saving Graphic Images on Disk   284
- 13.6 Loading a Graphics Image from Disk   285
- 13.7 Printing Graphic Displays   286
- 13.8 Adding Text to your Graphics   289
- 13.9 Appendix   292

APPENDICES   294
- A Algorithmic Language Summary   A1
- B Library of Subroutines   B1
- C ASCII Codes   C1
- D The Editor and Cross-Reference Table Generator   D1
- Index   I1

PREFACE

We wrote this book hoping that it would help a wide variety of people to learn to program a computer using the BASIC language. We were motivated partly by the belief that the ability to program a computer will become increasingly important in the future—even for people who do not consider themselves to be computer scientists. There is a tendency for many people to view learning how to program as a vocational skill—much like the ability to use a calculator or typewriter. But there is a growing body of opinion that suggests that the ability to develop and debug a computer program contributes to the development of human problem solving skills—to the improvement of the thinking process itself.

The text is intended for use in a beginning level one-semester BASIC course and also by individuals desiring to teach themselves to program. In addition to teaching BASIC, we also attempt to introduce the learner to problem-solving techniques, which include the use of a simple flexible algorithmic language. In creating even a moderately complicated program, the process is always complicated by the idiosyncrasies of the dialect of the language available. For that reason, we prefer to teach one how to develop a solution in a simple but flexible algorithmic language and then translate it into BASIC (Chapter 3). We have found such an approach indispensable in developing large scale research and administrative applications in other languages.

In presenting the BASIC language, we have attempted to stay as close as possible to ANSI minimal BASIC. We do cover a number of matters—strings, files and graphics—which are not defined in the minimal standard. We chose to focus on microcomputers because of their greatly increasing popularity. We are convinced that they will become increasingly important in the future. Most of the BASIC syntax that we present is common to the Apple, the PET and the TRS-80. On some occasions, we must treat one machine separately. Such treatment is indicated clearly as boxed material. We should point out, that while we focus attention on the three microcomputers, some of our own students have satisfied some course requirements with other systems, including Digital's MUBASIC and BASIC PLUS. On such systems, string handling is different and high resolution graphics is not supported at all.

We assume only that users of this book have an understanding of arithmetic. Since this text is intended to be useful to a wide audience including people with backgrounds and interests in the sciences as well as those interested in the social sciences and humanities, some may find occasional sections that require more detailed mathematical treatments. Sections 5.6, 6.7, 10.9, 10.10 and 10.11 are such sections and can be omitted. We also realize that persons who have neither a background nor interest in mathematics will from time to time discover some equation that will be useful to them. With this in mind, we present in sections 6.5 and 6.6 some simple techniques whereby the nonmathematician can convert a useful equation into one or more BASIC statements.

We give considerable attention to graphics in the belief that graphics techniques will continue to increase in importance. We treat "teletype" graphic techniques that can be used with any version of BASIC. We also treat low resolution graphics on the Apple, the PET and the TRS-80 individually. Finally, we treat Apple high resolution graphics separately. We end the book with a treatment of computer mapping (Chapter 13) using Apple high resolution graphics.

The chapters of this text are intended for use in linear order. We discuss simulation and modeling in chapter 12 and computer mapping in chapter 13. We believe both these chapters present interesting and useful applications that will interest many students. However, they may be omitted if necessary.

The programs displayed here were developed and tested on the Apple II Plus using Applesoft BASIC, the 8k PET, and the TRS-80 with Level II BASIC. Some programs were also tested on other machines. Therefore, we believe that the book can be useful in connection with a wide range of BASIC dialects.

Finally, in Appendix B, we present a number of useful subroutines that we use from time to time in various chapters.

In the process of writing this book we have benefited from the assistance of a number of people. We are glad to have an opportunity to express our gratitude to Dennis J. Clayton, Bethune Cookman College, who read the manuscript and offered numerous useful suggestions; to Nancy G. Haigh, who read and reread drafts of the manuscript in order to improve its clarity and style; to Sara Waller of PWS Publishers, who was a patient and helpful production editor; and to our colleagues and others who have offered various suggestions: John Biros, Mark Goldstein, Shirley Rychlicki, Doris Simon, Victor Tenaglia and Tony Vavra. Appreciation is also extended to Jack R. Cimprich, Glassboro State College; Barry De Roos, Community College of Denver; Norman Licht, SUNY Potsdam; Donald A. Norton, University of California, Davis; and Richard L. Tangerman, Arkansas State University.

Roger W. Haigh
Loren E. Radford

1
COMPUTERS—COMPONENTS AND TERMINOLOGY

1.1 INTRODUCTION TO COMPUTERS

This is not a text about computers. Very little attention will be given to computer architecture. However, in this chapter we will develop, in a very qualitative way, some of the characteristics of a microcomputer. We do this to introduce terminology and to clarify the way humans interact with computers.

We have chosen to link the study of **BASIC** with microcomputers because we believe that language texts often fail to emphasize certain characteristics that make the microcomputer so valuable to its user. In particular, we will explore the *screen orientation* of the microcomputer output. We will also treat its unique graphics and file handling capabilities.

Because there are so many microcomputers, each with its own dialect of BASIC, it is difficult to discuss their capabilities without reference to a specific machine or machines. We chose to concentrate our attention on three machines: the Apple, the PET (8k) and the TRS-80 with Level II BASIC. Selection of a computer means accepting the resident BASIC dialect of that device. Typically, the programs presented in this text were developed on one of the three computers and then tested on the others. There are minor differences in the dialects of the BASIC language used by each of these computers. In most cases, we present programs that run correctly on all three machines. However, sometimes we must present a different version of a program for a specific machine. In the relatively few cases that a specific program is designed for only one computer, we enclose that program in a box indicating the specific computer.

Photos 1.1–1.3

The Apple (1.1), the Pet (1.2), and the TRS-80 (1.3) microcomputers. (Photo 1.1 courtesy of Apple Computer Inc.; 1.2 courtesy of Commodore Business Machines; and 1.3 courtesy of Radio Shack, a division of Tandy Corp.)

(1.1)

(1.2)

(1.3)

From time to time we also present other machine-specific information in similar boxes. In discussing the BASIC language we will try to emphasize standard rather than unique syntax. We will also consider important similarities and differences between the Apple, the PET and the TRS-80 in the area of graphics.

1.2 COMPONENTS OF A COMPUTER

The development of the microcomputer has been very rapid indeed. It has been little more than ten years since Intel Corporation marketed the first **microprocessor** (computer on a chip). Early microcomputers were experimental devices built around microprocessors of limited capability. Microprocessor capabilities have increased rapidly. The combination of improved microprocessors and the emerging BASIC language has proven to be fortunate. By 1975 low cost microcomputers began to show significant sales outside the experimental and hobbyist markets. Sales of microcomputers are now expected to increase tenfold between 1975 and 1985. Most impressive is the increase in capability of these small computers. As a result they have moved beyond the classification of *personal* and *home* computers and are beginning to challenge service areas formerly reserved for minicomputers. Equally impressive is their widespread use in education.

The microcomputer is similar to other computers in its basic architecture. All computers consist of three major components: a **central processing unit (CPU)**, a **memory**, and **input/output (I/O) devices**. The central processing unit consists of two parts: the **control unit** and the **arithmetic logic unit**. The control unit is a switching center through which the computer moves information to the appropriate places and in the proper sequence. The arithmetic logic unit is appropriately named to indicate the kinds of operations it can perform on the data. These operations consist of the standard arithmetic operations and logical comparisons. A schematic of the components is shown in Figure 1.1.

The central processing unit is often called the heart of the computer. If we want to describe the CPU in anatomical terms, central nervous system might be the most appropriate term. The CPU in your microcomputer is probably a single integrated circuit (a chip). Such a CPU is called a microprocessor. The CPU may constitute only a small percent of the cost of your microcomputer. The cabinet in which the computer is housed may cost as much. It is even possible to place the memory, CPU, and I/O functions on a single chip. However, such computers are rather limited in capability at present.

If you look inside your Apple, for example, you can identify two of the three major components quite easily. The CPU (microprocessor) is the largest chip and is marked with the number 6502. The memory is housed within the white bordered area and consists of 8 to 24 chips labelled **RAM**, an abbreviation for **Random Access Memory**. The memory capacity is dictated by the number of chips and is normally given in kilobytes. The **byte** is a storage location capable of holding the equivalent of a single character of information (for example, the letter *a* or the digit 7). If you have a

Figure 1.1
Schematic of Computer Components

```
                    ┌──────────────────┐
                    │    Arithmetic    │
┌───────────┐       │   Logic Unit     │       ┌──────────┐
│  Input–   │ ◄────►├──────────────────┤ ◄────►│  Memory  │
│  Output   │       │                  │       │          │
└───────────┘       │  Control Unit    │       └──────────┘
                    └──────────────────┘
```

CENTRAL PROCESSING UNIT

16K (kilobyte) Apple, you would expect to have 16,000 bytes of RAM available. Actually, you may have a little more since one thousand to a computer turns out to be 1024. This memory space must be shared by the instructions (your program) and by the data. In some cases, the CPU uses some of this memory as a "scratch pad" so that the available RAM is less than advertised. For example, the 8 Kilobyte PET has 7168 bytes of RAM available since the CPU uses 1 kilobyte. The Apple also uses part of RAM in certain modes of operation.

The interesting thing about memory is the way it is accessed by programs. Perhaps you have seen a large array of mail slots in a hotel or apartment complex. We might make an analogy between these slots and the memory locations in the computer memory. In early versions of computers the programmer was required to know how much space was used for the program and to select numbered storage locations for the data. The programmer kept track of these locations and the particular data stored in them. Essentially, the programmer made a memory map. Now the CPU takes care of that job for us. The CPU behaves like a desk clerk. We simply give the clerk our name and the mail is retrieved from the correct box. So long as the desk clerk is well and the mail boxes are not all used, we have no problems.

The input/output components of our microcomputer are the most visible parts.

Photo 1.4
The TRS-80 Model II microcomputer with line Printer III, external disk system, and system desk. (Photo courtesy of Radio Shack, a division of Tandy Corp.)

Besides being quite visible, they are also quite costly. They are expensive because they must either accommodate the limitations of a human's ability to send and receive information (for example, a typewriter keyboard and video monitor), or because they are rather sophisticated devices for information storage and retrieval (for example, a disk drive). I/O devices provide means of communicating with the computer. Most commonly, the I/O devices used are the keyboard and a television monitor, a disk drive and/or a cassette tape unit.

1.3 INTERACTION WITH THE COMPUTER

We mentioned earlier that the purpose of discussing computer components was to clarify the way human beings interact with computers—sometimes called the "human-computer interface." Let us consider a very simple program to illustrate this interface. Suppose we wish to execute a program that will add two numbers together. We must provide the following information to the computer:

1 The operation to be performed on the two numbers,
2 The source of the numbers,
3 The values of the numbers, and
4 The disposition of the result of the operation.

All of this information could be given to the computer in a set of instructions, which we call a **program**. Before these instructions can be executed, they must be in the computer's memory (an exception will be given in Section 1.4). We must go to the computer's input device and enter a program through the keyboard or instruct the computer to retrieve the program from some other storage device. This brings us to a method of information storage that differs from the memory we called RAM above. Disk storage and tape storage are forms of magnetic storage which have the advantage of permanency; the contents are not lost when the power is turned off. Suppose that the program is stored on a floppy disk. The program calls for the entry of the two numbers at the keyboard and the display of the sum on a video screen. Here is a possible sequence of events:

Step 1 User types an instruction at the keyboard telling the control unit to place the program in memory. (input)

Step 2 Control unit finds the program in disk storage and places it in memory (RAM). (input and storage)

Step 3 Control unit sends a message to user via video indicating that the program is stored. (output)

Step 4 User tells control unit to execute the program. (input)

Step 5 Control unit responds by bringing the program instructions from memory and executing each of them in turn. (processing instructions)

Step 6 During this execution the control unit will ask for input of two values from the keyboard by placing a prompt on the video screen. (output)

Step 7 User provides the values to control unit. (input)

Step 8 Control unit stores the values in memory (RAM). (storage)

Step 9 Control unit takes the values from memory and moves them to the ALU for addition. (processing data)

Step 10 Control unit stores the answer in memory (RAM). (storage)

Step 11 Control unit delivers the answer from memory to the video screen. (output)

A schematic of this process is shown in Figure 1.2.

The important thing to note from this example is the complexity of this apparently simple task. We observe that the control unit is involved in every step. With this example we hope to illustrate the essential steps in making the computer work for us. These steps are input, process, and output. Input steps involve giving the computer instructions and data. The process step involves the control unit carrying out the operations specified in the instructions. The output step involves the presentation of the results of the process to some device for viewing or for storage.

1.4 THE COMMUNICATION PROCESS

We would like to be able to communicate with the computer in a language that is natural to us. In computer jargon this is a *high level* language. BASIC is such a language. In the example above, we noted the critical role of the control unit. Its role is even more remarkable when we consider that it doesn't *understand* the BASIC language. The

Figure 1.2
Input, Process, and Output Events Involved in Executing a Computer Program

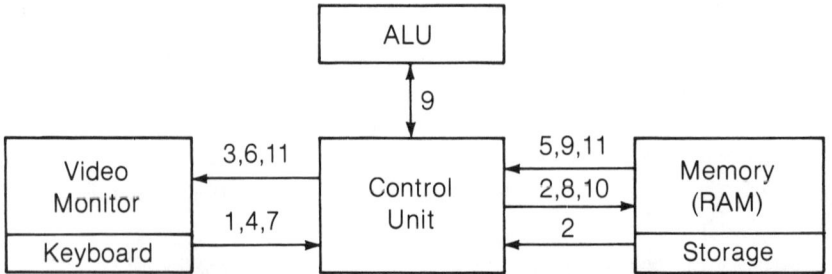

Sec. 1.4 The Communication Process **7**

Photo 1.5
The TRS-80 Line Printer VII, an I/O device which displays output. (Photo courtesy of Radio Shack, a division of Tandy Corp.)

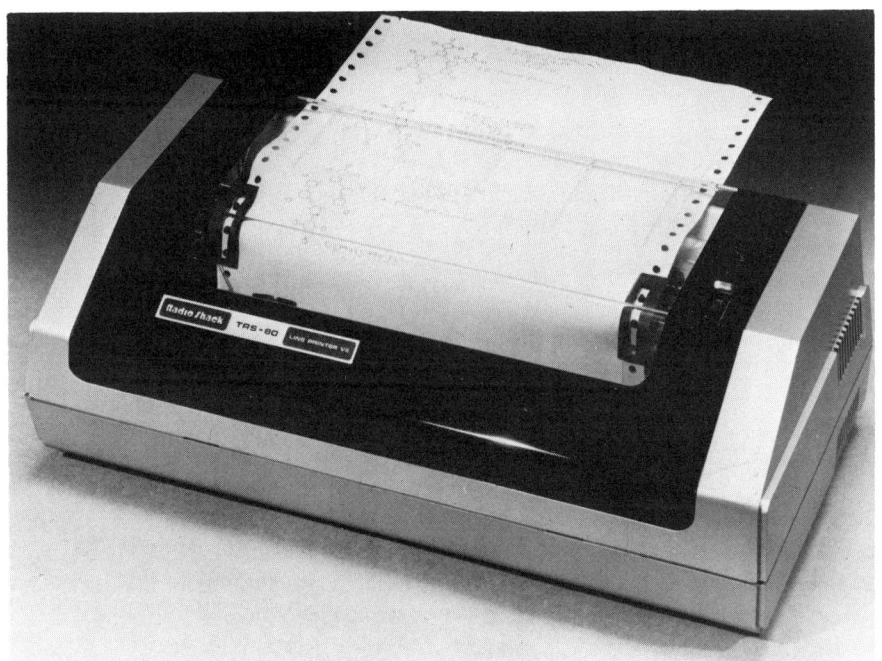

control unit cannot read the instructions we write in BASIC. It must have access to another set of instructions that translate these instructions into *machine language* to which the microprocessor can respond. This introduces additional complexities. For example, the control unit must keep track of where it is in the sequence of stored instructions. The entire high level language program is not retrieved from storage and translated at one time.

The computer, of course, does not translate languages the way humans do. The computer scans the instructions for certain key words and symbols. Each key word is translated into one or more machine operations. Only certain key words have meaning to the computer. When a key word is misspelled, the computer is unable to deduce our meaning. Humans can often deduce from context what others are trying to convey. Computers, at least in their present state of development, cannot deduce from context. Thus, we see the need for rather rigid rules of grammar (*syntax*) in dealing with the computer.

Earlier we noted that to add two numbers together we needed a set of instructions in the computer's memory. Then we discussed a mode of operation of the computer called **program mode**. In program mode we ask the computer to execute a prepared set of instructions, which are stored in its random access memory (RAM). A second mode of operation relays instructions for the performance of some arithmetic or logical operation directly to the CPU. In this mode, called **immediate mode**, we ask the computer to perform an operation by issuing an instruction at the keyboard. The computer performs in much the same way as a hand calculator. In immediate mode, if we type

PRINT 2 + 3

the computer responds with the number **5**.

Later, we will find the immediate mode convenient for checking the contents of memory locations in the process of debugging (correcting) a program. Of course, we also communicate directly with the CPU when we issue instructions to retrieve programs from disk storage, execute (**RUN**) programs, **LIST** programs, and so forth.

1.5 HARDWARE AND SOFTWARE

The technical terms, **hardware** and **software**, have become quite commonplace. The hardware in a computer system is generally considered to be all of the electronic equipment including those pieces of equipment that contain operating instructions and language translation instructions. The instructions for language translation on the microcomputer are contained in **read-only memory (ROM)**. The ROM is considered part of hardware, although its function is to provide instructions to the control unit. In contrast, software is a set of instructions which is resident in RAM as a result of placing a program there. The programs we write in BASIC will be computer software. As software is developed it is placed on disk or cassette tape so that it need not be entered through the keyboard each time the program is to be executed.

1.6 SCREEN CHARACTERISTICS

Throughout this text we will be concerned with the appearance of the output generated by our programs. We discuss the screen space available for that output in this section. The screen space is defined by the number of printing lines (rows) and the number of printing positions on each line (columns). This set of rows and columns defines the **screen grid**. Each computer must have some way of indicating that it is prepared for input and where the next input will be printed. This indication is given through the

Photo 1.6
The TRS-80 screen grid is divided into printing lines (rows), and the number of printing positions on each line determine columns. (Photo courtesy of Radio Shack, a division of Tandy Corp.)

prompt and the *cursor* location. These characteristics for each machine are discussed below:

=========================== APPLE ===========================

Screen space: 24 printing lines each 40 characters long
Prompt:] = Applesoft BASIC
          > = Integer BASIC
Cursor: a blinking square

=========================== TRS-80 ===========================

Screen space: 16 print lines each 64 characters long
Prompt: >
Cursor: an underline

━━━━━━━━━━━━━━━━━━━━ PET ━━━━━━━━━━━━━━━━━━━━

Screen space: 25 printing lines each 40 characters long
Prompt: the word **READY**
Cursor: a blinking square

The cursor locates the current position of the printing head. The next character entered at the keyboard will appear at the current cursor location. Successive characters entered at the keyboard will appear on the same line as in typing. If we continue to print beyond the permitted number of spaces on a line the computer will print the excess on the next line(s). If we print more than the number of lines per full screen, subsequent lines will be printed at the bottom of the screen with the preceding lines of text being moved upward one unit. This effect, called **scrolling**, can be troublesome. To avoid scrolling, we need to be aware of the characteristics of our output screen.

On some machines the cursor position can be moved to permit *editing* (fixing or modifying) programs. The Apple and the PET have such controls. The TRS-80 has a special *edit mode* so that movement of the cursor around the screen is not necessary. Cursor control on the Apple and PET is discussed below.

━━━━━━━━━━━━━━━━━━━━ APPLE ━━━━━━━━━━━━━━━━━━━━

We recommend *cursor control* through use of the four keys: **I**, **J**, **K**, and **M** whose relative positions suggest the moves they allow. To enter cursor control mode press the **ESC** key once. Thereafter, using either of the four keys will produce the movements indicated below.

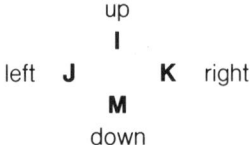

To get out of cursor control mode, press any key other than one of the four above or such special keys as **RESET** and **CTRL**. Cursor control moves may be repeated automatically by using the **REPT** key simultaneously with the appropriate move.

PET

Use the four arrow keys on the top of the number pad to move the cursor around. Note that two of the keys are accessed by using a shift key.

EXERCISE SET 1.1

These exercises are designed to give you some experience with the screen and storage characteristics of your computer. They require that you enter simple programs and immediate commands at the keyboard. You may not understand the programs until later.

1. The computer's memory (RAM) is used to store both instructions and data. This exercise is designed to illustrate space utilized during program storage. Follow the preliminary instructions step by step.

    (a) With the computer on, type **NEW** at the keyboard and then press **RETURN**. You have just issued an immediate command to the control unit to clear any program and data from RAM.

    (b) Type **PRINT FRE(0)** at the keyboard and then press **RETURN**. If you are using a TRS-80, type **PRINT MEM** and press **ENTER**. The computer will display a number that represents the number of bytes of RAM available at this time. If the computer is an Apple, the number displayed may be negative. In this case, add 65536 to it to obtain the number of bytes free. Record this number.

    Sometimes you will type the wrong character. If you discover the error before you press **RETURN**, you can easily delete the unwanted character or characters by using the delete key—the key with the left-pointing arrow, which is located at the right side of the keyboard. If you are using a PET, use the key in the far upper right corner with **DEL** on it. One character will be deleted each time you push the key. If you have already pushed **RETURN** when you discover the error, you can retype the entire line.

    (c) Type the following and then press **RETURN**

    110 READ A

    (d) Repeat step (b). The bytes of RAM available should have decreased by seven (eight for the TRS-80 and the PET). If the number was negative, it becomes more negative by seven. Memory space decreases because the computer stored one line of instructions. The seven (or eight) bytes were used as follows.

five for the line number (regardless of its size),

one for the word **READ**,

one for the character **A**, and

one for the blank space betwen **READ** and **A** (for the TRS-80 and the PET).

You will note that the Apple makes its own decisions about spacing at no cost in RAM. The PET and TRS-80 use RAM to store spaces except for the one after the line number. As you begin to format your programs, you will recognize that there are advantages and disadvantages to either feature.

(e) Now enter the line **120 READ B** and press **RETURN** (or **ENTER**).

(f) Repeat step (b) and the bytes available should decrease by seven (eight for the PET and the TRS-80).

(g) Enter the following. Press **RETURN** after each line.

```
130  LET C = A + B
140  PRINT C
150  DATA 4,5
```

(h) Compute the bytes that you think these three lines require and compare your answer with the computer's result by typing **PRINT FRE(0)** or **PRINT MEM**.

Now you should be able to evaluate the memory space requirements of programs. Recall that line numbers use five bytes, the word following the line number (a BASIC keyword) uses one byte and each other character or digit uses one byte. Evaluate the bytes required to store each of the following program lines:

```
100  INPUT X
200  LET Y = X + 5
300  PRINT "DOG"
400  PRINT Y
500  END
```

2. This exercise will illustrate the use of RAM for data storage. Follow the steps outlined below:

(a) Type **NEW** and then enter the following program, pressing **RETURN** after the entry of each line:

```
100  READ A
110  PRINT A
120  DATA 5
```

(b) Type **PRINT FRE(0)** or **PRINT MEM**, press **RETURN**, and record the number of bytes free.

(c) Type **RUN**, press **RETURN**, and observe the computer print the number five. Now type **PRINT FRE(0)** or **PRINT MEM**, press **RETURN**, and compare the bytes free with the value obtained in Step (b). There should be seven fewer bytes available as we now have data (the number five) in memory location **A**. Each numeric data storage location uses seven bytes of RAM.

(d) The immediate command **CLEAR** clears all data storage locations in the computer's memory but does not remove the program instructions. Type **CLEAR**, press **RETURN**, and again determine the number of bytes free. You should find that the seven bytes used for data storage are now available.

To compute the space required for data storage we must be able to determine the number of memory locations set aside for data by the program. This is usually determined by counting the variables used by the program. Variables will be discussed in more detail in Chapter 2. The demonstration program in problem 1 above used three variables: **A**, **B**, and **C**. It would require twenty-one bytes for data storage. Determine the space required for program and for data storage in the following program:

110 INPUT A
120 LET C = A + 5
130 PRINT C

3. Determine the program and data storage space needed for the programs below:

(a) **100 INPUT A,B**
110 LET C = A * B
120 PRINT C
130 END

(b) **100 READ A,B,C**
110 LET D = A * B + C + 75
120 PRINT C
130 DATA 4,5,6
140 END

4. This problem consists of three exercises designed to demonstrate screen characteristics.

(a) Type **NEW**, enter the following program pressing **RETURN (ENTER)** after each line, and then type **RUN** and press **RETURN (ENTER)**.

===== APPLE =====

```
100 HOME
110 FOR I = 1 TO 4
120 PRINT "0123456789";
130 NEXT I
140 PRINT
150 PRINT "40 COLUMNS ARE AVAILABLE - COUNT THEM"
160 END
```

===== PET =====

```
100 PRINT CHR$(147)
110 FOR I = 1 TO 4
120 PRINT "0123456789";
130 NEXT I
140 PRINT
150 PRINT "40 COLUMNS ARE AVAILABLE - COUNT THEM"
160 END
```

===== TRS-80 =====

```
100 CLS
110 FOR I = 1 TO 8
120 PRINT "12345678";
130 NEXT I
140 PRINT
150 PRINT "64 COLUMNS ARE AVAILABLE - COUNT THEM"
160 END
```

To see your program after it is entered, type **LIST** and then press **RETURN**

(b) Type **NEW**, enter the program below and follow the instructions of Step (a) above. Select the appropriate version of the program for the machine you are using.

Exercise Set 1.1

═══════════════════════════ APPLE ═══════════════════════════

```
100 HOME
110 FOR I = 1 TO 24
120 PRINT TAB(38) I;
130 IF I < 24 THEN PRINT
140 NEXT I
150 VTAB 1
160 HTAB 1
170 PRINT "24 ROWS ARE AVAILABLE - COUNT THEM"
180 END
```

═══════════════════════════ PET ═══════════════════════════

```
100 PRINT CHR$(147)
110 FOR I = 1 TO 25
120 PRINT TAB(35) I;
130 IF I < 25 THEN PRINT
140 NEXT I
150 PRINT CHR$(19)
160 PRINT "25 ROWS ARE AVAILABLE - COUNT THEM"
170 END
```

═══════════════════════════ TRS-80 ═══════════════════════════

```
100 CLS
110 FOR I = 1 TO 16
120 PRINT TAB(38) I;
130 IF I < 16 THEN PRINT
140 NEXT I
150 PRINT @ 1, "16 ROWS ARE AVAILABLE - COUNT THEM"
160 END
```

(c) Type **NEW** and enter the program below. If you are using a TRS-80, substitute **CLS** for **HOME**. If you are using a PET, substitute **PRINT CHR$(147)** for **HOME**. **LIST** and **RUN** the program.

```
100 HOME
110 FOR I = 1 TO 30
```

```
120 PRINT TAB(I)"SCROLLING"
130 FOR J = 1 TO 200  :  NEXT J
140 NEXT I
150 PRINT "NOTE THAT WHEN WE REACHED THE"
160 PRINT "BOTTOM OF THE SCREEN, THE LINES"
170 PRINT "BEGAN TO 'SCROLL' UPWARD."
180 END
```

Review

We summarize the new terms introduced in this chapter.

MICROCOMPUTER   a computer in which the central processing unit is a microprocessor. (Section 1.1)

BASIC   an acronym for a high level computer language entitled *Beginners' All-purpose Symbolic Instruction Code*. (Section 1.1)

BASIC DIALECT   a version of the BASIC language characteristic of a certain machine or software developer. (Section 1.1)

MICROPROCESSOR   a central processing unit on a single integrated circuit (chip). (Section 1.2)

CPU   an acronym for *Central Processing Unit*. The CPU consists of two subunits called the control unit and the arithmetic logic unit. (Section 1.2)

I/O   an abbreviation for input/output. I/O may refer to the processes of information exchange with the CPU or to the devices, which are used in these processes. (Section 1.2)

MEMORY   storage locations in which instructions (a program) or data may be located. (Section 1.2)

CONTROL UNIT   the part of the CPU that handles the flow of information during execution of a program. The control unit also handles functions relating to retrieval, storage, and displaying of instructions or data. (Section 1.2)

ARITHMETIC LOGIC UNIT (ALU)   the part of the CPU which performs arithmetic operations and makes comparisons. (Section 1.2)

RAM   an acronym for *Random Access Memory* that can be used for storage of program instructions and data during execution of a program. (Section 1.2)

KILOBYTE   a unit of storage capability containing 1024 memory locations. (two to the tenth power) (Section 1.2)

PROGRAM a set of instructions to the computer written in some language that the computer *understands* or can translate. (Section 1.3)

DISK STORAGE a form of permanent storage for programs or data that allows rapid recording and retrieval on a random basis. (Section 1.3)

TAPE STORAGE a form of permanent storage for programs or data that is accessed sequentially and that requires a longer access time than disk storage. (Section 1.3)

HIGH LEVEL LANGUAGE a language that allows computer instructions to be written in English-like statements. (Section 1.4)

MACHINE LANGUAGE a language to which the CPU can respond directly. (Section 1.4)

SYNTAX rules of expression for any language to which the computer is expected to respond. (Section 1.4)

PROGRAM MODE a mode of computer operation in which the control of the computer is given over to the instructions in a stored program. (Section 1.4)

IMMEDIATE MODE a mode of computer operation in which instructions are given directly to the CPU from the keyboard. (Section 1.4)

HARDWARE those built-in parts of the computer that permit it to function as advertised. (Section 1.5)

SOFTWARE computer programs that link with the hardware to adapt the computer to the needs of the particular user. (Section 1.5)

ROM an acronym for *Read Only Memory* that is used by the computer to store fixed instructions. ROM might contain instructions for translating a high level language to machine language. (Section 1.5)

SCREEN GRID a term that considers the screen to be composed of a grid of printing positions. (Section 1.6)

SCROLLING text movement up the screen as additional lines are printed at the bottom. (Section 1.6)

CURSOR CONTROL movement of the cursor (printing position) through the use of certain keys. (Section 1.6)

2
ELEMENTARY PROGRAMMING TECHNIQUES

2.1 INTRODUCTION TO ELEMENTARY PROGRAMMING TECHNIQUES

A computer is a machine that "manipulates symbols by following the instructions in a computer program."* A computer program is a sequence of instructions written in a language that the computer *understands*. A computer's native tongue is machine language, which consists entirely of numbers. In the last chapter we pointed out that higher level languages, such as BASIC, have been developed so that computer programs can be written in a language more easily understood by humans. Such programs are then translated into machine language by a compiler or translator. The computer will execute the machine language version of the program.

In this chapter we will concern ourselves with very rudimentary programs, which illustrate the following:

1. Storing data in memory under program control,
2. Output of data from memory under program control, and
3. Arithmetic operations on data.

The program is entered into the computer as a series of statements, each

*Rich Didday and Rex Page, FORTRAN FOR HUMANS, 2d ed., (St. Paul: West Publishing Co., 1976), p.3.

preceded by a number. The order of the **statement numbers** determines the order of their execution, unless the program itself dictates the altering of that order. In this chapter we will only consider programs that are executed in the sequence of their statement numbers.

2.2 PROGRAM ENTRY

We enter our program (sequence of instructions) by typing them on the microcomputer keyboard. Before beginning to enter a new program, type:

NEW and then press **RETURN**. (Apple and PET)
NEW and then press **ENTER**. (TRS-80)

This step clears any program that may be in memory. We are now ready to enter a program. Suppose we are preparing a program to accomplish the addition of two numbers as described in the last chapter. We write such a program as follows:

```
100  INPUT A
110  INPUT B
120  LET C = A + B
130  PRINT C
140  END
```

Our program contains five instructions. Each instruction consists of a statement number followed by a word. The word is called a *keyword*. The keyword makes it possible for the BASIC interpreter to identify the instruction to be performed. Sometimes more than one keyword is used in the same line. Certain letters and arithmetic symbols are also present within this program.

To enter this program we type each line just as it appears above. At the end of each line, press the **RETURN (ENTER)** key and enter the next line. To view the complete program when it is entered, do the following:

Type **LIST** and then press **RETURN (ENTER)**.

The computer will display what you have entered.

2.3 THE NATURE OF A VARIABLE

In the example program in Section 2.2 we see the letters **A**, **B**, and **C**. These letters are called **variables** in the program. A variable is a symbolic name for a memory location used to store an element of data in our program. In mathematics, we often consider a variable to be a symbolic representation of a whole range of values. In a computer program, the variable represents a single well-defined quantity. That quantity can change values under program control, but it cannot have more than one value at any given time.

It is common in scientific literature to distinguish between *dependent variables* and *independent variables*. A dependent variable is one that depends upon other variables and constants for its value. For example, in the statement

120 LET C = A + B

C is the dependent variable. In this statement, the value of **C** depends upon the values of **A** and **B**. In contrast, both **A** and **B** hold their values independently of whatever value **C** may have. For these reasons, **A** and **B** are classed as independent variables. Statement 120 above is characteristic of a class of statements called **arithmetic assignment statements**. In such statements, the dependent variable appears alone on the left hand side of the expression, and the independent variables appear on the right hand side.

The number of variable names which can be used in BASIC is limited. The variable names above consist of single letters. Longer names, involving *alphanumeric characters,* are permitted. An alphanumeric character is a letter or one of the ten digits. The computer usually ignores all but the first two characters. Thus, to the computer, the names **A12** and **A13** are identical. A variable name in BASIC must begin with a letter. It may be followed by other letters, other decimal digits, or a blank space (some BASICs require the second character to be a digit or a blank). Since there are twenty-six letters, one blank space, and ten decimal digits, we would expect to have 26 x 37 = 962 variable names. However, we fall slightly short of this number because certain **reserved words** cannot be used in variable names.

Reserved words are words that have special meanings in the BASIC language. The keywords discussed above are examples of reserved words. We noted that **LET** is a keyword. As a result, a variable name such as **BULLET** is not permitted. As another example, the word "TO" would appear to be a valid variable name. However, **TO** is a keyword and will not be accepted. Other examples will be given in the exercises. Use of a single character variable name or a single character and digit will avoid any conflict with reserved words. However, we will use longer, more descriptive names in this text to identify certain variables more precisely. We do need to be careful in the selection of these longer variable names.

The rules above imply that special characters such as # , $, %, &, (, and so forth are not permitted in variable names. We will find some exceptions to this general rule as we continue. For example, $ has a special meaning in a variable name.

EXERCISE SET 2.1

1. Determine which of the following are invalid variable names. Give a reason in each case.

BB	BALANCE	MONEY
3A	T&	FIVE+
LEGALTENDER	A1 #	C123
BOOKLIST	FORK	PAY RATE

   Note: A quick way to see if the computer will accept a variable name is to enter in immediate mode **PRINT NAME** where **NAME** is the test name. Unacceptable names will cause the printing of an error message. An important exception to this is an invalid variable name such as **3A**, which begins with a digit.

2. Enter and **LIST** the following programs.

   Program 1

   100 LET C = 7
   110 LET CSQR = C^2
   120 PRINT CSQR
   130 END

   Program 2

   100 LET SALESPRICE = 5.75
   110 LET TAXRATE = .04
   120 LET COST = SALESPRICE * (1 + TAXRATE)
   130 PRINT SALESPRICE, COST
   140 END

   Observe carefully the result of running these programs. In each case, error messages are generated, indicating that we have chosen illegal variable names. What new reserved words have you discovered?

2.4 STORING VALUES IN MEMORY

In the last chapter, we pointed out that the computer in program mode typically retrieves data from memory. We might logically ask how such data gets into memory in the first place. Three methods of data storage are possible. They are:

   1. The **LET** statement, also called the arithmetic assignment statement,
   2. The **INPUT** statement, which retrieves data values from the keyboard, and

3 The **READ** statement, which retrieves data values from **DATA** statements within the program itself.

We consider each of these methods in turn.

In the last chapter, we noted that every computer has a certain amount of memory (RAM) that is able to hold a representation of numeric or character values. Each memory location has a unique numeric address within the computer. Therefore, it is possible to store a specific value in a specific memory location. However, BASIC makes it easier for us by allowing the use of variable names to store values in the computer. Let us consider the following statement:

100 LET X = 19

This statement instructs the computer to select a memory location for the variable **X** and to store the value **19** in that location. Therefore, it is unnecessary for us to know the exact memory address of any particular value. The computer creates a cross reference table or memory map, which contains the memory address associated with each variable.

Consider one more example of an arithmetic assignment statement:

120 LET C = A + B

This statement instructs the computer to locate the value stored in the memory location associated with **A**, add it to the value stored in the memory location associated with **B**, and then store the resulting value in the memory location associated with **C**. The arithmetic assignment statement is then used not only for placing values in storage, but also to indicate the operations to be performed on independent variables.

We should note that statement 120 above looks like an equation. However, it should be viewed as an assignment statement—a method of giving a value to variable **C**. This distinction will become more important when we encounter arithmetic assignment statements that are nonsensical as equations.

The next form of entering information into memory is through the **INPUT** statement. In the example program shown earlier in this chapter, Section 2.2, two statements containing the keyword **INPUT** appeared.

100 INPUT A
110 INPUT B

When the computer encounters such a statement during program execution, it will print a question mark at the terminal. This question mark is a signal to the user that the computer is waiting for a value for **A** to be entered (line 100). The user responds by typing a value and pressing the **RETURN** key. The computer then moves to line 110 and repeats the process but then assigns the entered value to **B**.

The final form for entering data into storage is through the **READ** statement. The **READ** statement works in a manner similar to the **INPUT** statement except that values are retrieved from a data set within the program itself, rather than from the keyboard.

Consider our example addition program as modified here:

```
100  READ A
110  READ B
120  LET C = A + B
130  PRINT C
135  DATA 27,36
140  END
```

Notice the appearance of an additional line, (line 135). This line provides data internal to the program. The **DATA** line is necessary because of lines 100 and 110 that instruct the computer to seek data within the program. When line 100 is executed, the computer will find the first value on the **DATA** line and assign that value to the memory location associated with **A**. Upon execution of line 110, the value thirty-six will be assigned to the variable **B**.

In summary, there are four keywords associated with storage of values in memory. These are:

LET—for assigning constants or the results of operations,

INPUT—for entering values at the keyboard, and

READ and **DATA**—for entering values contained in the program.

At this point, we should mention that the use of the keyword **LET** is not necessary in most BASIC systems. That is, we might have written

120 C = A + B

in the preceding program and the same operations would have been performed. However, the use of **LET** reminds us that we are dealing with an assignment statement and not a statement of mathematical equality. Its use also preserves a certain symmetry, having all statements begin with a keyword. You may choose to dispense with the **LET**. When you do so, we hope you will read the equals sign as "is assigned the value of".

2.5 ARITHMETIC OPERATIONS

The example program in Section 2.4 indicates the operation of addition in statement 120. **Arithmetic operations** will appear only in arithmetic assignment statements in this text. It is possible to output the results of operations without the intermediate storage step, but we do not recommend such a practice. The permitted arithmetic operations are:

+ Addition
− Subtraction
* Multiplication
/ Division
^ Exponential (up arrow (↑) for the PET and the TRS-80).

In using the operators above we need to understand how the computer responds when combinations of operators appear in the same expression. For example, consider the following statement:

120 LET V = 3 + 5 * 2

When the computer executes this statement, what value will be stored for **V**? Will the computer add **3** to **5** to get 8 and then multiply the result by **2** to get 16? Or will it multiply **5** by **2** to get 10 and add 10 to **3** to get 13?

The computer is bound by a set of rules that answers these questions for us. This set of rules is called the **hierarchy of operations.** If you have studied this hierarchy in mathematics, you will find it the same here. The hierarchy of operations follows:

1. Quantities within parentheses are evaluated first using rules 2, 3, and 4 following. Innermost parentheses must be evaluated first.
2. Among the arithmetic operations, exponentiations are performed first.
3. Multiplications and divisions are performed next—the order is unimportant.
4. Additions and subtractions are performed last—the order is unimportant.

The following worked examples illustrate this hierarchy.

100 LET V = 3 * 2^3 + 4 evaluates in the following manner:

Step 1 2^3 = 8
Step 2 3 * 8 = 24
Step 3 24 + 4 = 28

100 LET C = (3 + 8) * 5 evaluates in the following manner:

Step 1 3 + 8 = 11
Step 2 11 * 5 = 55

100 LET A1 = (2 * (1 + 5)) + 12/2 evaluates in the following manner:

Step 1 1 + 5 = 6
Step 2 2 * 6 = 12
Step 3 12/2 = 6
Step 4 12 + 6 = 18

EXERCISE SET 2.2

1. Write BASIC statements to accomplish the following:
   (a) Obtain the value of **CASH** from the keyboard.
   (b) Enter data values **34**, **45**, and **79** into a program.
   (c) Obtain values for **X** and **Y** from within the program.
   (d) Assign to **BALANCE** the product of **PRINCIPAL** and **PERCENT**.
   (e) Assign to **QUOTA** the value **55**.

2. Write BASIC statements that will cause the following expressions to be evaluated and assigned to the variable **RESULT**:
   (a) **F** divided by the quantity **T** + **30**
   (b) the product of **A**, **B**, and **C**
   (c) the sum of **21** and **5** squared
   (d) the product of the quantities **S** and **R** + **1**

3. Evaluate the following expressions:
   (a) 3 + 4 * 5 ^ 2
   (b) (30 − 2 * 3) / 4
   (c) 20 − (15 + 2 * 3) / 3
   (d) (6 * (1 + 3))/3
   (e) 28/(5 + 4/2)
   (f) (4 * 9 − 6)/(1 + 3 * 3)

4. Evaluate each of the expressions in problem 3 in immediate mode by entering the command **PRINT** followed by the expression. Check to see that the results agree with your hand calculation.

2.6 OBTAINING OUTPUT FROM THE PROGRAM

Output from the computer to the video screen is accomplished through the use of statements with the keyword **PRINT**. We will use the **PRINT** statement for two purposes: to deliver values stored in memory to the screen and to deliver *character strings* found in the program to the screen. It should be clear that the operation of printing is nondestructive to the data in memory. That is, a value is printed and yet remains unchanged in memory. The term "character string" refers to any printable characters on the keyboard. Printable characters include the alphanumeric characters and special symbols. Delivery of data from memory allows us to see the results of a computation that may have been stored there. Such statements take the form:

130 PRINT C

This statement instructs the computer to deliver the value stored in the location associated with variable **C** to the screen.

The second common use of the **PRINT** statement is to place prepared messages, character strings, on the screen. Examples are:

110 PRINT "ENTER THE VALUE OF A"
120 PRINT "THE ANSWER IS"

Notice that the character string to be printed is enclosed within quotation marks. Combinations of data and character strings may be contained in a single **PRINT** statement. For example, we might write:

150 PRINT "THE ANSWER IS ";C

The BASIC language provides certain **punctuation** that can be used with our **output**. This punctuation is used with the **PRINT** statement to control the format of the output. The punctuation consists of commas and semicolons. The function of each is discussed below.

The comma "**,**" is used to control placement within groups of columns called fields. The following programs illustrate the use of the comma and field structure. They are different because the field structure is different on each computer.

APPLE

```
100 PRINT "0123456789ABCDE",
110 PRINT "0123456","0123456"
120 PRINT 1,2,3
130 PRINT ,2,
140 PRINT 3
150 PRINT 1,,3
```

A run of this program appears as follows:

```
0123456789ABCDE 0123456         0123456
1               2               3
                2               3
1                               3
```

You should note the presence of the three fields. The first two are sixteen characters wide and the third is eight characters wide. Access to the third field is denied if the string printed in the second field is too long.

PET

```
100 PRINT "012345678",
110 PRINT "012345678","012345678","012345678"
120 PRINT 1,2,3,4
130 PRINT,2,
140 PRINT 3
150 PRINT 1,,3,4
```

A run of this program appears as follows:

```
012345678 012345678 012345678 012345678
    1         2         3         4
              2         3
    1                   3         4
```

TRS-80

```
100 PRINT "0123456789ABCDE","0123456789ABCDE",
110 PRINT "0123456789ABCDE","01234567"
120 PRINT 1,2,3,4
130 PRINT ,2,
140 PRINT 3
150 PRINT 1,,3,4
```

A run of this program appears as follows:

```
0123456789ABCDE 0123456789ABCDE 0123456789ABCDE 01234567
    1                 2                 3             4
                      2                 3
    1                                   3             4
```

There is room for a full fifteen characters in the fourth field of the TRS-80.

Note that we were able to obtain blank fields by the appropriate use of commas. You will want to investigate the field characteristics of your computer for yourself.

Ordinarily, every execution of a **PRINT** statement causes BASIC to begin printing a new line. We say that a print statement is followed by a *line feed*. However, because the last character in statement 130 was a comma, the line feed was suppressed and the next value was printed by statement 140 on the same line.

The semicolon ";" used between variables or character strings causes minimum spacing between output. It also suppresses the line feed. The following program illustrates the effect of the semicolon.

Sec. 2.6   *Obtaining Output from the Program*

```
100 PRINT 1;2;3;"A";"B"
110 LET X = 20
120 PRINT "HE WAS";X;"YEARS OLD."
130 PRINT "HE WAS ";X;" YEARS OLD."
```

The program output is displayed below for each computer.

APPLE

```
123AB
HE WAS20YEARS OLD.
HE WAS 20 YEARS OLD.
```

PET AND TRS-80

```
 1  2  3 AB
HE WAS  20  YEARS OLD.
HE WAS  20  YEARS OLD.
```

Note that in order to intermix numbers with text we need to leave appropriate spaces. Some computers leave a space before and after a positive integer so that numbers are more easily integrated into the text. The PET and the TRS-80 provide this kind of spacing.

We began this chapter with a discussion of a program that illustrated the steps of input, processing, and output. Let us look at that program again.

```
100 INPUT A
110 INPUT B
120 LET C = A + B
130 PRINT C
140 END
```

When we run this program we see the following:

```
?21
?12
33
```

This is not very informative. Our program needs to be clarified so that a user may understand what is happening without looking at the program listing. We insert the following statements.

```
90  PRINT "THIS PROGRAM SUMS TWO NUMBERS"
95  PRINT "ENTER THE FIRST NUMBER";
105 PRINT "ENTER THE SECOND NUMBER";
130 PRINT "THE SUM OF ";A;" AND ";B;" IS ";C;"."
```

Omit extra blanks for PET and TRS-80.

With these statements a run of the program appears as follows:

```
THIS PROGRAM SUMS TWO NUMBERS
ENTER THE FIRST NUMBER ?21
ENTER THE SECOND NUMBER ?12
THE SUM OF 21 AND 12 IS 33.
```

The semicolons in lines 95 and 105 cause the prompts "**?**" to be printed on the same line as the request for data because the line feed was suppressed. We also repeat the input in the final line of output, using semicolons to construct a sentence with proper spacing.

In discussing punctuation, we should also note that the comma can be used with **READ** and **INPUT** keywords to store multiple values in memory with a single statement. For example,

```
100 READ X,Y
```

will cause the computer to seek values in a **DATA** line for two values and store them as variables **X** and **Y**.

Similarly,

```
100 INPUT X,Y,Z
```

will cause the computer to seek three values from the keyboard for assignment to **X**, **Y**, and **Z**.

EXERCISE SET 2.3

Write programs that will accomplish the following:

1. Read three values from a data line and print them in the three fields on a single line.
2. Input two values from the keyboard, add them together, and print the entered values in the first two fields and the sum in the third field.
3. Read a value from a data line and print the word TOTAL in the first field and the value read in the third field.
4. Print in the following order your last name, first name, and middle initial in the first three fields.

5. Input a value from the keyboard, multiply it by .05 and save this value as the variable **TAX**. Add **TAX** to the value entered and call the result **SPRICE**. Print the character strings **LPRICE**, **TAX**, and **SPRICE** in the three fields on one line. On the next line print the value entered, the value of **TAX** and the value of **SPRICE** in three fields.

6. Determine values for all variables in the following programs after they are run.
   (a) 100 **READ A**
       110 **LET C = 2 + 4 * A**
       120 **PRINT C**
       130 **DATA 6**
       140 **END**
   (b) 100 **READ X,Y**
       110 **LET Z = (X/Y + 30)/X^2**
       120 **PRINT X,Y,Z**
       130 **DATA 4,2**
       140 **END**
   (c) 100 **LET C = 5**
       110 **LET D = (C + 10)/3**
       120 **PRINT "D IS EQUAL TO ";D**
       130 **END**

7. Display the output of each preceding program in the format in which it will appear on the computer screen.

2.7 EDITING THE PROGRAM

For our uses, editing will indicate the process of making changes in a program already entered into the computer. Obviously, we review (edit) handwritten programs before entry into the computer. Editing should begin as soon as the program is entered. Before executing the newly entered program, verify that the program in the computer's memory is identical with what was supposedly entered. Do this by listing the program and checking for data entry errors.

Errors involving omissions of entire statements are corrected by typing in the missing statements. The computer is not concerned with the time sequence in which our statements are entered, only their numerical sequence is important.

To remove unwanted statements, we simply type the statement number and then press **RETURN (ENTER)**. This enters a blank statement, which replaces the existing statement. Most systems allow blocks of statements to be deleted. For example, on the Apple this is accomplished by typing **DEL 150,200** followed by a **RETURN**. This

32 *Elementary Programming Techniques*   Ch. 2

deletes statements 150 through 200. On the TRS-80, the command is **DELETE 150-200**. The PET has no command for deletion of blocks of statements.

    Correction of a program statement is somewhat more difficult. Correction by retyping the entire line is, of course, always acceptable and may be quicker with short lines. The alternative to retyping a statement is **editing** it on the **screen** (or in **edit mode** on the TRS-80).

    The following examples will illustrate the editing procedure:

1   Change of a character. Consider the line:

100 PRINT "MY NOME IS JOHN."

We want to correct the misspelling of NAME.

==================== **APPLE** ====================

1. Type **LIST 100** and press **RETURN**.
2. Press **ESC** to enter cursor control mode.
3. Move the cursor using the combination of **I**, **J**, **K** and **M** keys until it is over the **1** in **100**.
4. Copy line 100 using the right arrow key. Use this key to move the cursor over the **O** in **NOME**. Now press the **A** key to replace **O** with **A**. Continue to copy by pressing the right arrow key until the end of the statement is passed.
5. Press **RETURN** at this point and **LIST** to see that the line is corrected.

==================== **PET** ====================

1. Type **LIST 100** and press **RETURN**.
2. Use the cursor keys to move by the shortest path to the letter **O**. With the cursor over **O**, press **A** to replace **O** with **A**.
3. Press **RETURN** and **LIST 100** to see the correction.

==================== **TRS-80** ====================

1. Type **EDIT 100** and press **ENTER**.
2. Use the space bar to move the cursor between the letters **N** and **O** in **NOME**.
3. type **1CA**. This instructs the computer to replace the next single character with **A** (one change a).
4. Press **ENTER** to get out of **EDIT** mode.

Sec. 2.7   Editing the Program

2   Deletion of character(s). Consider the line:

    100 PRINT "MY NAME IS IS JOHN."

    We have inadvertently typed the word **IS** twice. Corrections are:

    ========================== APPLE ==========================
    | 1 | Follow steps 1, 2, and 3 above. |
    | 2 | Use the right arrow key to move to the space between the two **IS's**. Press **ESC** and the **K** key three times to move to the space in front of **JOHN**. |
    | 3 | Press the right arrow key to copy the remainder of the quotation. |

    ========================== PET ==========================
    | 1 | Type **LIST 100** and press **RETURN**. |
    | 2 | Use cursor moves to place the cursor between the two **IS's**. Press the **DEL** key three times. |
    | 3 | Press **RETURN** to copy the corrected line. |

    ========================== TRS-80 ==========================
    | 1 | Type **EDIT 100** and press **ENTER**. |
    | 2 | Use the space bar to move the cursor until it is between the two **IS's**. |
    | 3 | Type **3D** and press **ENTER** to get out of edit mode. **3D** means delete the next three characters. |

3   Addition of character(s). Consider the line:

    100 PRINT "MY NAME IS JOHN."

    Suppose we intended to include JOHN's last name of SMITH.

    ========================== APPLE ==========================
    | 1 | Follow Steps 1; 2, and 3 above to place the cursor over the number **1** in **100**. |
    | 2 | Use the right arrow key to move the cursor over the period after **N**. |

3   Press **ESC** and cursor to any blank space on the screen. Type **SMITH** with a blank in front of it. (Be careful doing this since the first key pressed causes no action other than termination of cursor mode.)
4   Press **ESC** and cursor back over the period.
5   Use the right arrow key to copy the rest of the line and then press **RETURN**.

====== PET ======

1   Cursor to the period.
2   Press the **INSERT** key six times to make room.
3   Type **SMITH** preceded by a blank and press **RETURN**.

====== TRS-80 ======

1   Type **EDIT 100** and press **ENTER**.
2   Move the cursor between the **N** and the period.
3   Type **I** followed by a space and then **SMITH**.
4   Press **ENTER** to finish the edit mode.

The need to edit may first come to our attention because of an error message given by the computer during an attempted **RUN** of the program. The error message will give a brief indication of the type of error and the line in which it occurred. You should consult the list of error messages (see Chapter 11) when you begin to write programs.

We include in this section a new BASIC keyword. This keyword **REM** is used to designate a **remark statement**. The remark statement is used to identify parts of a program. This statement permits the programmer to enter any text desired on the same line with the REM keyword. The computer ignores the contents of the remark statement during program execution. When the program is listed the remark statement appears in its normal line order. We illustrate the use of this statement as follows:

```
100  REM -- SQUARE 6-4-81
110  PRINT "NUMBER","SQUARE"
120  REM -- READ NUMBER
130  READ A1
140  REM -- SQUARE NUMBER
```

```
150 LET A2 = A1^2
160 REM -- PRINT TABLE
170 PRINT A1,A2
180 DATA 11
190 END
```

EXERCISE SET   2.4

1. The following exercises are intended to provide practice in screen editing.

    (a) Enter the following program line. Then type **NEW** to clear the memory and recover the line in memory by copying it off the screen. (PET and Apple only)

    100 PRINT "THIS IS AN EXERCISE IN COPYING."

    (b) Enter the following program lines and correct them as indicated by screen editing (or by using **EDIT** mode).

    100 LET C − A + B
    (Place = sign after **C**)

    110 LET R = (A + (B − C)/D
    (Insert missing parenthesis after **C**.)

    120 PRINT "THE ANSWERR IS";A
    (Correct the spelling of "**ANSWERR**" and insert a blank after "**IS**".)

2. Insert appropriate REM statements in the following program in order to identify the purpose of the program and the major steps involved.

    ```
    110 INPUT PRICE
    120 DISCOUNT = .20
    130 TAX = .05
    140 NET = (PRICE * (1 − DISCOUNT)) * (1 + TAX)
    150 PRINT NET
    ```

3. Insert appropriate character strings to prompt for the input and identify the output in the following program:

    ```
    120 INPUT LONG
    130 INPUT WIDE
    140 AREA = LONG * WIDE
    150 PRINT AREA
    ```

Review

We summarize the new terms and the new syntax introduced in this chapter.

STATEMENT NUMBER   the number preceding a program instruction. This number normally determines the order of execution of the statement. (Section 2.1)

VARIABLE   a symbolic name for a memory location. (Section 2.3)

ARITHMETIC ASSIGNMENT STATEMENT   a statement in which a variable receives a value by assignment within the program. The value received may result from the evaluation of combinations of other variables; that is, from a computation. (Section 2.3)

RESERVED WORD   a word that has special meaning in the BASIC language and is to be avoided in variable names. (Section 2.3)

ARITHMETIC OPERATION   one of the operations of addition, subtraction, multiplication, division, or exponentiation. (Section 2.5)

HIERARCHY OF OPERATIONS   a set of rules that dictates the order of arithmetic operations in a mathematical expression. (Section 2.5)

OUTPUT PUNCTUATION   semicolons and commas used to pack output or to arrange it in fields. (Section 2.6)

SCREEN EDITING   correction of BASIC statements by combinations of cursor control and copying. (Section 2.7)

EDIT MODE   a special mode of operation that permits the correction of errors in program statements (TRS-80). (Section 2.7)

BASIC SYNTAX

LET   a keyword designating that an assignment of a variable value will follow. (Section 2.4)

INPUT   a keyword indicating that a variable value will be entered at the keyboard. (Section 2.4)

READ   a keyword indicating that a variable value will be found within the program. (Section 2.4)

DATA   a keyword preceding data values stored within the program. (Section 2.4)

REM   a keyword preceding remarks internal to the program. (Section 2.7)

NEW   an immediate command used to clear the memory of program instructions and data. (Section 2.2)

3 PREPARING A COMPLETE PROGRAM

3.1 INTRODUCTION TO PREPARING A COMPLETE PROGRAM

In this book our purpose is to help the reader develop the ability to use a computer as a problem-solving tool. This process—usually called **programming**—consists of two unique tasks. The first is the formulation of an unambiguous and logically correct procedure for solving a given problem, and the second is the translation of such a procedure into a form acceptable to a computer. The first of these tasks is far more challenging and intellectually demanding, while the second is more mechanical. Too often computer programming—and efforts to teach it—tend to concentrate on the second task. "A computer programmer is first and foremost a solver of problems."*

Developing the ability to use a computer as a problem-solving tool leads us to consider programming in a different context. The programming process becomes an opportunity to develop our skills in problem analysis. "With the advent of computers, the task of constructing and debugging programs has provided an ideal domain for students to develop their problem-solving skills."† Therefore, we suggest that programming has value that extends beyond the solution of specific problems with a

---

*Jean-Paul Tremblay and Richard D. Bunt, *An Introduction To Computer Science: An Algorithmic Approach.* (New York: McGraw-Hill, 1979,)p. 34.

†*Technology In Science Education—The Next Ten Years,* a publication prepared for the National Science Foundation, 1979, p. 23.

computer. We hope to develop an approach to programming that will emphasize this value. For the student of programming who lacks the prerequisite training in problem solving, "the approach and method of analysis are .. more significant than the details of the programming language."*

In this chapter, we will suggest a procedure for problem-solving that is specifically adapted to the development of a computer program. We have been influenced in this effort by the often-cited work of G. Polya.† Polya suggests a four-step sequence for solving problems:

Step 1 Understand the problem,
Step 2 Devise a plan,
Step 3 Carry out the plan, and
Step 4 Look back.

Each of the steps outlined by Polya is relevant to the preparation of a computer program. However, for purposes of program development, we will expand these four steps into seven steps. These seven steps, presented in Section 3.2, will more accurately reflect the problem-solving sequence as it applies to the development of a computer program.

3.2 A PROBLEM-SOLVING MODEL

We have identified two unique tasks for the programmer. Here we attempt to place these tasks in the context of a general problem-solving model. It is not important that you accept this specific model in all its details. However, you should develop some systematic scheme for attacking a problem. Such a scheme must defer coding until the solution procedure is at hand. Too often we hasten to the coding phase without having developed a procedure for solving the problem.

Our model consists of the following seven steps:

Step 1 Clarify the problem.   } Step 1 (Polya)
Step 2 Identify input and output.
Step 3 Develop a procedure for the solution of the   } Step 2 (Polya)
       problem.

---

*Richard Conway, David Gries, and David Wortman, *Structured Programming Using* PL/1 *and* SP/K. (Cambridge: Winthrop, 1977) preface by Wortman.

†G. Polya, *How To Solve It.* (Princeton, New Jersey: Princeton University Press, 1971), pp. 1-29.

Step 4 Hand check the procedure and revise as necessary.
Step 5 Code the algorithm.   } *Step 3* (Polya)
Step 6 Run the program with trial data, debugging as necessary.
Step 7 Refine and document the program.   } *Step 4* (Polya)

Steps 3 and 5 (algorithm development and coding) will receive the most attention in this text, since they are the tasks normally associated with programming.

3.3 THE NATURE OF AN ALGORITHM

Programming is a form of communication. Weinberg has written that "programming is at best a communication between two alien species,"* the two species being human kind and computers. But computer programming is also a form of communication between humans. The author of a program is communicating with those who will use the program and with those who will later modify it, which includes the author. Such communication is a matter of major concern to those professionally involved in programming.

We noted above that programming consists of two unique tasks, commonly called algorithm development and coding. An **algorithm**, which is a fundamental concept in computer science, can be informally described as a series of steps used to solve a problem. More formally, an algorithm has been defined as "a sequence of operations that, when executed, will produce a result and terminate in a finite amount of time."† An algorithm is the product of a systematic analysis of the problem to be solved. It is a document expressed in an English-like language that indicates the detailed operations to be followed in solving the given problem. The algorithm is then coded or translated into a language that the computer understands, such as BASIC or FORTRAN. Schematically, algorithm development can be depicted as follows:

Problem ⟶ Analysis ⟶ Algorithm ⟶ Coding ⟶ Program

In summary, an algorithm is a procedure for performing a particular task. The procedure must have the following characteristics:

---
*Gerald M. Weinberg, *The Psychology Of Computer Programming*, (New York: Van Nostrand Reinhold, 1971), p. 214.
†Schneider, Weingart, and Perlman, *An Introduction to Programming and Problem Solving with Pascal*, (New York: John Wiley & Sons, 1978), p. 20.

1 "Upon completing the execution of each step, we will always know the identity of the step to be executed next.

2 There is a single clearly defined starting point and one or more clearly defined stopping points.

3 In all cases, the algorithm will terminate after a finite number of steps.

4 The algorithm is composed of primitives whose meaning is clear and unambiguous to the person or machine executing it."*

Initial formulations or drafts of an algorithm usually do not conform to this definition, but an algorithm will have to be successively refined until it does conform. **Primitive operations** are "the most sophisticated and complex operations that the person or machine executing the algorithm is capable of directly performing and that do not have to be broken down into more basic steps." †

Since another purpose of this book is to assist the reader in developing the ability to code programs in the BASIC language, readers may wonder why we consider it necessary to use an **algorithmic language** as well. Several reasons exist. First of all, BASIC is not the only programming language and many readers of this book will eventually find themselves learning another language. The algorithmic approach is independent of BASIC and every other computer language (although it bears a resemblance to several of them). Once you develop the algorithmic technique, you can use it to write programs that you may then code in languages other than BASIC. Secondly, the algorithmic language is designed to accommodate the human mental process rather than computer hardware. It avoids the syntactic restrictions of various programming languages, which tend to complicate the process of problem-solving. As we will soon see, our algorithmic language has some fairly strict rules, but it is flexible and easy to use. Algorithmic languages are superior to English (or French, for that matter) because they are less ambiguous. We have chosen to use an algorithmic language because it "represents a compromise between the representational extremes of natural language (the language we speak and write) and . . . [a] programming language."‡

A summary of the elements of our algorithmic language, also called pseudocode, can be found in Appendix A. Readers familiar with other computer languages will detect the influence of such languages as Pascal, C and PL/1. §

---

*Schneider, et al., pp. 22-23.
† Schneider, et al., p. 22.
‡ Schneider, et al., p. 31.
§ The following works have significantly influenced our thinking on this matter and upon programming generally.
Brian W. Kernighan and P. J. Plauger, *The Elements of Programming Style,* Second edition (New York: McGraw-Hill, 1978).
Brian W. Kernighan and P. J. Plauger, *Software Tools,* (Boston: Addison-Wesley, 1976).

3.4 PSEUDOCODE ILLUSTRATED

To introduce our algorithmic language (which we will sometimes call AL for short), we solve a sample problem. Suppose we are to write a program that computes and displays the value of the area of a circle. We first look at our problem-solving model.

Step 1 is concerned with problem clarification. Although the stated problem is relatively straightforward, a programmer may have to make decisions about such things as the source and nature of input data, the output desired, the degree of precision desired, and so on. In the case of professional programmers, such decisions will probably be made in consultation with eventual users of the program. In this simple problem, we might ask what information is needed to compute the area of a circle. In the process of problem clarification, we find a formula that relates area to radius and the value of π (3.14 . . .). That formula is,

$$\text{area} = \pi r^2$$

where r represents the circle radius. It appears that our problem is to input values for π and the radius and then compute the area. Step 1 is complete when we understand the problem and select a name for our algorithm.

PSEUDOCODE RULE 1

The first statement in each algorithm both names it and marks its starting point. This name is written in upper case followed by a colon.

We choose CIRCLE: as the first statement in our algorithm.

Step 2 in our model concerns identification of input and output quantities. This identification includes choosing names for variables representing those quantities. This step is frequently referred to as identifying knowns and unknowns in the solution of mathematical problems. Knowns are the input; unknowns are the output. We recognize

---

Gerald M. Weinberg, *The Psychology of Computer Programming,* (New York: Van Nostrand Reinhold, 1971).
Kenneth L. Bowles, *Problem Solving Using Pascal,* (New York: Springer-Verlag, 1977)
Brian W. Kernighan and Dennis W. Ritchie, *The C Programming Language,* (Englewood Cliffs: Prentice-Hall, 1978).

that we must provide two knowns as input (π and r) in order to compute the unknown area. We select variable names that suggest the quantities they represent (AREA, RADIUS, and PI).

================= PSEUDOCODE RULE 2 =================

All variables in a program must be declared as to type and size. Variable names are written in upper case.

In our algorithmic language, there are two types of variables: numeric and string. The latter will be discussed in Chapter 8. For the present, we will limit ourselves to variables of standard size, temporarily ignoring size specifications. From the above, we can see that our program will require three variables, all numeric. Our algorithm now looks like this:

CIRCLE:
declare numeric AREA, RADIUS, PI

Step 3 requires that we develop a procedure to solve the problem. That is, we must arrive at the unknowns (output) by manipulating the knowns (input) in some fashion. As noted above, we must supply values for PI and RADIUS. Thereafter, the program should display the value of the area. We establish the value of PI, a constant in our program, by use of the algorithmic statement: set PI to 3.14. We generalize this with the following rule:

================= PSEUDOCODE RULE 3 =================

All constants to be used in a program receive their value by a "set . . . to . . ." statement.*

In our algorithmic language, there is only one input instruction and one output instruction.

---

*This statement will also be used to assign initial values to counters and accumulators.

PSEUDOCODE RULE 4

Input and output of variables is expressed generically, without reference to particular input/output devices.

The format is:

    get(VARIABLE)
    put(VARIABLE)
    put("MESSAGE")

For example:

    get (RADIUS)

means that the program should get a value for the variable RADIUS without indicating where that value should come from. Similarly,

    put(AREA)

means to display the value of AREA on some output device to be specified later. In addition to displaying the values of variables, the put instruction can be used to display messages. We can cause a program to identify itself and give directions to its user by printing messages such as:

    put("THIS PROGRAM COMPUTES AND DISPLAYS THE AREA OF A CIRCLE")
    put("ENTER THE RADIUS")
    put ()

Anything enclosed within quotation marks will be displayed on the output device exactly as written. The last of the three put statements prints a blank line.

In our algorithmic language both the get and put statements are generic; that is, they do not imply any specific input or output device. As a result, we are able to postpone making such device selections until we translate our pseudocode to BASIC.

Combining all these statements, our program expressed in algorithmic language is as follows:

    CIRCLE:
    declare numeric AREA, RADIUS, PI
    set PI to 3.14
    put("THIS PROGRAM COMPUTES AND DISPLAYS THE AREA OF A CIRCLE")
    put ()
    put ("ENTER RADIUS")
    get (RADIUS)

We now have all the known information (PI and RADIUS) in memory and are ready to compute the area.

=================== **PSEUDOCODE RULE 5** ===================

Variables will receive new values within the program by use of the arithmetic assignment statement ($\leftarrow$).

==

In our example, we write:

AREA $\leftarrow$ PI * RADIUS ^ 2

If we were to read this statement out loud, we would say, "AREA gets the value of PI times the RADIUS squared." If it is more convenient, you can use the equal sign (=) in place of the replacement symbol ($\leftarrow$) but the latter is preferred. Having computed the area, we are ready to display the result.

put("THE AREA IS",AREA)

Note the combination of message and numeric output.
To signify the end of the algorithm, we write "end."

=================== **PSEUDOCODE RULE 6** ===================

The end of every program unit is marked by "end."

==

Finally, our algorithm is complete.

```
CIRCLE:
declare numeric AREA, RADIUS, PI
set PI to 3.14
put("THIS PROGRAM COMPUTES AND DISPLAYS THE AREA OF A CIRCLE")
put()
put("ENTER RADIUS")
get(RADIUS)
AREA ← PI * RADIUS ^ 2
put("THE AREA IS", AREA)
end.
```

In Step 4 we indicated that it was necessary for us to handcheck the algorithm. That is, we should follow the steps in the algorithm and generate the output by hand calculation. As we follow the program, we note that the value of PI has been set. A message about the program's purpose has been displayed. The program then asks for a value for radius and accepts that value. Let us assume that we entered the value 5. The program computes AREA as:

AREA ← 3.14 * 5 ^ 2
AREA ← 78.5

The program then displays a message, as follows:

THE AREA IS 78.5

and terminates. We seem to be able to follow the program through and deliver the output.

So far our efforts in developing this small program are completely independent of all programming languages. At this point, we could decide to translate our algorithm into any programming language with which we were familiar (our Step 5). Because we are also concerned here with teaching readers to use the BASIC language, we will now address ourselves to the second part of the programming task, the translation of our algorithm into BASIC.

3.5 CODING THE ALGORITHM

To accomplish Step 5 in our problem solution, we must translate the algorithmic representation of our program into BASIC. It should be borne in mind that both the algorithmic version and the BASIC version to be created, are of equal importance. The BASIC version can be executed but the algorithmic version helps us to understand what our program is supposed to do. We can consider our algorithmic version to be a blueprint for the BASIC program to be created, a written record of our problem-solving procedure. This may seem to be a duplication of effort, but the independent value of both versions of a program will become apparent as we move on to more complicated problems. Next, we will take each line of our algorithm and translate it into BASIC adding commentary as required.

AL

CIRCLE:

BASIC

100 REM---CIRCLE 9-1-80

Since BASIC does not provide syntax for naming programs (except when saving them on disk or tape), we use a **REMARK** statement to indicate the program's name. We also follow the practice of including the date when the program was written. As you may recall, anything may follow the characters **REM** in a BASIC statement. This feature provides us with a simple way of inserting an explanation into the program itself. The contents of a **REM** statement are not scanned for syntactic validity.

AL

declare numeric AREA, RADIUS, PI

BASIC

110 REM   INPUT VARIABLES: PI, RADIUS
120 REM   OUTPUT VARIABLES: AREA

This instruction in our algorithm has no counterpart in the BASIC language. All variables are numeric unless their names end with a dollar sign, in which case they are string variables. We translate the statement for documentation purposes again by using the **REM** statement.

AL

set PI to 3.14

BASIC

130 PI = 3.14

In the BASIC language there is no separate syntax for initializing constants so we use the ordinary arithmetic assignment statement. We still prefer to use the different syntax in our algorithmic language because we believe that it enhances our understanding of the algorithm. The next three statements all display information and can be treated as a group.

AL

put("THIS PROGRAM COMPUTES AND DISPLAYS THE AREA OF A CIRCLE")
put()
put("ENTER RADIUS")

BASIC

140 PRINT "THIS PROGRAM COMPUTES AND DISPLAYS THE AREA OF A CIRCLE"
150 PRINT
160 PRINT "ENTER RADIUS"

The translation here is rather straightforward. The middle statement merely prints a blank line.

AL

get(RADIUS)

BASIC

170 INPUT RADIUS

By choosing to use the BASIC input statement, we have opted to retrieve the value of the radius from the keyboard.

AL

AREA ← PI * RADIUS ^ 2

BASIC

180 AREA = PI * RADIUS ^ 2

The translation here takes the form of a standard arithmetic assignment statement like those you have seen in the previous chapter.

AL

put ("THE AREA IS",AREA)

BASIC

190 PRINT "THE AREA IS",AREA

Here again the translation is simple.

AL

end.

BASIC

200 END

Our translation work has gone smoothly and now we can look at the BASIC version in its entirety:

```
100 REM---CIRCLE 9-1-80
110 REM     INPUT VARIABLES: PI, RADIUS
120 REM     OUTPUT VARIABLES: AREA
130 PI = 3.14
140 PRINT "THIS PROGRAM COMPUTES AND DISPLAYS THE AREA OF A CIRCLE"
150 PRINT
160 PRINT "ENTER RADIUS"
170 INPUT RADIUS
180 AREA = PI * RADIUS ^ 2
190 PRINT "THE AREA IS",AREA
200 END
```

We are now ready for Step 6, which is to run the program. A run with the trial data used earlier is shown:

```
RUN
THIS PROGRAM COMPUTES AND DISPLAYS THE AREA OF A CIRCLE
ENTER RADIUS
? 5
THE AREA IS 78.5
```

As a result of the agreement between this answer and the hand calculation plus the absence of error messages, we are reasonably certain that our program is working correctly.

3.6 COMPLETING THE JOB—DOCUMENTATION

Finally we are ready for Step 7—the refinement and documentation of our program. This example program is certainly of limited value, so we probably would not refine it further. *Documentation* refers to the production of explanatory material that helps a user understand the program. If we follow the procedure of variable identification within the program, we have already accomplished some of the documentation work. Further use of **REM** statements may be appropriate in more complex programs. It is helpful to conceive documentation as being of two types: internal and external. Documentation found within a program, is called **internal documentation**. Internal documentation usually takes the form of **REM** statements. But careful choice of variable names also contributes to internal documentation.

External documentation is found outside the program, usually in the form of written explanatory material. There are two types of external documentation, which we believe foster good programming habits: the **cross-reference table** and the **variable list**. A cross-reference table is a list of variable names with the line numbers of the statements in which the variables are used. A cross-reference table for CIRCLE appears below. For a small program such as this one, a cross-reference table can be easily created by hand. In Appendix D we describe a BASIC program which will create a cross-reference table by reading and processing your program.

CROSS-REFERENCE TABLE

AREA	180	190
PI	130	180
RADIUS	170	180

A variable list is a kind of program dictionary that defines each variable used in a program. A variable list must be created by hand. Its contents may differ depending upon the programming language used and other factors. We consider the following approach to be a minimal one. You may find it useful to add other attributes to the list.

Variable List for CIRCLE

AREA   The area of a circle to be computed by the program.

PI   A constant with the value 3.14.

RADIUS   A variable retrieved from the keyboard containing the value of the radius of a circle.

EXERCISE SET 3.1

1. Consider the completion of Step 1 (clarify the problem) and Step 2 (identify the input and output) for the following problems and list specific decisions you must make:
   (a) Write a program in algorithmic language that computes the volume of a sphere.
   (b) Write a program in algorithmic language that computes the area of a triangle.
   (c) Write a program in algorithmic language that computes the sales price of an item whose list price is reduced by 25 percent.

2. Develop algorithms for the solutions of problems 1(a), 1(b), and 1(c) based on your work in problem 1.

3. Code the algorithms in problem 2.

50 *Preparing a Complete Program*   Ch. 3

4. Complete the seven-step sequence begun in problem 1 by running and documenting the three programs.

5. Translate the following pseudocode into BASIC:
   (a) get(PRICE)   data source is the program
   (b) get(TAX,DISCOUNT)   data source is the keyboard
   (c) put("THE ANSWER IS",TOTAL)
   (d) set RATE to 0.05
   (e) VOLUME ← PI * RADIUS ^ 2 * HEIGHT
   (f) PRICE ←(LIST − DISCOUNT) * TAXRATE
   (g) put (PRICE,DISCOUNT)

6. Translate the following algorithms to BASIC:
   (a) TEMPERATURE:
      declare numeric FTEMP, CTEMP
      put("THIS PROGRAM CONVERTS FAHRENHEIT TO CENTIGRADE")
      put("ENTER THE FAHRENHEIT TEMPERATURE")
      get(FTEMP)
      CTEMP ← 5 * (FTEMP − 32)/9
      put("THE CENTIGRADE TEMPERATURE IS",CTEMP)
      end.

   (b) PRINCIPAL:
      declare numeric RTE, COMP, DEP, NBALANCE, YEARS
      put("THIS PROGRAM COMPUTES THE BALANCE ON AN INTEREST DRAWING DEPOSIT")
      put("ENTER DEPOSIT")
      get(DEP)
      put("ENTER ANNUAL INTEREST RATE")
      get(RTE)
      put("ENTER FREQUENCY OF COMPOUNDING PER YEAR")
      get(COMP)
      put("ENTER YEARS ON DEPOSIT")
      get(YEARS)
      NBALANCE ← DEP * (1+RTE/COMP) ^ (YEARS * COMP)
      put("THE NEW BALANCE IS", NBALANCE)
      end.

Review

We summarize the new terms and syntax introduced in this chapter.

ALGORITHM   a sequence of primitive operations that will produce a result in a finite number of steps. The algorithm is expressed in an English-like language. (Section 3.3)

PRIMITIVE OPERATION   a step in an algorithm whose meaning is clear, unambiguous and ready for execution without further refinement. (Section 3.3)

ALGORITHMIC LANGUAGE   the language used to express an algorithm. (Section 3.3)

PSEUDOCODE   another name for an algorithmic language. (Section 3.3 and 3.4)

INTERNAL DOCUMENTATION   explanatory material entered within the text of a program through the use of remark statements. (Section 3.6)

EXTERNAL DOCUMENTATION   explanatory material developed by the programmer to help a user understand and modify the program. (Section 3.6)

CROSS-REFERENCE TABLE   a form of external documentation, which includes the names of all variables used in a program and the line numbers in which they occur. (Section 3.6)

VARIABLE LIST   a form of external documentation that defines each variable used in the program. (Section 3.6)

4
SIMPLE LOOPS AND DECISIONS

4.1 INTRODUCTION TO LOOPS AND DECISIONS

Although the computer is extremely fast, we would probably not see it in such widespread use if each step in a process had to be separately programmed. For example, if a separate program had to be written to determine each customer account balance in a large business, the program size would soon become overwhelming. Fortunately, only the numerical entries differ from account to account. The process of arriving at a balance is the same for each account. Once the process is programmed it is only necessary to devise a method by which the program will repeat itself until all accounts have been analyzed. Such an internal repetition process within a program is called a *loop*. Without loops to perform repetitive processes our computing ability would be severely limited.

4.2 THE SIMPLE LOOP

We wish to develop a program that accepts as input the shelf price of an item, adds sales tax, and computes a total price. The pseudocode might look like this:

PSEUDOCODE

PRICE:
declare numeric SHELFP, TAXR, SALESP

```
set TAXR to 5
get (SHELFP)
SALESP ← SHELFP + SHELFP * TAXR / 100
put ("SALES PRICE IS $" SALESP)
end.
```

We code this as follows:

BASIC

```
100  REM -- PRICE---11-20-80
110  REM      INPUT VARIABLES: SHELFP
120  REM      LOCAL VARIABLES: TAXR
130  REM      OUTPUT VARIABLES: SALESP
140  LET TAXR = 5
150  INPUT SHELFP
160  LET SALESP = SHELFP + SHELFP * TAXR / 100
170  PRINT "SALES PRICE IS $"; SALESP
180  END
```

When we run this program with sample data we obtain:

? 25.40
SALES PRICE IS $26.67

If we want to use the computer as a sort of cash register at a checkout stand in a grocery store, we could modify this program to handle more than one item. We add a line 175:

175 GOTO 150

Here we encounter a new keyword **GOTO** which has the effect of transferring control from line 175 to line 150. Upon entry of a second price the computer will add tax and print out the sales price for the new item and again ask for a price. In fact, this process will continue indefinitely because we have produced an infinite loop from which we cannot escape. The *loop* portion of the modified program and its pseudocode follow:

PSEUDOCODE	BASIC
loop	
get (SHELFP)	150 INPUT SHELFP
. . .	. . .
end loop	175 GOTO 150

The pseudocode for this new structure consists of the terms *loop* and *end loop*. However, our inability to escape from the loop is unsatisfactory. We should be able to develop an instruction that will allow the program to terminate under the user's control. Let us change the program to provide a means of exiting the loop. We show the essential parts of this change in pseudocode and in BASIC.

```
PSEUDOCODE              BASIC
loop
    get (SHELFP)        150  INPUT SHELFP
    if (SHELFP < 0) break   155  IF SHELFP < 0 THEN 180
        .                       .
        .                       .
        .                       .
end loop                175  GOTO 150
                        180  ...
```

We have introduced a pseudocode expression

if (condition) [break]

that gets us out of the loop. Such an expression translates into BASIC as

IF condition **THEN** line number

The **IF-THEN** is BASIC syntax, which gives us a means of making a conditional transfer. The **GOTO** introduced earlier is an unconditional transfer. Study the relation between the pseudocode version and the BASIC version of the simple loop. Note that the "end loop" in pseudocode becomes a **GOTO** (unconditional transfer). The beginning of the simple loop is not specifically translated into code, because in the coded version both the loop beginning and its end are specified in the **GOTO** statement. The beginning of the loop is the destination of the **GOTO** statement.

A run of this program for three items might look like this:

```
? 25.40
SALES PRICE IS $26.67
? 5.60
SALES PRICE IS $5.88
? 9.20
SALES PRICE IS $9.66
? −1
```

We have managed to get out of the loop by entering a negative number. Note that statement 155 reads:

155 IF SHELFP < 0 THEN 180

This statement causes the computer to determine if the input value is less than zero. If it is less than zero, the program transfers control to line 180, which is the end statement. In the **IF-THEN** syntax a line number following **THEN** is interpreted as **GOTO** the line number. If the price is not less than zero, the program control passes to the next program statement (160 in this case). A negative value has been chosen to terminate the program since it is unlikely that the price of an item would be negative. A value that causes a program to exit a loop is called a *trailer value*.

The program above illustrates what we will call a **simple loop**. The rules for writing such a loop in pseudocode are given here.

PSEUDOCODE RULE 7

Simple loops will be delineated by the words loop and end loop. Between these markers are the pseudocode statements for the repetitive operations. The simple loop must contain an additional structure called a loop exit. The parts are shown below.

    loop
      . . .
      loop contents
      loop exit
    end loop

The loop exit can be anywhere in the loop depending upon the program.

PSEUDOCODE RULE 8

In pseudocode simple loops may be exited by use of the break statement—either as part of a logical if statement or standing alone.
    if (condition) [break]
          or
    [break]

4.3 THE IF-THEN STATEMENT

The **IF-THEN** statement used in the simple loop permits branching within a program depending upon the evaluation of a logical expression. This capability is central to the information processing power of computers. Computer programs can contain instructions that change the path through the program.

IF-THEN statements are really compound statements containing two segments: (1) a logical expression and (2) a dependent statement. Consider the following example:

	Logical Expression		Dependent Statement
155 IF	SHELFP < 0	THEN	180
160			
.			
.			
.			
180 END			

The logical expression involves a statement of the relative size of two quantities. In the BASIC syntax the logical expression is found between the **IF** and **THEN**. Typical logical expressions are:

WIDTH > LENGTH

X^2 + 2 * X < 3

Y > 0

SUM = 0

Note that every logical expression contains a relational operator (<, >, or =). A list of relational operators can be found in Section 4.4. In **IF-THEN** statements, the logical expression is evaluated in order to determine whether it is true or false. Only if the logical expression evaluates as true is the dependent statement executed. In the case **SHELFP < 0** in our example program, control passed to statement 180 when −1 was entered as **SHELFP**. In the previous three entries the condition **SHELFP < 0** evaluated as false and control passed to statement 160 (the next statement).

4.4 RELATIONAL OPERATORS

When we compare two variables and/or expressions, three results are possible:

1 The two may be equal,
2 The first may be greater than the second, or
3 The second may be greater than the first.

But while there are three alternatives for describing the relation between the two variables and/or expressions, a logical expression can only be evaluated in terms of two alternatives—true or false. For this reason relational operators (>, =, <) are combined to describe the two alternatives. Operator combinations and their complements are shown in Table 4-1. We will see the need to understand these complements when we begin to implement decision structures later in the chapter.

Table 4-1
Operators and Their Complements

Operator	Meaning	Complement
<	Less than	>=
>	Greater than	<=
=	Equal	<>
<>	Not equal	=
<=	Less than or equal to	>
>=	Greater than or equal to	<

EXERCISE SET 4.1

1. Translate the following pseudocode (fragments of programs) into BASIC.

    (a) loop
        get (ACCT,OBAL,PAYMENT)
        NBAL ← OBAL * (1 + SURCHG) − PAYMENT
        put (ACCT,OBAL,NBAL)
        OBAL ← NBAL
    end loop

    How would you describe this loop? What is being done in the loop?

    (b) loop
        get (SCORE)
        if (SCORE < 0) break
        ADJSCORE ← SCORE + (100 − SCORE) / 3
    end loop

    How would you describe this loop? What is being done?

2. Write programs in pseudocode to accomplish the following:

    (a) Determine the discounted prices of items reduced by 25% using a simple loop. Allow for an exit from the loop.

    (b) Determine the new balance of accounts subject to additional monthly charges, interest, and reduction by payments. Use a simple loop.

3. Identify the logical expression, relational operator, and the dependent statement in each of the following:
   (a) **150 IF Y <> 0 THEN 200**
   (b) **150 IF 3 * X + 1 > 10 THEN 300**
   (c) **150 IF X ^ 3 <= 1 THEN 100**
   (d) **150 IF PAYM < .1 * BAL THEN 200**
4. Translate the pseudocode fragments in problem 2 above into BASIC.
5. Write the correct pseudocode to accomplish the following:
   (a) Transfer out of a loop when Y is greater than ten.
   (b) Transfer out of a loop when $Y + 1$ is greater than or equal to X.
   (c) Transfer out of a loop when N is greater than your age.
   (d) Transfer out of a loop when the payment received (P) is at least $50.
   (e) Transfer out of a loop if X is less than or equal to ten.

4.5 VARIATIONS ON LOOPS—COUNTERS

We have considered terminating the simple loop by entry of a number (called a trailer value) in a given range. In the example in Section 4.4, this was accomplished by entering a negative price.

In some cases we may want the loop to repeat a specified number of times. To accomplish this we may enter a counter in the loop. Consider the following algorithm, which is designed to print the first nine integral multiples of five. An *integral multiple* is a product of the number and an integer.

```
MULTIPLE:
declare numeric NUMBER, MULTIPLE
set NUMBER to 0
loop
    increase NUMBER by 1
    if (NUMBER = 10) break
    MULTIPLE ← 5 * NUMBER
    put(MULTIPLE)
end loop
end.
```

The variable NUMBER serves as a counter. Its value on any pass through the loop represents the number of times the loop has been executed. Note that the counter was set at an initial value of zero before the loop was entered.

We have introduced a new bit of pseudocode above that involves the phrase "increase ... by ...". The BASIC translation of such an expression will be an arithmetic assignment statement with the named variable (NUMBER in this case) appearing on both sides of the equal sign. The exact translation:

PSEUDOCODE	BASIC
increase NUMBER by 1	**LET NUMBER = NUMBER + 1**

The BASIC translation of the entire program would look like this:

```
100 REM -- MULTIPLE 11-24-80
110 REM     INTERNAL VARIABLE: NUMBER
120 REM     OUTPUT VARIABLE: MULTIPLE
130 LET NUMBER = 0
140 LET NUMBER = NUMBER + 1
150 IF NUMBER = 10 THEN 190
160 LET MULTIPLE = 5 * NUMBER
170 PRINT MULTIPLE
180 GOTO 140
190 END
```

The use of counters in programs will always be accompanied by a process of initialization of these counters. The term initialize means to give a variable an initial value. Under ordinary circumstances, counters and accumulators are initialized by setting them to zero. Some computers will initialize all variables to zero automatically, but it is good practice to include the initialization step whether required or not. Thus, in our pseudocode version, whenever we use an "increase ... by ..." we will expect to find a "set ... to ..." earlier in the program. In Section 4.6 we will write the rule for this new pseudocode syntax.

In the example program above we used the statement **LET NUMBER = NUMBER + 1**. Writing this statement without the **LET** would give the appearance of an equation that does not make sense; that is,

NUMBER = NUMBER + 1

It is for this reason that we have stressed that the equal sign in arithmetic assignment statements signifies assignment (in this case reassignment) of value to a variable.

4.6 VARIATIONS ON LOOPS— ACCUMULATORS

Accumulators are frequently used in loops to carry a running total. Consider the problem of summing a specified number of positive integers. We write a program in pseudocode as follows:

Sec. 4.6 Variations on Loops—Accumulators

```
INTEGERSUM:
declare numeric LARGE, NUMBER, SUM
put("HOW MANY INTEGERS")
get(LARGE)
set NUMBER to 0
set SUM to 0
loop
   increase NUMBER by 1
   increase SUM by NUMBER
   if (NUMBER = LARGE) break
end loop
put("THE SUM OF THE FIRST" LARGE "INTEGERS IS" SUM)
end.
```

Note that this program treats SUM in much the same way as NUMBER. From the last section we recognize NUMBER as a counter. The variable SUM is known as an accumulator. It differs from a counter in that it is incremented by the value of a variable rather than a fixed amount each time the loop is executed. The accumulator should be initialized just as the counter was in Section 4.5. We translate the pseudocode above into BASIC:

```
100 REM -- INTEGERSUM 11-24-80
110 REM    INPUT VARIABLE: LARGE
120 REM    LOCAL VARIABLE: NUMBER
130 REM    OUTPUT VARIABLES: LARGE, SUM
140 PRINT "HOW MANY INTEGERS";
150 INPUT LARGE
160 LET NUMBER = 0
170 LET SUM = 0
180 LET NUMBER = NUMBER + 1
190 LET SUM = SUM + NUMBER
200 IF NUMBER = LARGE THEN 220
210 GOTO 180
220 PRINT "THE SUM OF THE FIRST ";LARGE;" INTEGERS"
230 PRINT "IS ";SUM;"."
240 END
```

Again note that the BASIC translation of the "increase ... by ..." syntax involves an expression with the quantity being incremented on both sides of the equal sign. The key lines here are 170 and 190.

```
170 LET SUM = 0
190 LET SUM = SUM + NUMBER
```

We should now recognize that the counter introduced in Section 4.5 is a special form of an accumulator. The pseudocode for counters and accumulators is described here.

62 Simple Loops and Decisions Ch. 4

PSEUDOCODE RULE 9

Counters and accumulators will be incremented using the expression,

increase VARIABLE by AMOUNT

or the expression

decrease VARIABLE by AMOUNT

where AMOUNT will usually be the value 1 for counters.

One more example may serve to illustrate the functions of counters and accumulators. To compute the arithmetic mean of a series of values we must compute the accumulated total of the values and divide that total by the number of values. Suppose we wish to enter the values to be averaged at the terminal. If we are using grades in the range from 0 to 100, we could use any negative value or any value above 100 for a trailer value. Remember that the trailer value serves to trigger the exit from the loop. Consider the following program in pseudocode form:

```
AVERAGE:
declare numeric NUMBER, SUM, AVERAGE, VLUE
set NUMBER to 0
set SUM to 0
loop
    get (VLUE)
    if (VLUE < 0) [break]
    increase NUMBER by 1
    increase SUM by VLUE
end loop
AVERAGE ← SUM / NUMBER
put (AVERAGE)
end.
```

This program translates into BASIC as follows:

```
100  REM -- AVERAGE 11-30-80
110  REM     INPUT VARIABLE: VLUE
120  REM     LOCAL VARIABLES: NUMBER, SUM
130  REM     OUTPUT VARIABLE: AVERAGE
140  LET NUMBER = 0
150  LET SUM = 0
160  INPUT VLUE
170  IF VLUE < 0 THEN 210
```

Sec. 4.6   Variations on Loops—Accumulators

```
180  LET NUMBER = NUMBER + 1
190  LET SUM = SUM + VLUE
200  GOTO 160
210  LET AVERAGE = SUM / NUMBER
220  PRINT AVERAGE
230  END
```

Below is a sample run of the program:

?23
?34
?45
?56
?67
?78
?−9
50.5

Note that the last value of **VLUE** is not a "real" data value. It differs from all the other values in that it is not intended to be accumulated into the sum, but merely to serve as a trailer value or a flag indicating that there is no more data to be read. For that reason, our program must test the value before, not after, it is added to the running total **SUM**. In this program, any negative value will serve as trailer value.

The exits illustrated above were triggered by entering a number in a specified range. This required the user to have knowledge of the program in order to select an appropriate trailer. However, we could arrange to exit by printing instructions to the user. As an example, consider a modification of our program **AVERAGE**. In this modification the user enters the data at the keyboard. The size of the data set is determined by the user terminating the data entry loop at the appropriate time.

```
AVERAGE:
declare numeric NUMBER, SUM, VLUE, AVERAGE
set NUMBER to 0
set SUM to 0
loop
   put ("NOW ENTER A VALUE")
   put ("A NEGATIVE VALUE WILL TERMINATE DATA INPUT")
   get (VLUE)
   if (VLUE < 0) [break]
   increase SUM by VLUE
   increase NUMBER by 1
end loop
AVERAGE ← SUM / NUMBER
put (AVERAGE)
end.
```

The addition of a single line of pseudocode has advised the user of the method of terminating the program. Some precautions are necessary to avoid accidental termination. More careful methods of screening responses may be necessary. For example, 99 can not serve as a trailer value if the range of expected input values is from 1 to 100. So too, any negative value cannot be interpreted as an end of data trailer if the range of expected input values runs from -100 to 100. In this case any value less than -100 can serve as a trailer or flag value.

EXERCISE SET 4.2

1. Write programs in pseudocode to accomplish the following:
   (a) Generate the first twelve integral multiples of 3; that is, 3, 6, . . . , 36, using a simple loop.
   (b) Generate the first N integral multiples of X, where N and X are positive integers to be entered at the keyboard. This is a generalization of the program requested in problem 1(a).
   (c) Generate the course averages for students each of whom has taken four examinations of equal weight. Use the number 9999 as a trailer value.
   (d) Modify example program **PRICE** (Section 4.2). The modified program should do the following:
      (1) Print the shelf price of each item without adding tax.
      (2) Keep a running total of the shelf prices.
      (3) Allow for a conditional transfer from the loop upon entry of a trailer value.
      (4) Total the shelf prices, add tax, and determine a total price.
      (5) Output the number of items purchased, the total shelf price, the total tax, and the total price.

2. Convert each of the pseudocode programs above into BASIC.

3. Convert the following pseudocode (program fragments) into BASIC.
   (a) put ("ENTER MARK FOR EACH COURSE USING THE CODE:")
       put ("A = 4")
       put ("B = 3")
       put ("C = 2")
       put ("D = 1")
       put ("F = 0")
       put ("TO STOP ENTER A NEGATIVE NUMBER")
       set GVLUE to 0
       set TCRED to 0

```
            loop
               get (MARK)
               if (MARK < 0) break
               get (CREDIT)
               increase GVLUE by MARK * CREDIT
               increase TCRED by CREDIT
            end loop
            GPA ← GVLUE / TCRED
            put ("GRADE POINT AVERAGE IS" GPA)
   (b)   get (NS)
         loop
            set TNUM to 0
            set TMARK to 0
            set GSUM to 0
            set NBR to 0
            loop
               get (MARK)
               if (MARK < 0) break
               increase TNUM by 1
               increase TMARK by MARK
            end loop
            AVE ← TMARK / TNUM
            put (AVE)
            increase GSUM by AVE
            increase NBR by 1
            if (NBR = NS) break
         end loop
         CLAVE ← GSUM / NBR
         put (CLAVE)
```

4. Identify the counters and accumulators in problem 3(b).
5. Construct the additional pseudocode to make complete programs of the fragments in problem 3.

4.7 DECISION STRUCTURES— SINGLE ALTERNATIVE

One factor that contributes to the utility of computers is their ability to perform different tasks depending upon specific conditions. For example, it is common for a program to perform a logical test and, as a result, select one of several alternative courses of action. Those parts of programs, which perform such steps, are commonly called **decision structures** or control structures because they govern the flow of control within a program. They are also the most common locus of confusion and error within a program. All computer languages provide some facility for decision structures; but some provide a variety of well-designed structures while others provide only a few awkward ones. Unfortunately, BASIC is in the latter category. For that reason we present some basic generic decision structures in our algorithmic language and demonstrate how they can be translated into BASIC.

While we have stressed using the **IF-THEN** statement to terminate a simple loop, we will probably find it used more frequently to select a particular path within the program. To understand its use in this manner we introduce some new terminology.

Single Alternative Decision Structure

A program segment that causes a group of statements to be executed only if a certain condition exists.

We introduced single alternative decision structures at the end of Section 4.3. At that point we did not show their relation to the remainder of a program. A single alternative decision structure in a real-life situation might serve as an example. Suppose you receive these instructions: "On your way home, stop at the pizza parlor. If it is open, bring home a large pepperoni pizza and a pint of tossed salad."

No alternative action has been specified. You would assume that if the pizza parlor is closed, you will proceed home in the normal manner. You would also assume that after buying the pizza (if the parlor is open) you are to proceed home in the normal manner. Buying the pizza and the salad is the single alternative that delays your movement home. We can represent such a structure in the following manner.

```
if (pizza parlor is open)
    [buy a large pepperoni pizza
    buy a pint of tossed salad]      (task if condition is true)
continue home
```

Although this is the most natural way to consider the problem, the BASIC syntax we are using does not support this structure (at least without introducing multiple statements on a line). Recall that we can use a transfer in conjunction with the **IF-THEN** statement. If our logical condition is false we need to transfer over the true tasks. But the transfer occurs only if the logical condition is true. Thus, we need to use the complement of the original relational operator in the logical expression to effect the proper transfer. If BASIC had a larger vocabulary, we might be able to make the following translation:

```
100  IF PIZZA PARLOR IS NOT OPEN THEN 130
110  BUY A LARGE PEPPERONI PIZZA
120  BUY A PINT OF TOSSED SALAD
130  CONTINUE HOME
```

Assuming that we could execute such a program, the fragment above should do the job. But we have had to change the logical condition. The logical condition "PIZZA PARLOR IS NOT OPEN" is the complement of "PIZZA PARLOR IS OPEN". We are suggesting that the more logical order, in which the original true tasks follow the **IF-THEN,** can be retained by choosing the complement of the relational operator.

We have encountered the first case in which the BASIC translation is not a straightforward conversion of the algorithmic representation. We will tolerate this inconvenience in coding because other structured languages, as well as advanced versions of BASIC, do permit a more literal translation of the structure.

================ PSEUDOCODE RULE 10 ================

Single alternative decision structures will be indicated by one of the following:

    if (condition) [statement]
           or
    if (condition)
      [. . .
      block of statements
      . . .]

When a task consists of more than one statement, the entire task is enclosed within a pair of square brackets. Single statement tasks may be so enclosed if you wish.

_____

Consider another example. At a certain point in a program, if the variable X is greater than zero, we are to set the variable Y equal to zero and increment the counter N by one. We may write:

PSEUDOCODE	BASIC
if $(X > 0)$	200 IF X <= 0 THEN 230
[Y ← 0	210 LET Y = 0
N ← N + 1]	220 LET N = N + 1
. . . continue	230 (NEXT INSTRUCTION)

The complement of $>$ has been used in the logical expression in the program.

There is another case in which the more logical order may be retained. If the true tasks consist of a single instruction, then we may write:

if (logical condition) [true task]

and translate this almost literally. Consider the following examples:

1   PSEUDOCODE
if (X > 0) [put ("POSITIVE")]

BASIC
200 IF X > 0 THEN PRINT "POSITIVE"

2   PSEUDOCODE
if (X < Y) [Z ← X + Y]

BASIC
200 IF X < Y THEN LET Z = X + Y

3   PSEUDOCODE
if (AREA > 0) [put (AREA)]

BASIC
200 IF AREA > 0 THEN PRINT AREA

4   PSEUDOCODE
if (A < B)
  [if (B < C)]
    [L ← A]

BASIC
200 IF A < B THEN IF B < C THEN LET L = A

In each case, line 200 contains the entire single alternative decision structure. The correct relational operator is used (not its complement). Additional true tasks may be added as multiple statements providing the permitted line length is not exceeded. Multiple statements may be placed on a single line providing the proper symbol of separation is used. This symbol is the colon. For example, we may write:

120 PRINT X: PRINT Y: PRINT Z

All three instructions will be executed in the order written. If one of the instructions, such as **PRINT X**, is an **IF-THEN** statement, the subsequent instructions on the line will be executed only if the logical expression evaluates to true. For example, consider the following:

120 IF X > 0 THEN PRINT X: PRINT Y: PRINT Z

Suppose **X** = −1. Then the program would not execute **PRINT X**. Furthermore, the instructions **PRINT Y** and **PRINT Z** will not be executed. However, if **X** = 1 (or any positive number) **X**, **Y**, and **Z** will all be printed. There are three true tasks.

Consider the following line of BASIC:

200 IF X > 0 THEN PRINT "POSITIVE": LET Q = 1

The true task in this structure consists of the statements: **PRINT "POSITIVE"** and, **LET Q = 1**. They constitute a block of statements that will be treated as a unit. Both or neither will be executed.

4.8 DECISION STRUCTURES— DOUBLE ALTERNATIVES

The double alternative decision structure allows a second set of tasks to be introduced. This structure is defined as follows:

Double Alternative Decision Structure

A program segment that causes one group of statements to be executed if a certain condition is true. A second group of statements is executed if the condition is false.

Returning to our example, suppose we receive these instructions: "On your way home stop at the pizza parlor and buy a large pepperoni pizza and a pint of tossed salad. If the pizza parlor is closed, get a frozen pizza and a head of lettuce at the grocery store."

We may represent our alternatives as follows:

```
if (pizza parlor is open)
    [buy a large pepperoni pizza      } true
     buy a pint of tossed salad]        task
else
    [go to the grocery store
     buy a frozen pizza               } false
     buy a head of lettuce]             task
continue home
```

We can partially solve the problem of programming these instructions by taking the complement of the relational operator as before. However, we must be careful not to stop at both the pizza parlor and the grocery store. We need an unconditional transfer to our route home once we have completed our business at the pizza parlor. Consider the following:

100 IF PIZZA PARLOR IS NOT OPEN THEN 140
110 BUY A LARGE PEPPERONI PIZZA
120 BUY A PINT OF TOSSED SALAD
130 GOTO 170

140 GOTO THE GROCERY STORE
150 BUY A FROZEN PIZZA
160 BUY A HEAD OF LETTUCE
170 CONTINUE HOME

Line 130 is very important. It is the unconditional transfer referred to in Section 4.2. It assures that we buy only one pizza.

PSEUDOCODE RULE 11

Double alternative decision structures will be indicated by the following pseudocode:

>   if (condition)
>   [. . .
>   true task
>   . . .]
>   else
>   [. . .
>   false task
>   . . .]

Whenever the true task and/or the false task consists of more than a single statement, those statements must be grouped together by enclosing them within a pair of square brackets. Tasks consisting of single statements may also be so enclosed if you wish.

Consider an example involving variables. At a certain point in our program we test X. If it is less than zero, we increment it by one. If it is greater than or equal to zero, we decrement it by one and increment Y by one. We write:

PSEUDOCODE	BASIC
if $(X < 0)$	200 IF X >= 0 THEN 230
$\quad[X \leftarrow X + 1]$	210 LET X = X + 1
	220 GOTO 250
else	
$\quad[X \leftarrow X - 1$	230 LET X = X - 1
$\quad Y \leftarrow Y + 1]$	240 LET Y = Y + 1
	250 (NEXT INSTRUCTION)

As with single alternative decision structures, it may be possible to retain the more logical order without inverting the relational operator. We rewrite the problem above as follows:

200 IF X < 0 THEN LET X = X + 1: GOTO 230
210 LET X = X − 1
220 LET Y = Y + 1
230 (NEXT INSTRUCTION)

Note the transfer over the false task. This technique is limited to cases where the true tasks can be fitted on a single line with an unconditional transfer.

EXERCISE SET 4.3

1. Convert the following statements to pseudocode:
   (a) Compare Y to L. If Y is greater than L, then let L take on the value of Y.
   (b) Compare X to 0. If X is greater than 0, then add X to the accumulator T and increment K by 1.
   (c) Compare X to 0. If X is less than 0, then add X to the accumulator S and increment N by 1. Otherwise, decrement N by 1.
   (d) Compare $X1$ to $X2$. If $X1$ is greater than $X2$, then interchange the values of $X1$ and $X2$. (Hint: This process is an essential step in ordering numbers. You will need to introduce an additional variable to accomplish the interchange.)

2. Code the algorithms developed in problem 1.

3. Convert the following pseudocode to BASIC:
   (a) if (PAYM > .1 * BAL)
   　　　[put ("THANK YOU")]
   　　else
   　　　[put ("INSUFFICIENT PAYMENT")]
   (b) if (X > B)
   　　　[X ← X − 1
   　　　 B ← B + 1]
   (c) if (X > 0)
   　　　[Y ← 1
   　　　 Z ← 0]
   　　else
   　　　[X ← X + 1]

4. Identify the true task(s) and false task(s) in each of the exercises in problem 3.

Review

We summarize the new terms and the BASIC syntax introduced in this chapter.

DECISION STRUCTURE program segments containing alternate paths. The path taken is determined by the evaluation of a logical expression that heads the structure. (Section 4.7)

SIMPLE LOOP a series of instructions that is repeated by placement of a combination of conditional **IF-THEN** and unconditional **GOTO** transfers. (Section 4.2)

BASIC SYNTAX

GOTO (line number) a BASIC keyword that causes an unconditional transfer to the designated line number. (Section 4.2)

IF-THEN BASIC keywords that connect a logical expression with a dependent BASIC statement. When the logical expression evaluates as true, the dependent statement is executed. When the logical expression evaluates as false, control passes to the next statement in the program. The **IF-THEN** statement is written as follows:

    IF logical expression **THEN** dependent statement (Section 4.2)

5
INDEXED LOOPS

5.1 INTRODUCTION TO INDEXED LOOPS

The conditional transfer discussed in Chapter 4 provides a means for terminating a simple loop. The indexed loop can be considered a more sophisticated structure for handling repetitive processes within a program. It has certain characteristics, a built-in counter and automatic termination, that make it very useful in many applications.

The **indexed loop** is more complex than other structures we have encountered so far. To specify the behavior of the loop we introduce a variable called the **loop index** (or **loop control variable**) and three values of that variable. The three values are the **initial value of the loop index** (value when the loop is first entered), the **final value of the loop index** and the **step value** (the amount by which the index is incremented or decremented on each pass through the loop). We introduce the loop structure in pseudocode first.

PSEUDOCODE RULE 12

Indexed loops will be specified by the following structure:
loop while INDEX goes from START to STOP by STEP
   . . .
   loop contents
   . . .
end loop

The pseudocode above displays the loop index and the three values critical to the loop control. Several instructions are implied in the indexed loop. When the loop is entered, INDEX receives the value of START. If START is already greater than STOP, the loop contents are not executed at all and execution continues with the first statement after the end loop statement. When "end loop" is encountered, the value of STEP is added to INDEX. The value of INDEX is then compared with the value of STOP (the final value of the loop index). If the value of the index exceeds the specified end value (or is less than it in case the loop index proceeds from high to low values), execution of the loop terminates and the statement after end loop is executed. Otherwise, execution of the loop contents is repeated.

As an example, suppose we encounter the following loop in pseudocode.

```
loop while INDEX goes from 1 to 3 by .5
    put (INDEX)
end loop
```

Upon entry into this loop, INDEX will be assigned its starting value of 1. The pseudocode "put (INDEX)" will then result in the output of the value 1. When "end loop" is encountered INDEX will be increased by .5 and will then have the value of 1.5. Since 1.5 is not greater than 3 (the final value of INDEX) we will repeat the loop contents, which call for the output of the current value of INDEX (1.5). We then increment 1.5 by .5 to get 2, compare 2 with 3 and repeat the loop contents. This process continues until INDEX receives the value 3.5 at the end of the loop. Exit of the loop then occurs. The output of this loop is the series of numbers:

1, 1.5, 2, 2.5, 3

The result above could have been obtained with the following simple loop:

```
set INDEX to 1
loop
    put (INDEX)
    increase INDEX by .5
    if (INDEX > 3) break
end loop
```

The corresponding simple loop requires six lines of pseudocode. Furthermore, its operation is less clear than the indexed loop.

5.2 THE INDEXED LOOP IN BASIC

Consider again the example above:

```
loop while INDEX goes from 1 to 3 by .5
    put (INDEX)
end loop
```

We translate the header statement in the loop as follows:

140 FOR INDEX = 1 TO 3 STEP .5

The terminator statement translates into:

160 NEXT INDEX

Here we see a new keyword pattern

FOR . . . TO . . . STEP

and a new keyword

NEXT

The indexed loop in BASIC is called a **FOR-NEXT** loop, naming the words that serve as its boundaries. The number of times the **FOR-NEXT** loop is executed is determined by the values of START, STOP and STEP. We may write an equation for this number as follows:

Number of repetitions = (STOP − START) / STEP + 1

If the value calculated for the number of repetitions is not an integer, ignore the decimal part of the value.

As we shall see later, this is the maximum number of repetitions. It is possible to include a conditional transfer in the loop, which causes premature exit from the loop.

It is permissible to omit the reference to a step value in the **FOR-NEXT** loop. Doing so causes the computer to use a value of one as the step value. Values assumed for unspecified quantities are referred to as default values. We say that the default step size is one. If the loop index is to be incremented by one, we need not specify a step size. Default values are for the convenience of the programmer and reflect most commonly used values.

Several precautions are necessary when using **FOR-NEXT** loops:

1   **FOR-NEXT** loops should be entered at the top; that is, at the **FOR . . . TO . . . STEP** statement. This means that transfers into the interior of a loop, from either above or below the loop, should be avoided. Doing so would bypass the step that initializes the loop counter. Some dialects of BASIC may permit such a transfer, but the results will be unpredictable. The PET, the TRS-80 and the Apple will permit the transfer, but an error message will be generated when the **NEXT** statement is encountered because the associated **FOR** statement had not been previously encountered.

2   Operations that alter the value of the loop index within a loop should also be avoided. Many dialects of BASIC permit such an action, but the results are unpredictable. The PET, the TRS-80 and the Apple are in this category. This type of procedure may well create an infinite loop. Here is a sample program to illustrate:

```
140 FOR I = 1 TO 10
150 PRINT I
160 LET I = I - 1
170 NEXT I
```

Here statement 160 modifies the value of the loop index thus producing an infinite loop.

3   Finally, care should be taken so that a **FOR-NEXT** loop is not entered accidentally. American National Standards Institute specifications for minimal BASIC indicate that a loop should not be entered at all if the beginning value of a loop index is already past the ending value of the loop index as shown:

200 FOR I = 4 TO 1

Most versions of BASIC comply with this specification and such a loop will not be entered at all. However, the PET, the TRS-80, and the Apple will execute such a loop once. In this respect these dialects of BASIC provide a loop that is much like the FORTRAN DO loop. An **IF . . . THEN** statement just before the header statement can prevent accidental entry into the indexed loop.

5.3 USING THE LOOP INDEX

There are numerous situations in which we need to count the number of repetitions of a loop or we need to identify data by its order of presentation. The loop index can serve this purpose without introducing an additional counter as we were required to do with the simple loop. As an example, consider the following problem:

Write a program that will read six successive yearly values of population from a data line and print these values along with an identifying year. The data starts in 1973. We display a pseudocode solution first.

```
POPULATION:
declare numeric YEAR, POPULATION
put ("YEAR", "POPULATION")
loop while YEAR goes from 1973 to 1978
   get (POPULATION)
   put (YEAR, POPULATION)
end loop
end.
```

Converted to code this becomes:

```
100 REM -- POPULATION 12/5/80
110 REM -- INPUT VARIABLE: P
120 REM -- OUTPUT VARIABLES: YEAR, P
130 PRINT "YEAR", "POPULATION"
140 FOR YEAR = 1973 TO 1978
150 READ P
160 PRINT YEAR, P
170 NEXT YEAR
180 DATA 49500, 50100, 51210, 52225, 51875, 51760
190 END
```

The program output appears below:

YEAR	POPULATION
1973	49500
1974	50100
1975	51210
1976	52225
1977	51875
1978	51760

The loop index is also available to serve as an independent variable in an equation. Consider the following problem:

Write a program that generates points on the curve $Y = 2 * X^2 + X - 3$ from $X = 1$ to $X = 7$. Pseudocode and BASIC versions are shown below.

```
X-Y PAIRS:
declare numeric X, Y
put ("X-VALUE", "Y-VALUE")
loop while X goes from 1 to 7
   Y ← 2 * X^2 + X - 3
   put (X, Y)
end loop
end.
```

```
100 REM -- X-Y PAIRS
110 REM -- OUTPUT VARIABLES: I, Y
120 PRINT "X-VALUE", "Y-VALUE"
130 FOR X = 1 TO 7
140 LET Y = 2 * X^2 + X - 3
150 PRINT X,Y
160 NEXT X
170 END
```

The output is:

X-VALUE	Y-VALUE
1	0
2	7
3	18
4	33
5	52
6	75
7	102

If we were to plot these points on a set of X-Y axes, we would see the shape of the curve Y = 2 * X ^ 2 + X − 3 in the interval from X = 1 to X = 7.

5.4 SUMMATION NOTATION

Another use of the **FOR-NEXT** loop is to translate mathematical **summation notation** into calculated values. We frequently see expressions such as:

$$\Sigma X$$

This is mathematical notation in which the Greek letter sigma (Σ) means add. The combination of sigma with a variable means add together all indicated values of the variable X. Suppose X represents the scores a student receives on tests in a course. Then ΣX designates the total score on all tests taken. We could designate the total as XSUM.

Let us generate the average (or mean) score on a set of tests. That is, we will evaluate the expression

XMEAN = XSUM / NTEST

where NTEST is the number of tests taken. The following pseudocode indicates a possible solution to the problem.

```
MEANGRADE:
declare numeric I, X, XSUM, XMEAN, NTEST
set XSUM = 0
get (NTEST)
loop while I goes from 1 to NTEST
    get (X)
    increase XSUM by X
end loop
XMEAN ← XSUM / NTEST
```

put ("AVERAGE GRADE IS ";XMEAN)
end.

This translates into:

```
100 REM -- MEANGRADE 12/5/80
110 REM -- INPUT VARIABLES: X, NTEST
120 REM -- LOCAL VARIABLES: I, XSUM
130 REM -- OUTPUT VARIABLE: XMEAN
140 LET XSUM = 0
145 READ NTEST
150 FOR I = 1 TO NTEST
160 READ X
170 LET XSUM = XSUM + X
180 NEXT I
190 LET XMEAN = XSUM / NTEST
200 PRINT "AVERAGE GRADE IS ";XMEAN
210 DATA 5,70,84,92,81,76
220 END
```

Note that the summation of X occurs in line 170 through the use of the accumulator **XSUM**. You should enter and **RUN** this program.

In some cases the permitted values to be summed over are indicated explicitly on the summation sign. For example,

$$\sum_{i=1}^{5} i$$

means add together all values obtained when **i** runs from 1 to 5. Thus,

$$\sum_{i=1}^{5} i = 1 + 2 + 3 + 4 + 5 = 15$$

The following pseudocode fragment will express this result.

set ISUM to 0
loop while I goes from 1 to 5
   increase ISUM by I
end loop
put (ISUM)

You will often see loop indices given as the letters I, J, K, L, M, or N. This follows standard mathematical usage. These loop indices usually assume only integral (whole number) values. The FORTRAN language has taken advantage of this usage by requiring a class of integer variables to have names beginning with one of these letters.

EXERCISE SET 5.1

1. Write header and terminator statements in BASIC for indexed loops with the following characteristics:

Loop Index	Start	Stop	Step
COUNT	2	50	2
J	10	−5	−1
NUMBER	5	10	0.2
I	2	49	2

    Determine the number of times each of these loops will be executed.

2. Construct pseudocode fragments to solve the following problems:
    (a) Read the balance of 100 different accounts receivable that are entered on data lines. Print out a number that identifies each account by its place in the data list, print out each account balance, and accumulate the total accounts receivable for the 100 accounts.
    (b) Sum all the integers from 1 to 25 inclusive.
    (c) Print out the first twelve multiples of 5 (a multiple of a number is a product of the number and an integer). First multiples of a number are formed by multiplying the number by one, then by two, etc.
    (d) Find the average of all even numbers from 16 to 38 inclusive.

3. Convert the pseudocode fragments in problem 2 to BASIC program fragments.

4. Write BASIC program fragments that will evaluate the dependent variable Y for the specified values of X in the following equations. Print the X and Y pairs in columns.
    (a) $Y = 3 * X + 7$ (X ranges from 1 to 7 in unit steps)
    (b) $Y = X - 4$ (X ranges from −4 to 5 in steps of .5)
    (c) $Y = X \wedge 2 - 3$ (X ranges from −8 to 8 in steps of 2)

5. Write **FOR-NEXT** loops to evaluate the dependent variable in the following equations:

    (a) $$Y = \Sigma X \wedge 2$$

    where the values of **X** are on data lines. Assume there are eleven values of **X**.

    (b) $$Y = \sum_{I=1}^{5} I \wedge 3$$

(c) $$Y = \sum_{i=1}^{6} I\text{\textasciicircum}2$$

6. Write program fragments to accomplish the following:
   (a) Print the integers from 7 to −3 starting with 7.
   (b) Print every fifth year starting with 1900 and ending with 1980.

7. Enter and **RUN** the following program fragments.
   (a) ```
       100 FOR I = 1 TO 5
       110 PRINT I
       120 NEXT I
       130 PRINT I
       ```
   (b) ```
       100 FOR I = 2 TO 3 STEP .2
       110 PRINT I
       120 NEXT I
       130 PRINT I
       ```
   Observe the final value of the loop index (printed by line 130).

8. Verify the validity of the following relation:

   $$\sum_{i=1}^{n} i\text{\textasciicircum}2 = n * (n + 1) * (2n + 1) / 6$$

   for values of **n** from 1 to 7.

   Hint: Use a loop to evaluate the left side. Program the equation on the right side for each **n** and compare results.

5.5 LOOPS WITH CONDITIONAL TRANSFERS

In certain applications, it may be necessary to transfer out of a **FOR-NEXT** loop before the loop index reaches the end value. For example, the loop may be accumulating a sum whose value is to be used to terminate the loop. Or we may be using the loop to read and print data sets of variable length that are terminated by a trailer value.

As an example consider the following problem. We are to develop pseudocode that reads account balances, determines the number of accounts, and accumulates the balance payable. Assume a negative number is used as a trailer. The total number of accounts payable will not exceed 100. Here is a solution.

82 Indexed Loops   Ch. 5

```
ACCTPAYABLE:
declare numeric BAL, TBAL, I
set TBAL to 0
loop while I goes from 1 to 100
    get (BAL)
    if (BAL < 0) break
    increase TBAL by BAL
end loop
put (I— 1;" ACCOUNTS WITH A TOTAL BALANCE OF ";TBAL)
```

Can you see why $I - 1$ is the number of accounts payable rather than I?

5.6 LOOPS TO CALCULATE AREA

We consider one problem that illustrates the power of the **FOR-NEXT** loop in numerical analysis. Suppose we are asked to evaluate the area under a curve (a typical problem in introductory calculus). To illustrate the technique of a computer solution we will select an area for which the value can be determined by elementary means.

Consider the equation $Y = .5 * X + 2$. This equation can be represented by the straight line in Figure 5.1.

If we are asked to find the area under the curve between $X = 1$ and $X = 5$, we would be concerned with the shaded area in the Figure 5.2.

That area is a trapezoid of height 4 and average base 3.5. Thus, the area must

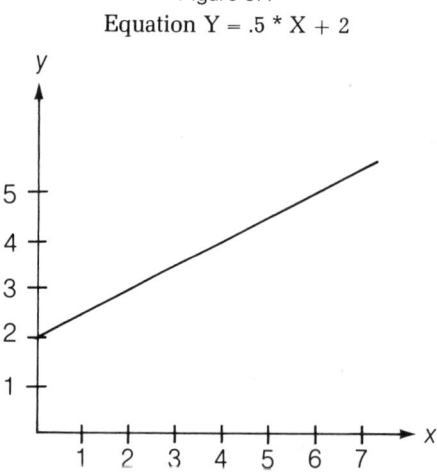

Figure 5.1
Equation $Y = .5 * X + 2$

Figure 5.2
Area Under Curve Between X = 1 and X = 5

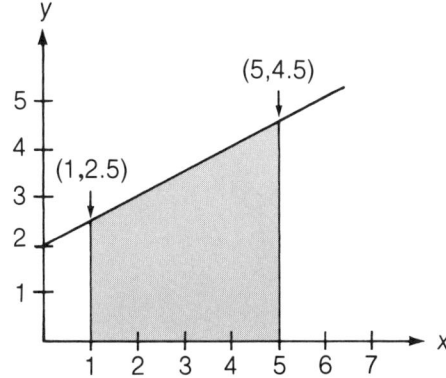

be (4)(3.5) = 14 units. To evaluate this by computer, we can subdivide the area into rectangles as shown in Figure 5.3.

The area of each rectangle is obtained by multiplying its base width (1) by its height. But the height is the value of *Y* corresponding to the left corner of the rectangle. This method would yield:

$$\text{Area} = 1(2.5) + 1(3) + 1(3.5) + 1(4)$$
$$= 2.5 + 3 + 3.5 + 4 = 13 \text{ square units}$$

The discrepancy between this and the correct answer (14) results from the neglect of the small triangles shaded in Figure 5.3. We could reduce this error by using

Figure 5.3
Area Subdivided into Rectangles 1 Unit Wide

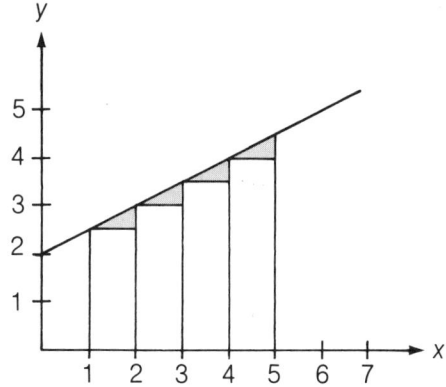

narrower rectangles. Suppose we choose the rectangles to be .5 units wide. Since the arithmetic is getting complicated, we can write a program to do the calculation of the new area.

```
AREA:
declare numeric I, X, HEIGHT, WIDTH, RECT, AREA
set AREA to 0
set WIDTH to .5
loop while I goes from 1 to 8
    X ← 1 + (I − 1) * WIDTH
    HEIGHT ← .5 * X + 2
    RECT ← HEIGHT * WIDTH
    increase AREA by RECT
end loop
put ("APPROXIMATION TO AREA IS ";AREA)
end.
```

When we convert this to code and run it we find an approximation to the area of 13.5. The situation is depicted in Figure 5.4.

In this approximation we have neglected the eight small triangles shaded in Figure 5.4. These triangles apparently have a total area of .5 square units. This suggests that we might be able to continue to improve our computer approximation by increasing the number of rectangles. Perhaps we can generalize this program to allow a variable number of rectangles. Consider the following:

100 REM -- AREA 12/9/80
110 REM -- INPUT VARIABLES: NUMRECT
120 REM -- LOCAL VARIABLES: I, WIDTH, X, HEIGHT, RECT
130 REM -- OUTPUT VARIABLE: AREA

Figure 5.4
Area Subdivided into Rectangles ½ a Unit Wide

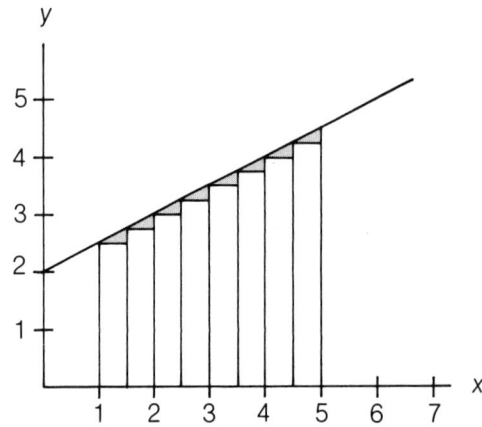

```
140 PRINT "ENTER THE NUMBER OF RECTANGES"
150 INPUT NUMRECT
170 LET AREA = 0
160 LET WIDTH = 4 / NUMRECT
180 FOR I = 1 TO NUMRECT
190 LET X = 1 + (I − 1) * WIDTH
200 LET HEIGHT = .5 * X + 2
210 LET RECT = HEIGHT * WIDTH
220 LET AREA = AREA + RECT
230 NEXT I
240 PRINT "APPROXIMATION TO AREA IS  ";AREA
250 END
```

This is a coded and generalized form of the preceding algorithm. As we increase the value of **NUMRECT** we should see the approximation approach fourteen.

We have gone to a lot of work to approximate the answer to a problem whose answer is already known. However, it might not be possible to calculate the area under more complicated curves so easily. Our general method will work in such cases. Consider the following problem:

Calculate the area under the curve $Y = -X^2 + 16$ from $X = 0$ to $X = 4$. We can use the program above to solve this problem by simply changing lines 190 and 200 to read

```
190 LET X = 0 + (I − 1) * WIDTH
200 LET HEIGHT = −X * X + 16
```

The area being evaluated is shown in Figure 5.5. The exact value of this area is 42⅔ units. Run the program to find an approximation to this area. Increase **NUMRECT** and note that the approximation improves.

Figure 5.5
Area Under the Curve $Y = -X^2 + 16$ from $X = 0$ to $X = 4$

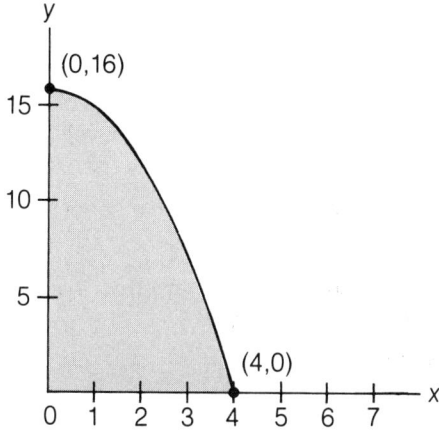

A word of warning concerning the evaluation of areas may be in order. If the expression being evaluated (Y in our case) does not stay positive over the range of X, the value obtained for the area does not have the interpretation that it has been given above.

EXERCISE SET 5.2

1. Write **FOR-NEXT** loops with conditional transfers to accomplish the following:
   (a) Read data values from a data line and terminate when a data value is greater than 100.
   (b) Read data values from a data line, accumulate them, and terminate when the sum is greater than 200.
   (c) Evaluate the expression $Y = 2*X + 3$ as X ranges from -5 to 20. Terminate the evaluation if Y gets larger than 25.

2. Develop **FOR-NEXT** loops that will approximate the area under the following curves. Include a statement to print the approximate value of the area.
   (a) $Y = X^3 + 1$ from $X = 0$ to $X = 4$
   (b) $Y = -2*X + 12$ from $X = 0$ to $X = 3$
   (c) $Y = -X^2 + 8$ from $X = -2$ to $X = 2$

3. Develop a program to evaluate areas by using the loop step value as the rectangle width.

4. Further generalize program **AREA** to allow the starting and ending values of X to be designated at the keyboard.

5. Code program ACCTPAYABLE, which is written in algorithmic form in Section 5.5.

Review

FOR-NEXT loops simplify the process of handling repetitive processes by providing automatic controls over the operation of the loop. We summarize the new terms and concepts introduced in this chapter.

INDEXED LOOP   a loop in which the maximum number of repetitions is controlled by a counter. (Section 5.1)

LOOP INDEX   the name for the variable that holds the count of the number of repetitions of a **FOR-NEXT** loop. (Section 5.1)

LOOP CONTROL VARIABLE   another name for the loop index. (Section 5.1)

INITIAL VALUE OF LOOP INDEX   the value given the loop index upon entry into the loop. (Section 5.1)

FINAL VALUE OF LOOP INDEX   the value which determines when the loop is exited. It is important to note that the loop index may never actually hold the specified final value. (Section 5.1)

STEP VALUE   the amount by which the loop index is increased (or decreased) on each pass through the loop. (Section 5.1)

DEFAULT VALUE   the value assumed for a certain quantity if it is not specified. (Section 5.1)

SUMMATION NOTATION   an abbreviated mathematical notation used to indicate the sum of permitted values of a certain variable. (Section 5.4)

BASIC SYNTAX

FOR . . . TO . . . STEP   the header statement for an indexed loop. (Section 5.2)

NEXT   the terminator statement for an indexed loop. (Section 5.2)

6
FUNCTIONS

6.1 INTRODUCTION TO FUNCTIONS

A **function** can be considered to be a processor that performs some type of computation and returns a single value as a result. Programming languages generally provide a series of built-in functions that perform useful tasks. Such languages also allow users to write their own functions. All functions receive values called **arguments** as input, perform computations, and return results. Functions are quite useful; they make it possible to eliminate repetitive segments from programs and to simplfiy complex programming tasks by breaking them up into smaller and more manageable modules. Kernighan and Ritchie have written: "Functions are really the only way to cope with the potential complexity of large programs. With properly designed functions, it is possible to ignore HOW a job is done; knowing WHAT is done is sufficient."[*]

A common function is **SQR** which extracts the positive square root of its argument. Just about all dialects of BASIC support this built-in function. Here is an example:

```
OUTPUT    PROCESSOR    INPUT
  5    ←     SQR    ←    25
```

To implement this function in a program we might write:

200 LET X = SQR(25)

---
[*]Brian W. Kernighan and Dennis M. Ritchie, *The C Programming Language.* (Englewood Cliffs, NJ; Prentice-Hall, 1978) p.22.

In this case, the argument passed to the function is **25** and the returned value is **5**. The argument and **returned value** are synonymous with input and output in the previous schematic. The returned value may be assigned to a variable as in line 200 above where it is assigned to **X** and hence stored. The returned value may also be used in a computation or immediately printed out as shown.

```
210  LET X = 10 + SQR(Y + 3)
220  PRINT SQR(X)
```

Note that either constants (line 200), variables (line 220), or expressions (line 210) may be used as arguments of functions.

BASIC keeps a list of built-in function names. Indeed, we cannot use **SQR** as a variable name since the CPU has reserved it as a built-in function name. We cannot see the built-in function, nor can we list it. We do not know what statements are in the function. We only know the value of the argument we have passed to the function and the value it returned.

6.2 FUNCTIONS THAT MODIFY OUTPUT VALUES

We introduce two additional functions that process numerical values. These functions are useful in a variety of problem situations.

We have previously developed a program that accepts as input the shelf price of an item, adds sales tax, and computes a total sales price (Section 4.2). A portion of this program is shown below.

```
140  LET TAXR = 5
150  INPUT SHELFP
160  LET SALESP = SHELFP + SHELFP * TAXR / 100
170  PRINT "SALES PRICE IS $";SALESP
```

When we ran this program before we were careful to enter values that caused the results to come out in even dollars and cents. Let us run it again.

```
?49.97
SALES PRICE IS $52.4685
```

We are not accustomed to recording prices to the hundredths of cents. In fact, we would like to avoid such complications. For this purpose the **INT** function determines the largest integer less than or equal to the argument and returns that integer. This process is often called truncation (when dealing with positive numbers). Suppose we write

```
LET X = INT(52.4685)
```

52.4685 is the argument. **INT** is the function. **X** accepts the **function value** which will equal 52.

Schematically, this process appears as follows:

```
OUTPUT        PROCESSOR         INPUT

[  52  ]  ←    [  INT  ]  ←   [ 52.4685 ]
```

It may seem as if this will not help us with our dollars and cents problem since this function would delete the entire decimal part. However, if we multiply 52.4685 by 100 and then use the **INT** function, the function value will be 5246. To get the decimal part back we can divide by 100 to obtain 52.46. The statement,

LET SALESP = INT(SALESP * 100) / 100

will truncate all decimal parts beyond the second decimal.

There are situations in which we would prefer to round a value to a certain number of decimal places. *Rounding* means retaining the nearest approximation to the calculated value upon truncation. For example, 52.4685 is closer to 52.47 than to 52.46. To round, add .5 to the argument of the **INT** function. The statement,

LET SALESP = INT(SALESP * 100 + .5) / 100

will return 52.47 rather than 52.46. This procedure rounds positive numbers according to the following Rules for Rounding:

If the first digit discarded is zero through four, the last digit retained is unchanged.

If the first digit discarded is five through nine, the last digit retained is increased by one.

We can generalize on the procedure of rounding in the following manner. To round a number to the *N*th decimal place use the expression:

LET ROUND = INT(NUMBER * 10 ^ N + .5) / 10 ^ N

Unwanted digits to the left of the decimal point may also be removed with the **INT** function.

The **INT** function may appear to behave differently for negative numbers. For example, **INT(−7.5) = −8**. This is the way the function is supposed to work. Truncation does not occur with negative arguments. To effect truncation of negative numbers special steps must be taken.* (See exercise 1 in Exercise Set 6.1.)

---

*TRS-80 BASIC has a special function called **FIX()** which truncates both positive and negative numbers.

The **INT** function provides another capability that is very useful. Suppose we wish to determine if a number is evenly divisible by another number. The test of divisibility is the absence of any decimal parts in the answer after the division has occurred. For example, eight is divisible by four since the answer, two, has no decimal parts. This means that the value of **INT(8 / 4)** is also two, so that **8 / 4 = INT(8 / 4)**. We can generalize this to write:

Y is evenly divisible by X if **Y / X = INT(Y / X)**

But nine is not evenly divisible by two. Note that $9/2 = 4.5$ and that **INT(9/2) = 4**. Thus, **9/2 <> INT(9/2)**. We can generalize this to write:

Y is not evenly divisible by X if **Y / X <> INT(Y / X)**

Another function that modifies numerical output is the **ABS** function. **ABS** is an abbreviation for absolute value. The absolute value of a number refers to its size without regard to its mathematical sign. That is, the absolute value of -9 is greater than the absolute value of -7, although -7 is greater than -9. The absolute value of -9 is also greater than $+7$. The absolute value of a number is a measure of its distance from zero on the number line.

In many cases, we are concerned only with the size of number and not whether the number is positive or negative. Running a number through the **ABS** function removes its negative sign if it has one. The processor does nothing to positive numbers. The statement, **LET X = ABS(−7.32),** will return **7.32** as the function value. In symbolic notation:

OUTPUT	PROCESSOR	INPUT
7.32	← ABS ←	−7.32

EXERCISE SET 6.1

1. Write a BASIC statement that will accomplish each of the following:
    (a) Evaluate the square root of $X + 4$ and assign the value to Y.
    (b) Assign the absolute value of $X + Y$ to Z.
    (c) Compute the largest integer less than $X + Y$ and assign the value to Z.
    (d) Compute the smallest integer greater than X if X is negative. Assign this computed value to Y. This statement will truncate negative numbers.

2. Predict the values of X that would be generated in each case below.
    (a) **LET X = SQR(49)**
    (b) **LET X = INT(−32.31)**
    (c) **LET X = INT(39.94 * 10 + .5) / 10**
    (d) **LET X = INT(2.316 * 100 + .5) / 100**
    (e) **LET X = ABS(−3.2)**
    (f) **LET X = ABS(2 − 3 ˆ 3)**
    (g) **LET X = INT(SQR(30))**
    (h) **LET X = ABS(INT(−7.5))**

3. Insert a statement in program **AVERAGE** (Section 4.6) to round the average to one decimal place.

4. Write statements that will perform the following operations:
    (a) Truncate variable Y to two decimal places and assign the new value to X.
    (b) Round variable Y to three decimal places and assign the new value to X.
    (c) Replace the 1's and 10's digits in the number 5628 with zeros. You are to change this number to 5600 using the computer.
    (d) Retain only three non-zero digits in the number 41267 but round before discarding digits. That is, you are to use the computer to obtain the number 41300.

5. Write program fragments to accomplish the following:
    (a) Determine if Y is evenly divisible by seven. If so, print the message **"Y IS DIVISIBLE BY 7"**
    (b) Determine if both X and Y are evenly divisible by Z. If so, print the message **"X AND Y ARE DIVISIBLE BY Z"**
    (c) Print a line of dashes with every fifth dash replaced by an asterisk. Use a loop to produce a line sixty-one units long beginning and ending with an asterisk.

6.3 RANDOM NUMBERS

The computer has the capability to generate a series of random numbers. This is provided by another function, which is designated as **RND**. The **RND** function is somewhat different from those we have discussed. For example, the program fragment below will generate ten random numbers in the interval zero to one (excluding one).

```
100  FOR I = 1 TO 10
110  LET X = RND(1)       ← Use RND(0) on TRS-80.
120  PRINT X
130  NEXT I
```

A run of the program might yield the following:

```
.040731921
.528293158
.803172316
.064391512 1
.157805367
.367305924
.783585386
.395769807
.322348213
.372165689
```

As in other built-in functions, the **RND** function is designated by three letters followed by a set of parenthesis in which an argument is placed. However, the argument may have no fixed relation to the output as in other functions. The functions are usually designed so that the value of the argument determines whether the sequence of random values can be reproduced from run to run. Positive arguments, negative arguments and a zero argument may produce different results. We suggest you consult the documentation for your computer.

You may wonder what purpose these numbers serve. Probably their most common use is to simulate the results of processes that depend on random events. A familiar experience might be the tossing of a coin. We expect that a fair coin will show heads or tails with equal probability. Since the numbers generated by the **RND** function are supposed to be uniformly distributed in the interval from zero to one, we could consider any number less than .5 to represent a head and any number greater than or equal to .5 to represent a tail. With this criteria the preceding run would represent seven heads and three tails. Let us insert a double alternative decision structure in the program above to tabulate the heads and tails.

```
COINTOSS:
declare numeric I, X, TAIL, HEAD
set TAIL to 0
set HEAD to 0
loop while I goes from 1 to 10
    X ← RND
```

```
         if (X >= .5)
           [increase TAIL by 1]
         else
           [increase HEAD by 1]
      end loop
      put ("YOU TOSSED ";HEAD;" HEADS AND ";TAIL;" TAILS.")
    end.
```

In code, this might appear as follows:

```
100  REM -- COINTOSS 12/14/80
110  REM -- LOCAL VARIABLES: I, X
120  REM -- OUTPUT VARIABLES: HEAD, TAIL
130  LET T = 0
140  LET H = 0
150  FOR I = 1 TO 10
160  LET X = RND(1)      RND(0) for TRS-80
170  IF X >= .5 THEN LET T = T + 1 : GOTO 190
180  LET H = H + 1
190  NEXT I
200  PRINT "YOU TOSSED ";H;" HEADS AND ";T;" TAILS."
210  END
```

This procedure illustrated by statements 170 and 180 works well for two alternatives. Suppose there are six alternatives as in the roll of a die. The division of the interval zero to one into six subdivisions is more difficult, so we expand the range of the random numbers by multiplying **RND(1)** by six. The range of the output now runs from zero to six (excluding six) so that we could consider any number from zero to one to represent a one, any number from one to two to represent a two, etc. This is still not very satisfactory as we would like output that more closely simulates the actual experiment of rolling the die. Consider the effect of the following statement:

LET X = INT(6 * RND(1) + 1)

The argument of the **INT** function is **6 * RND(1) + 1**. This argument will be a number between one and seven since **6 * RND(1)** was a number between zero and six. The argument has the decimal part removed by the **INT** function. X is thus one of the integers 1, 2, 3, 4, 5, or 6. The value of X may be interpreted as the count on the die face. The tabulation of 1s, 2s, etc. would appear to be a more difficult problem requiring several decision structures. A simple method of tabulation will be available when we introduce subscripted variables in Chapter 7.

From this discussion it evolves that we may generalize the problem to produce **random integers** in any range. The generalized statement is:

LET X = INT((R2 − R1 + 1) * RND(1) + R1)

where **R1** is the smallest integer (lower value) generated and **R2** is the largest (upper value) of the integers.

TRS-80

The TRS-80 BASIC provides a convenient method of generating random integers in the range from one to N. Simply use the maximum integer desired as the argument of **RND**. That is, **LET X = RND(6)** will generate a random integer in the range one to six. Extension to any range then becomes an easy matter. For example, **LET X = RND(6) + 2** will provide random integers in the range three to eight.

A valuable application of random number generation occurs in the **Monte Carlo method** of simulation. The purpose of a Monte Carlo simulation is to solve problems in which only the statistical distribution of certain problem variables is known. Specific variable values from within that distribution can be produced using the random number generator.

One of the simplest problems to solve using the Monte Carlo method is the simulation of a one dimensional random walk. In such a walk, motion is limited to a straight line with the direction chosen randomly. The purpose of the simulation is to determine how far the walker will be from the starting point after N steps. We have a probability distribution (equal probability of right or left) and a random number generator to select one of the two options so the problem should be solvable. Let us develop a program in pseudocode for its solution.

```
RANDOMWALK:
declare numeric MOVE, DISTANCE, NTRIES, I
get (NTRIES)
set DISTANCE to 0
loop while I goes from 1 to NTRIES
   if (RND < .5)
      [MOVE ← −1]
   else
      [MOVE ← 1]
   increase DISTANCE by MOVE
end loop
DISTANCE ← ABS(DISTANCE)
put ("DISTANCE AFTER ";NTRIES;" STEPS IS ";DISTANCE)
end.
```

We convert this to code:

```
100 REM -- RANDOMWALK 9/15/80
110 REM -- INPUT VARIABLES:NTRIES
120 REM -- LOCAL VARIABLES: MOVE, I
130 REM -- OUTPUT VARIABLES: DISTANCE, NTRIES
140 INPUT NTRIES
150 LET DISTANCE = 0
160 FOR I=1 TO NTRIES
170 IF RND(1) < .5 THEN LET MOVE = -1: GOTO 190
180 LET MOVE = 1
190 LET DISTANCE = DISTANCE + MOVE
200 NEXT I
210 LET DISTANCE = ABS(DISTANCE)
220 PRINT "DISTANCE AFTER ";NTRIES;" STEPS IS "; DISTANCE
230 END
```

The repetition of this program should lead you to some sort of generalization about the relation between distance and number of steps. Such a generalization is the purpose of the experiment. You should find that the distance can be approximated by the square root of the number of steps. Do not expect to see this result in a single walk but only if you average many walks for a reasonably large number of tries.

As we noted earlier, the random number distribution is essentially uniform in any interval. We can, however, generate a peaked distribution using a series of such functions. We illustrate such a procedure in the Library of Subroutines. (Appendix B).

6.4 USER-DEFINED FUNCTIONS

A *user-defined function* is, as its name suggests, a function that the user constructs. For example, if we wish to convert a number of values to percent from decimal we might define a function that multiplies the function argument by 100 as follows:

200 DEF FN Y(X) = 100 * X

This function then acts as a processor, which multiplies the argument by 100 and delivers that value as output. We display the function below:

OUTPUT   PROCESSOR   INPUT

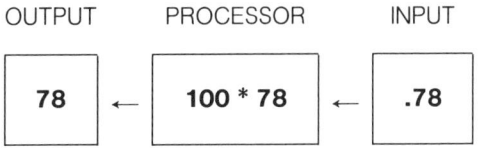

There is some variation in the type of user-defined functions allowed by the various dialects of BASIC. Some dialects allow multi-line user-defined functions. Some allow more than one argument. Since none of our microcomputers allow these special options we will not consider them further.

Let us begin with a simple example of a user-defined function in a single variable. Assume that we need to round numbers to one decimal place at several places in a program. A function can satisfy this need quite easily. Before a function can be used, it must be defined as in the following example:

```
150  DEF FN R(Z) = INT(Z * 10 + .5) / 10
      .
      .
      .
200  X = 127.68
210  PRINT FN R(X)
```

DEF is a BASIC keyword that identifies the statement purpose and **FN** is an abbreviation for the word function. The keywords **DEF FN** define **R** as a function rather than as a variable. It is possible to use **R** as a variable in the same program without confusing the computer. There is a greater risk, however, that this practice may confuse humans. The function definition must be logically prior to its use; in other words, the definition statement must be executed first.

The role of the variable **Z** in statement 150 may be the most difficult to understand. It is sometimes called a *dummy argument* or a *parameter variable*. It doesn't do anything; in reality it is only a stand-in or place holder for the real argument that will be passed to the function when it is invoked. **Z** can be thought of as a local variable since its value is not known outside the function itself. Thus, you could use another variable called **Z** elsewhere in your program without getting the values mixed up. Again, this may be a confusing practice for humans. You will also note the presence of a reference to **INT** with which you are already familiar. It demonstrates that one function can call another. All other values in the function statement are numeric constants. Statement 210 invokes or calls the function by using or referencing its name.

Let us now consider a slightly more complex version of the preceding program. Assume that we want the same rounding function with the additional consideration that we need to be able to vary the number of decimal digits to be retained. In this case, we need to pass an additional argument to the function. However, the dialects of BASIC that we are working with allow only one function argument. We accomplish our goal, nevertheless, with the use of a second variable as follows:

```
120  DEF FN RR(A) = INT(A * 10 ^ DP + .5) / 10 ^ DP
      .
      .
      .
```

```
200  X = 129.196
210  DP = 1
220  PRINT FN RR(X)
230  DP = 2
240  PRINT FN RR(X)
```

Here our function name is **RR**. As with variable names, function names can be of any length but only the first two characters are significant. This function is very similar to the previous one except for the substitution of the variable **DP** to indicate the number of decimal places desired. **DP** is called a *global variable* because its value is simultaneously known to the function and the main program. If the value of a global variable is changed in one program unit, this change affects its value in all program units. In fact, in BASIC, all variables are global except dummy variables. This contrasts with the practice of other languages, such as FORTRAN, where all variables are normally *local*, that is, known only to the program unit in which they occur. In FORTRAN, a programmer must explicitly declare a variable to be global.

It is important to note that if more than one variable appears in a function definition, the dummy (local) variable is immediately identified as the one that appears on the left side of the equation.

Finally, let us look at a simple program that is designed to illustrate the independence of global variables, functions, and local variables with the same name. This program is designed to discount by 10% the list price of any item valued at $100 or more and then add 5% sales tax to obtain a sales price.

```
100  REM -- FUNCTION TEST
110  REM
120  DEF FN TC(X) = X * 1.05
130  DEF FN RR(TC) = INT(TC * 100 + .5) / 100
140  PRINT "LIST","DISCOUNT","PRICE"
150  FOR I = 1 TO 5
160  DISC = 0
170  READ LP
180  PRINT LP,
190  IF LP >= 100 THEN DISC = LP * .1: LP = LP * .9
200  TC = FN RR(FN TC(LP))
210  PRINT FN RR(DISC),TC
220  NEXT I
230  DATA 55.71, 121.15, 69.95, 259.42, 86.20
240  END
```

This program produces the following output:

LIST	DISCOUNT	PRICE	
55.71	0	58.49	
121.15	12.12	114.49	(continued)

69.95	0	73.45
259.42	25.94	245.15
86.2	0	90.51

The program works correctly. The listing demonstrates the following:

1   **TC** is used as a function name in line 120, as a dummy variable in line 130, and as a global variable in lines 200 and 210. They are three completely separate entities.

2   **TC** is used as a function name and as a global variable in the same line, line 200.

3   **FN RR**, a user-defined function has as an argument another user-defined function in line 200.

4   **X** appears only as a local variable in this program, in line 120.

We certainly do not recommend this kind of programming practice but it does illustrate the distinctions between local variables, global variables, and function names.

EXERCISE SET 6.2

1. Write BASIC program fragments to accomplish the following:
   (a) Produce twenty random integers in the range from five to ten.
   (b) Produce 200 random integers in the range one to six. Have the program count those integers less than or equal to three.

2. Simulate the experiment of drawing colored balls from a box. Assume there are two white balls and three black balls in the box. Develop a program that will count the number of successes in drawing two white balls in sequence. The program must also tally the total number of attempts. Hint: generate random integers over a range of five allowing two values to represent white and three values to represent black. Solve the problem with and without replacement of the white ball.

3. Generalize the program **COINTOSS** to allow for input at the keyboard of the number of trials. Investigate the ratio of heads to tails as the number of trials increases.

4. Write user-defined functions to accomplish the following:
   (a) Convert a percentage value to a decimal.
   (b) Convert Fahrenheit temperature to Celsius.
   (c) Add 6% sales tax and round the result to two decimal places.

(d) Convert inches to feet and express the result to the nearest hundredth of a foot.

5. Consider the following BASIC statement:

100 DEF FN C(Z) = P0 * (1 − Z) ^ N

In this statement identify:

(a) the function name

(b) the dummy variable

(c) the global variable(s).

6. Simulate the crossing of two hybrid (mixed gene) characteristics. Assume that one of the genes is dominant and that the other is recessive. Count the percentage of double recessives, of hybrids, and of double dominants in the offspring for a large number of crossings.

6.5 CODING MATHEMATICAL FUNCTIONS

We have been careful to present mathematical expressions in coded form. However, we frequently face the task of coding such an expression. For example, the principal value (P) of a fixed amount of money deposited in a bank is given by the equation:

$$P = P_0 (1 + r)^n$$

where P_0 = initial deposit

r = annual interest rate in decimal form

n = number of years on deposit

This expression assumes that the interest is compounded annually. To code this expression we need to know something about the abbreviated notation of mathematics. Here is some of that notation.

$3x$ (a constant and a variable written side by side) implies 3 multiplied by x.

xy (two variables written side by side) implies x multiplied by y.

x^y (one symbol as a superscript) implies x raised to the y power—that is, exponentiation.

$x(y + 3)$ (one quantity in parenthesis) implies multiplication of the quantity outside the parenthesis with that inside.

The BASIC language does not recognize the mathematical conventions noted above. As a result, **implied operations,** those operations that are indicated by the placement of mathematical symbols, must be written out using the appropriate operators. However, the language does recognize parentheses. Such parentheses in a mathematical expression should be retained in the coded expression.

Looking again at the principal equation we see two implied operations and one set of parentheses. To change the implied operations to correct BASIC syntax, proceed as follows:

$$(1 + r)^n \quad \text{becomes } \mathbf{(1 + R)\wedge N}$$

$$P_0(1 + r)^n \quad \text{becomes } \mathbf{P0 * (1 + R)\wedge N}$$

We retain the parentheses.

Consider a modification of the problem. If the bank compounds interest more frequently than annually, the equation for principal becomes:

$$P = P_0\left(1 + \frac{r}{m}\right)^{mn}$$

where *m* is the number of compounding periods per year.

There are three implied operations in this equation. The additional one introduced is:

mn which converts to **M * N**

Note that the fraction bar (—) is an explicit expression for division, which equates to the division symbol (/).

We might be tempted to make the following literal translation of:

$$P = P_0\left(1 + \frac{r}{m}\right)^{mn}$$

LET P = P0 * (1 + R / M) ^ M * N

But note that BASIC will treat this expression as:

$$P = P_0\left(\left(1 + \frac{r}{m}\right)^m n\right)$$

BASIC has no way of knowing that we intended to raise $(1 + (r/m))$ to the *mn* power. As a result of the hierarchy of operations, the code as written above will raise $(1 + r/m)$ to the *m*th power and then multiply the result by *n*. In this case, we need to add a set of parentheses to avoid an error in the code. We write:

LET P = P0 * (1 + R / M) ^ (M * N)

This is another example of implied operations. By writing *mn* as an exponent we implied that it was to be treated as a unit.

6.6 RULES FOR CODING

Based on our experiences above, we might formulate a set of rules for programmers converting algebraic expressions to code. These rules are based on the hierarchy of operations discussed in Section 2.5. However, they provide more explicit instructions on how to code algebraic expressions involving implied mathematical operations.

Rules for Converting Expressions to Code

1 Parenthesize those units whose parenthesization is implied in the algebraic expression. Look specifically for exponents involving operators and numerators or denominators having more than one term.* BASIC function arguments should be parenthesized.

2 Convert all implied multiplications to explicit multiplications and fraction bars to division symbols.

3 Convert all implied exponentiations to explicit exponentiations.

4 Add the necessary assignment or print statement. The result should be a correct code representation.

Consider the following example problems:

1. Convert the expression, $y = 3^{2x}$ to code.
   Rule 1 yields $y = 3^{(2x)}$
   (Note that we have parenthesized the exponent.)
   Rule 2 yields $y = 3^{(2*x)}$
   (Implied multiplications are converted to explicit multiplications.)
   Rule 3 yields $y = 3 \text{^} (2 * x)$
   (Implied exponentiation has been converted to explicit exponentiation.)
   Rule 4 yields **LET Y = 3 ^ (2 * X)**
   (An assignment statement has been added and variables rewritten in upper case.)

2. Convert the expression, $y = \dfrac{x}{x^3 - 3}$, to code.

   Rule 1 yields $y = \dfrac{x}{(x^3 - 3)}$

   (Note the addition of a set of parentheses. Numerators and denominators of fractions must be treated as units. If they consist of more than one term, parenthesization is necessary.)

---

*A term in an algebraic expression is a unit of the expression separated from other units by addition or subtraction. In the expression $3x^2 + 2x + 2$, $3x^2$ is a term, $2x$ is a term, and 2 is a term.

Rule 2 yields $y = x / (x^3 - 3)$
(One fraction bar has been replaced by a division symbol.)
Rule 3 yields $y = x / (x \wedge 3 - 3)$
(One implied exponentiation has been converted to an explicit exponentiation.)
Rule 4 yields **LET Y = X / (X ^ 3 - 3)**

6.7 NUMERIC INPUT AND OUTPUT

The computer will accept numbers in whole number form, decimal form, or in **scientific notation.** Scientific notation refers to a form of notation in which a number is written as the product of two numbers. The first number has a single digit left of the decimal point. The second number is ten raised to a power. All numbers may be written in scientific notation.

To convert a number to scientific notation, move the decimal point so that only one nonzero digit appears left of the decimal point. The number of places the decimal point is moved determines the exponent on the power of ten. Right moves give negative exponents and left moves give positive exponents. For example, to write 521.5 in scientific notation we move the decimal point left two places to get 5.215. Next we multiply by 10 ^ 2 since the move was left two places. The final result is

5.215 x 10 ^ 2

To enter a number into the computer in scientific notation, it must be written in a special way. The value above would be entered as:

5.215E2

The **E** takes the place of "x 10 ^". Here are some additional examples:

$-0.0361 = -3.61$ x $10 \wedge -2 =$ **−3.61E−2**

$30 = 3.0$ x $10 \wedge 1 =$ **3.0E1**

Although we can enter a number in any form, the computer will print the number in scientific notation if the value is outside a certain range. That is, if the number is very small (less than 0.01) or very large (greater than or equal to 1,000,000,000), it will be printed in scientific notation.

This varies from computer to computer so that you should check the range for your system. The following immediate **PRINT** commands along with their output display this characteristic.

COMMAND	RESULT
PRINT .0052	5.2E−03
PRINT .052	.052
PRINT 520000000	520000000
PRINT 5200000000	5.2E+09

```
PRINT 5.21E5         521000
PRINT -3.21E-2       -.0321
```

We should note some other eccentricities in the numerical output of most machines. First, the computer will not retain trailing zeros after a decimal point unless forced to do so. This is illustrated in the following immediate commands:

COMMAND	RESULT
PRINT 512.0	512
PRINT .000320	3.2E-04
PRINT "$";25.20	$25.2

If the trailing zeros are present because they have meaning, as in the case of printing a value in dollars and cents, we may not be happy with the appearance of the output. More importantly, if the trailing zeros are present because they represent significant digits in a measured value, they will be lost during the computer operation. We will cover this problem in more detail in Section 11 of Chapter 10.

A second problem concerns the way the computer performs exponentiations. If you enter

PRINT 7 * 7

you are likely to obtain forty-nine as the answer. On the other hand, if you enter

PRINT 7 ^ 2

you are likely to obtain 49.0000001 as the answer. You may be surprised to find that seven squared is not the same as seven multiplied by seven. This result, of course, must be explained in terms of the way the computer performs exponentiation. It does so by multiplying the exponent by the logarithm of the base (seven in this case) and then exponentiating this result. Those who are mathematically inclined might try the following immediate command:

PRINT EXP(2 * LOG(7))

Both the Apple and the PET have this exponentiation characteristic. However, TRS-80 owners will be happy to learn that seven squared is still forty-nine.

EXERCISE SET 6.3

1. Write a BASIC statement that will evaluate the dependent variable in the following equations.

   (a) $v = \sqrt{\dfrac{3kT}{m}}$ k = Boltzmann constant
   T = absolute temperature
   m = molecular mass

(b) $v = 1.41 \sqrt{\dfrac{kT}{m}}$ k, T, and m as in problem 1(a)

(c) $v = c \sqrt{1 - \left(\dfrac{L}{2a}\right)^2}$ c = velocity of light
L = wavelength
a = guide width

2. Write a BASIC statement that will evaluate the dependent variable below for any assigned value of the independent variables.

(a) $V = \dfrac{4\pi r^3}{3}$

(b) $y = \dfrac{2x - 3}{x + 1}$

(c) $y = 2x^3 + 3x^2 - 1$

(d) $H = \dfrac{(5 - t)^2}{t} + \dfrac{1}{(5 - t)^2}$

(e) $z = (x + y)^{3x} + x^2 y$

3. Write a BASIC program fragment that will output the value of the dependent variable in the following equations. Use the given values for the independent variables.

(a) $V = \dfrac{4\pi r^3}{3}$ $\pi = 3.14$, $r = 2.5$

(b) $A = \dfrac{h(a + b)}{2}$ $h = 6$, $a = 2$, $b = 3$

(c) $y = \dfrac{3x^2 + 1}{x - 2}$ $x = 5$

(d) $R = 3t^2 - \dfrac{(t + 1)^2}{2t}$ $t = 2$

(e) $y = 4(x + h)^{3x}$ $x = 2$, $h = 5$

4. Write program fragments that include keyboard input of independent variables, as well as evaluation and output of the dependent variable, for each of the following equations.

n = number of moles
R = universal gas constant
(a) $P = \dfrac{nRT}{V}$ T = absolute temperature
V = volume
P = pressure

(b) $y = mx + b$
$\quad m$ = slope
$\quad b$ = y-intercept
$\quad x$ = x-coordinate
$\quad y$ = y-coordinate

(c) $Re = \dfrac{(R1)(R2)}{R1 + R2}$
$\quad R1$ = resistance 1
$\quad R2$ = resistance 2
$\quad Re$ = equivalent parallel resistance

5. Convert the following numbers to scientific notation:
   (a) 0.0032
   (b) −52
   (c) 2156000000
   (d) 4215
   (e) −0.000452
   (f) 6

   Which of these numbers would the computer place in scientific notation?

6.8 A CAUTION ABOUT FUNCTIONS

While functions are valuable shortcuts, they can also cause problems in our programs. For example, it is not possible to find the square root of −4 (at least not in the real numbers with which the computer deals). Thus, if a negative number is entered as the argument of the **SQR** function, some sort of error message will be generated depending upon the computer system. Some programmers may prefer to pass their arguments through a screening system before passing them to the **SQR** function to avoid such problems. In any case, one should be aware of this limitation and other limitations, which we will introduce as we encounter new functions. The **INT** and **ABS** functions have no restrictions on their arguments, as long as those arguments are numeric values.

Review

We summarize the new terms and BASIC syntax introduced in this chapter.

FUNCTIONS special operations of limited scope that process input values into output values bearing a known relation to the input. (Section 6.1)

ARGUMENT OF A FUNCTION the input value that is to be processed by the function. (Section 6.1)

RETURNED VALUE the output value after processing of the argument by the function. (Section 6.1)

RANDOM INTEGER integers generated randomly in any interval (R1 → R2 inclusive) through the use of the following expression:

LET X = INT(RND(1) * (R2 − R1 + 1) + R1)

(Section 6.3)

MONTE CARLO METHOD a method of simulation in which the problem variables receive random values that are dictated by a known statistical distribution. (Section 6.3)

IMPLIED OPERATIONS operations that are indicated by placement of symbols (for example, raising a symbol above the line implies exponentiation). (Section 6.5)

RULES FOR CODING ALGEBRAIC EXPRESSIONS rules designed to assist the programmer in converting algebraic expressions to code. (Section 6.6)

SCIENTIFIC NOTATION a special power of ten notation. Most BASIC dialects use this notation for the output of numeric values outside a given range. (Section 6.7)

Basic Syntax

SQR(X) a function that extracts the positve square root of X. X must be >= 0. (Section 6.1)

INT(X) a function that returns the largest integer less than or equal to X. (Section 6.2)

ABS(X) a function that returns the absolute value of X. (Section 6.2)

RND(X) a function that returns a random number with certain reservations depending upon the value of X. (Section 6.3)

DEF FN NA( ) = *(function)* a function to be defined by the user. The function name in this example is **NA**. A local variable must appear in the parentheses and in the function defined. The defined function may consist of any legal operations involving the local variable and global variables as well as other standard or user-defined functions. (Section 6.4)

7
SUBSCRIPTS AND ARRAYS

7.1 INTRODUCTION TO SUBSCRIPTS AND ARRAYS

In Chapter 2 we discussed the fact that values must first be stored in computer memory before they can be manipulated by the computer. We pointed out that values are inserted in memory locations by means of one of three methods:

1. Assigning values in a program statement (**LET**).
2. Reading values from an internal data set (**READ** and **DATA**).
3. Entering values at the keyboard (**INPUT**).

If we have a large number of related variables, which must be handled and kept distinct by the computer, we would be confronted with the problem of inventing enough variable names to represent the data and writing enough statements to assign data to the variables. In such circumstances, we would soon be overwhelmed by the task. Fortunately, there is an easier way to handle related variables.

Subscript notation allows us to organize related data into lists and tables. Such lists and tables are called **arrays**. The subscript serves as part of the variable name. The subscript also places a numerical identification on specific locations in the array which makes it very convenient to manipulate the data in the array with **FOR-NEXT** loops. With an understanding of arrays and their manipulation, we begin to realize the power of the computer in organizing and handling large data sets.

7.2 SUBSCRIPTS

When scientists work with a series of related numbers, they often use subscripts to indicate which item in the series is being referenced. For example:

$$X_1, X_2, X_3, X_4, X_5, X_6, X_7, X_8$$

represents a series of eight values of the quantity X. The use of subscripted variables in programming is a great convenience when handling large series of numbers. However, when we program, subscripts cannot be written below the line as their name implies because terminals and keypunches have no half-line carriage control. Therefore, we enclose subscripts within parentheses; for example, X_1, X_2, X_3 becomes **X(1)**, **X(2)**, **X(3)**. Programmers refer to such a series of numbers as an array. All elements of an array are referenced by the same variable name together with the appropriate subscript.

7.3 USING ARRAYS

Let us illustrate the utility of arrays by solving a simple problem. Our task is to write a program that will read and print a list of student grades, compute and print the average of those grades, print the lowest and highest grades, and list all those grades that are above the class average. The first part of the task, reading and printing the grades and computing and printing the average, is a relatively simple task. We need a loop to read and print the grade values, to accumulate the count of grades, and to keep a running total of the grades all at the same time. Once the loop is finished, we merely compute and print the average. The following program in pseudocode illustrates:

```
MEANGRADE:
declare numeric GRADE,SUM,COUNT,MEAN
set SUM to 0
set COUNT to 0
loop
   get(GRADE)
   if(GRADE < 0) [ break ]
   put(GRADE)
   increase SUM by GRADE
   increase COUNT by 1
end loop
MEAN ← SUM/COUNT
put("THE MEAN IS ",MEAN)
end.
```

However, this program only does half the job. At first glance it may seem as if we could add some modifications in order to satisfy the remaining requirements. But, in fact, there is a fundamental flaw in our approach. This program is fine for computing the mean, but since it does not retain individual scores as separate values for later comparison with the mean, we must devise a different approach. Not only do we wish to count and sum the grades, but we must also retain a copy of each grade. An array is well suited for such an application.

We can summarize our programming task as follows:

Step 1 Read a list of grades.
Step 2 Print the list of grades.
Step 3 Compute the mean grade.
Step 4 Select and print the lowest grade.
Step 5 Select and print the highest grade.
Step 6 Print the mean grade.
Step 7 Print all grades above the average or mean.

Upon careful study, we can determine that Step 7 requires a second pass through the data. This is so because we cannot know the mean grade in the same loop that is computing it. Thus we will need two loops. The first will read all the data and accumulate the count and sum of the grades; and, the second will select the above average grades. Since we must have two loops, a reasonable division of labor would be for the first loop to perform Steps 1, 2, and 3 and for the second loop to perform the rest of the steps. Below we present a second attempt at formulating a program in pseudocode. It bears some resemblance to the previous attempt.

```
MEANGRADE2:
declare numeric GRADE,SUM,COUNT,MEAN
declare numeric HIGH,LOW,INDEX,TABLE(20)
set SUM to 0
put("GRADES:")
loop while COUNT goes from 1 to 20
   get(GRADE)
   if(GRADE < 0) [ break ]
   TABLE(COUNT) ← GRADE
   put(GRADE)
   increase SUM by GRADE
end loop
decrease COUNT by 1
MEAN ← SUM / COUNT
put("MEAN GRADE IS ",MEAN)
LOW ← TABLE(1)
```

```
        HIGH ← TABLE(1)
        put("LIST OF ABOVE AVERAGE GRADES")
        loop while INDEX goes from 1 to COUNT
           if(TABLE(INDEX) > MEAN ) [ put (TABLE(INDEX)) ]
           if(TABLE(INDEX) < LOW) [ LOW ← TABLE(INDEX) ]
           if(TABLE(INDEX) > HIGH) [ HIGH ← TABLE(INDEX) ]
        end loop
        put("HIGH GRADE IS ",HIGH)
        put("LOW GRADE IS ",LOW)
        put("COUNT OF GRADES IS ",COUNT)
        end.
```

As in our first attempt, MEANGRADE2 makes two basic assumptions about the data: first, that no more than twenty grades will need to be processed; and, second, that legitimate grade values will be nonnegative and therefore any negative number can be properly used to indicate end of file. There are some important differences between the two versions of the program. They are as follows:

1   The second declare statement indicates TABLE to be an array of size twenty. This means that TABLE will have twenty memory locations assigned to it rather than merely one. Those memory locations will be numbered from one to twenty. Many versions of BASIC actually allow a subscript of zero and thus would provide room for a total of twenty-one data elements. Since this feature is not available in all dialects of BASIC and because it can greatly complicate an algorithm, it is best to avoid use of the zero array element.

2   The first loop in MEANGRADE2 is an indexed loop rather than the simple loop of the earlier version. Since we are dealing with an array, it makes sense to use the loop index as an automatic subscript index. You will also note that our algorithm gets a value for GRADE, which is inserted into the array TABLE only after it is determined to be a real grade value—that is, not a negative trailer value.

3   You will notice that COUNT is decreased by one after the first loop is exited. This is necessary because COUNT will always be one value too high. When the negative trailer value is encountered, COUNT will already have been incremented before GRADE is tested. Similarly, when the loop is executed twenty times, the index will be first increased to twenty-one before it is tested and found to exceed the limit for the loop.

4   In order to select the high and low scores we begin by arbitrarily declaring the first value in TABLE to be both the highest and the lowest.

5   Then the program enters the second loop in which it compares successive elements of TABLE with the current value of HIGH, substituting the current TABLE value for HIGH when it is the greater. A similar approach is used to select the

smallest value. It is true that the loop performs one unnecessary iteration—the first—but it is easier to waste a little computer time than create a more complicated algorithm. Had the loop index begun with two, we would not have been able to list element 1 of TABLE if it were greater than the MEAN.

With our pseudocode program complete, it only remains for us to translate it into BASIC. We have decided to get our data from data statements within the program itself. Here is the BASIC version:

```
100  REM -- MEANGRADE2 1-1-81
105  REM -- INPUT VARIABLES: G
110  REM -- LOCAL VARIABLES: INDEX, SUM
115  REM -- OUTPUT VARIABLES: MEAN, HIGH, LOW, COUNT, TABLE( )
120  DIM TABLE(20)
125  SUM=0
130  PRINT "GRADES:"
135  FOR COUNT = 1 TO 20
140     READ G
145     IF G < 0 THEN 170
150     TABLE(COUNT) = G
155     PRINT G
160     SUM = SUM + G
165  NEXT COUNT
170  COUNT = COUNT - 1
175  MEAN = SUM / COUNT
180  PRINT "MEAN GRADE IS ";MEAN
185  LOW = TABLE(1)
190  HIGH = TABLE(1)
195  PRINT "LIST OF ABOVE AVERAGE GRADES"
200  FOR INDEX = 1 TO COUNT
205     IF TABLE(INDEX) > MEAN THEN PRINT TABLE(INDEX)
215     IF TABLE(INDEX) < LOW THEN LOW = TABLE(INDEX)
220     IF TABLE(INDEX) > HIGH THEN HIGH = TABLE(INDEX)
225  NEXT INDEX
230  PRINT "HIGH GRADE IS ";HIGH
235  PRINT "LOW GRADE IS ";LOW
240  PRINT "COUNT OF GRADES IS ";COUNT
500  REM -- DATA SET
505  DATA 70,67,89,88,78,98,84,85
510  DATA -99
999  END
```

The translation has gone smoothly. The only unexpected change is that the variable name for the student grade was GRADE in the algorithmic language version, while **G** is used in the BASIC version. This was made necessary because **GR** is a reserved keyword on the Apple. Statement 120 contains new syntax which we will discuss next. Here is some sample output:

RUN MEANGRADE2
GRADES:
70
67
89
88
78
98
84
85
MEAN GRADE IS 82.375
LIST OF ABOVE AVERAGE GRADES
89
88
98
84
85
HIGH GRADE IS 98
LOW GRADE IS 67
COUNT OF GRADES IS 8

7.4 DECLARING ARRAYS

BASIC assumes that all variables are simple variables, sometimes called *scalars*, with only a single memory location associated with them unless we specify otherwise. We declare a variable to be an array by specifying its dimension or size in a dimension statement. Consider the following:

120 DIM ALPHA(50)

This statement declares the variable alpha to be an array and instructs BASIC to set aside fifty memory locations for it. **DIM** is a BASIC keyword—an abbreviation for dimension. We may declare an array to have as many elements as we wish within the limit of available computer memory. The early 8K PETs impose a maximum array size of 255. Generally speaking, it is best not to request more array space than needed. If we were to use an array name in a program without formally declaring its size in a dimension statement, BASIC will arbitrarily assign it a size of ten. This means that subscript values from one to ten will be legal. As mentioned earlier, some dialects of BASIC provide a zero array element as well. This automatic dimensioning feature can produce an error on some computers if we reference an array before we dimension it. For example:

```
    . . .
200 X(I) =A*B+C
    . . .
    . . .
220 DIM X(25)
```

In this case, BASIC automatically sets aside ten memory locations when it encounters statement 200. However, when statement 220 is reached, BASIC is told to change the size to twenty-five. Many versions of BASIC will consider such a sequence to be an error and interrupt the program with a message. The PET, the Apple, and the TRS-80 all permit this redimensioning of arrays. However, a **CLEAR** statement must be executed before the redimensioning statement is encountered on both the Apple and the TRS-80. While such a technique has some limited use, it should be avoided.

Sometimes arrays are known by other names, such as: vector, matrix, table, and list. Sometimes the term array is used to refer to a **one-dimensional array** and the term **matrix** is reserved for an array with more than one dimension. However, this is not a rule and you will find many exceptions to it. We declare an array or matrix to have two or three dimensions as follows:

```
110 DIM TABLE(5,10)
120 DIM MAT(2,3,2)
```

The first statement declares **TABLE** as a **two-dimensional array** or matrix with five horizontal rows and ten vertical columns. Array **MAT** is a three-dimensional array with dimensions of two, three, and two. More about multi-dimensional arrays will be presented later in Section 7.9.

EXERCISE SET 7.1

1. Write a program that loads the following arrays:
    (a) Array Y to contain the series of numeric values between one and fifteen. Begin with memory location one.
    (b) Array XRAY to contain all positive odd values between zero and twenty-five inclusive.
    (c) Array A to contain the first twelve multiples of seven.

2. Write a program that loads the matrix B with the squares of the first fifteen integers. Include a second loop which prints each integer followed by its square.

The output should look like this:

```
1    1
2    4
3    9
.    .
.    .
.    .
```

3. Answer the following questions about this program.

   100 DIM X(13)
   110 FOR I=1 TO 13
   120 LET X(I) = I+1
   130 NEXT I

   (a) What is the value of **X(1)**?
   (b) What is the value of **X(13)**?

4. Simulate a computer by hand-tracing the following programs. Write the appropriate values in the boxes below. The boxes are intended to be a visual representation of computer memory.

   (a) **100 DIM X(12)**
       110 FOR I=1 TO 12
       120 LET X(I) = I * 2 + 5
       130 NEXT I

   X(1) X(2) X(3) X(4) X(5) X(6) X(7) X(8) X(9) X(10) X(11) X(12)

   (b) **100 DIM X(12)**
       110 FOR I = 12 TO 1 STEP −1
       120 LET X(I) = I
       130 NEXT I

   X(1) X(2) X(3) X(4) X(5) X(6) X(7) X(8) X(9) X(10) X(11) X(12)

7.5 USING AN ARRAY AS AN ACCUMULATOR

In Section 6.3, we discussed the use of the random number generator to simulate the toss of a coin and the roll of a die. There we presented a program called **COINTOSS** that simulated the coin tossing process and kept track of how many heads and tails had been tossed. We also said that the toss of a die could be simulated in the same manner, but did not illustrate doing so because we would need six accumulators—one for each die face. An array provides an easy solution to this problem. Following we present an algorithm for a program which simulates a die toss. This algorithm follows very closely the model of **COINTOSS**, except for the use of the array as an accumulator.

```
DIETOSS:
declare numeric I,X,FACE(6),R1,R2
loop while I goes from 1 to 6
    set FACE(I) to 0
end loop
set R1 to 1
set R2 to 6
loop while I goes from 1 to 50
    X ← RND(R1-R2)*
    increase FACE(X) by 1
end loop
put("FACE","COUNT")
loop while I goes from 1 to 6
    put(I,FACE(I))
end loop
end.
```

Notice how we use X as the subscript in the increase statement within the first loop, rather than the loop index. In the previous statement, X was randomly assigned a value in the range of 1 to 6. If, for example, a five were *tossed* FACE(5) would be incremented by one. This program translates into BASIC easily:

```
100 REM -- DIETOSS 1-1-81
105 REM -- INPUT VARIABLES: R1, R2
110 REM -- LOCAL VARIABLES: X
115 REM -- OUTPUT VARIABLES: I, FACE(I)
```

*We use RND(R1-R2) to indicate the algorithm for generating random integers in the range R1 to R2.

```
120 DIM FACE(6)
125 R1 = 1
130 R2 = 6
135 FOR I = 1 TO 6
140     FACE(I) = 0
145 NEXT I
150 FOR I = 1 TO 50
155     X = INT((R2 - R1 + 1) * RND(1) + R1)
(Use 155 X = RND(6) on TRS-80.)
160     FACE(X) = FACE(X) + 1
165 NEXT I
170 PRINT "FACE","COUNT"
175 FOR I = 1 TO 6
180     PRINT I,FACE(I)
185 NEXT I
999 END

RUN
FACE    COUNT
1       10
2       6
3       4
4       6
5       12
6       12
```

When we simulated the die toss fifty times we tossed ten 1's, six 2's, four 3's, six 4's, twelve 5's, and twelve 6's.

7.6 SORTING WITH AN ARRAY

We have discussed the process of computing the mean of a data set in Section 5.4 and again in this chapter. A second measure of the *central tendency* of a data set is the *median* or middle value of the data. In order to find the middle value, the data set must be arranged in ascending or descending order. Consider the following data set:

$$2 \quad 34 \quad 42 \quad 30 \quad 32 \quad 12 \quad 29 \quad 34 \quad 22 \quad 98 \quad 99$$

We can easily sort this array by hand, which would then look like this:

$$2 \quad 12 \quad 22 \quad 29 \quad 30 \quad 32 \quad 34 \quad 34 \quad 42 \quad 98 \quad 99$$

Since there are eleven data values the center value is in position six. But suppose we have 1000 data values. A hand sort becomes tedious. We will consider how the computer can conduct a sort and locate the median.

When we compute the arithmetic mean of a series, we merely add each item into a running total. Only three variables are required: (1) the input item, (2) the accumulator or running total, and (3) a counter to keep track of the number of individual items actually accumulated. To compute the median, however, each individual value must be stored in the computer. This will require that data be read into an array.

Let us look at the unordered sequence:

2   34   42   30   32   12   29   34   22   98   99

One way to sort this data is to start by looking at the second element (34). Determine if it is smaller than the first element. If it is, interchange the two numbers. In pseudocode we can express this task as follows:

if (X(I) > X(I+1)) [interchange]

What we desire here is to interchange two values in an array whenever the leftmost one is larger than the rightmost one of the pair. The interchange procedure is ambiguous and requires refinement. Imagine the following situation:

X(1)		X(2)
4	↔	1

In our example X(1) has the value 4 and X(2) has the value 1. The logical expression will evaluate to true and the interchange procedure should be performed. If we move 4 from X(1) to X(2) then the value 1 will be destroyed and both memory cells will contain the same value. Thus, we will have to save the value 1 somewhere before the value 4 is transferred to X(2). We can accomplish this by adding a temporary variable called **TEMP**.

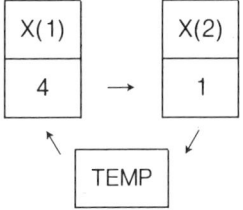

If we move the contents of X(2), to TEMP, the contents of X(1) to X(2), and the contents of TEMP to X(1) in that order, the exchange will occur correctly. Algorithmically, we would write:

TEMP ← X(2)
X(2) ← X(1)
X(1) ← TEMP

Now the interchange procedure is expressed unambiguously. This block is the heart of the *bubble sort* algorithm whereby the larger values *bubble* to the top of the array. Here is a complete bubble sort programmed in BASIC:

```
190  REM -- SORT ARRAY X
200  FOR I = 2 TO N
210      FOR J=1 TO I - 1
220          IF X(I) > X(J) THEN 260
230          LET TEMP = X(I)
240          LET X(I) = X(J)
250          LET X(J) = TEMP
260      NEXT J
270  NEXT I
```

To understand this sort routine we need to extend our treatment of loops slightly to include the concept of **nested loops**. Notice that there is a loop with the index **I** beginning at statement 200 and ending at statement 270. Within this loop is a second loop with index **J** beginning at statement 210 and ending at statement 260. The inner **J** loop is entirely enclosed within the outer **I** loop; in other words, it is nested within the outer loop. Loops can be nested in this way any number of times, as long as each loop has a different index, and is completely nested within all outer loops.

With this background, we will find it easier to understand the working of the sort routine. For each pass through the outer loop we will list I, the range of J and the rearranged array X(I). First let us recall the unsorted array:

2 34 42 30 32 12 29 34 22 98 99

Pass	I	Range of J	Rearranged X(I)
1	2	1 to 1	The inner loop has one iteration. The value to the left of 34 is less than 34. Therefore no exchange occurs. 2 34 42 30 32 12 29 34 22 98 99
2	3	1 to 2	The inner loop has two iterations. The values to the left of 42 are both less than 42 so no exchanges occur. 2 34 42 30 32 12 29 34 22 98 99

Pass	I	Range of J	Rearranged X(I)
3	4	1 to 3	The inner loop has three iterations. On the first iteration nothing happens because 30 is bigger than 2. On the second iteration 30 and 34 are exchanged. On the third iteration 34 and 42 are exchanged. 2 30 34 42 32 12 29 34 22 98 99
4	5	1 to 4	2 30 32 34 42 12 29 34 22 98 99

You may complete this sequence if you like. It should be clear that the outer loop moves along the array starting at position 2. At each position of the outer loop, the inner loop orders everything to the left of that point. For example, when I = 5 the inner loop has sorted the first five elements of the array. When I = N (11 in our case) the sort is complete. This process of sorting illustrates the power of the **FOR-NEXT** loop used in conjunction with subscripted variables.

7.7 THE MEDIAN

Now that we know how to sort an array, we are prepared to find the median of a data set. Recall that we said the median was the middle value. Data sets with an odd number of elements will always have a middle element. If the number of elements is even we average the values of the two "middle" elements. We will start by assuming that the data set has an odd number of elements and assign the middle value to the median. If the number of elements is even, we correct this assignment. The procedure can be expressed in pseudocode as follows:

$I9 \leftarrow INT(N / 2 + 1)$ (I9 is the center element when N is odd.)
$MEDIAN \leftarrow X(I9)$
if (N is even)
[$MEDIAN \leftarrow (X(I9) + X(I9-1)) / 2$]

Here we assume that the array X contains the sorted vector and that N indicates the operational size of X. The logical expression, (N is even), requires further refinement. Divisibility by two is a test for evenness. In Section 6.2 we developed a divisibility test. Using this test, we can refine the logical expression as follows:

if $N / 2 = INT(N / 2)$

An alternate and simpler expression that will test for N even in this special case is:

if $N = 2 * (I9 - 1)$

Our algorithm can be translated into BASIC as follows:

```
305  REM -- DETERMINE THE MEDIAN
310  I9 = INT (N / 2 + 1)
320  LET MEDIAN = X(I9)
330  IF N / 2 <> INT(N / 2) THEN 360
340  LET MEDIAN = (X(I9) + X(I9 − 1)) / 2
360  PRINT "THE MEDIAN IS  ";MEDIAN
```

Here is the completed program in BASIC:

```
100  REM -- MEDIAN
101  REM
102  REM     PROGRAM TO SORT AN ARRAY
103  REM     AND DETERMINE ITS MEDIAN
104  REM
105  DIM X(11)
110  LET N = 11
115  REM -- LOAD AND ECHO ARRAY
120  FOR I = 1 TO N
130     READ X(I)
135     PRINT X(I);" ";
140  NEXT I
145  PRINT
190  REM -- SORT ARRAY X
200  FOR I = 2 TO N
210     FOR J = 1 TO I − 1
220        IF X(I) > X(J) THEN 260
230        LET S = X(I)
240        LET X(I) = X(J)
250        LET X(J) = S
260     NEXT J
270  NEXT I
275  REM -- PRINT SORTED ARRAY
277  PRINT "HERE IS THE SORTED ARRAY:"
280  FOR I = 1 TO N
290     PRINT X(I);" ";
300  NEXT I
305  REM -- DETERMINE MEDIAN
310  I9 = INT(N / 2 + 1)
320  LET MEDIAN = X(I9)
330  IF N / 2 <> INT(N / 2) THEN 360
340  LET MEDIAN = (X(I9) + X(I9 − 1) ) / 2
350  REM -- PRINT MEDIAN
```

```
360 PRINT "THE MEDIAN IS ";MEDIAN
500 DATA 2,34,42,30,32,12,29,34,22,98,99
510 END
```

Here is a run of the program:

```
RUN
2 34 42 30 32 12 29 34 22 98 99
HERE IS THE SORTED ARRAY:
2 12 22 29 30 32 34 34 42 98 99
THE MEDIAN IS 32
```

EXERCISE SET 7.2

1. Write a program that generates the dependent variable values in the following equations. Store each value in an array Y. Add loops to the program to find the largest and smallest values of y. Print out these values.

    (a) $y = 3x^3 + 2x + 5$ from $x = -5$ to $x = 10$ in integer steps
    (b) $y = 4x^3 - 3x^2 + 1$ from $x = -20$ to $x = 4$ in integer steps

2. Generalize the program **MEDIAN** so that it does the following:

    (a) Reads a data set of any size determined by the user (maximum of 100 data elements),
    (b) Prints the data set in the order read,
    (c) Sorts the data set in ascending order,
    (d) Prints the sorted data set,
    (e) Computes the median of the data set.

3. Modify program **MEDIAN** so that it accepts data from the keyboard. A negative value should terminate input. The program should sort and print the array in descending order and evaluate the median and mean.

7.8 READING A DATA SET MORE THAN ONCE

In more complex programs, it may be convenient to read a data set more than once. The computer uses a pointer to indicate which value in the **DATA** statements will be read next. We can reset the pointer within our program by inserting a **RESTORE** statement. This moves the data set pointer to the first data value. It should be kept in mind that BASIC considers all the data values in all the **DATA** statements within a given program as a single data set, no matter where those statements may be—even if we consider them to be several data sets. The only control we have of the data set pointer is to move it to the beginning. However, it is possible to use a loop that will read and waste (that is, ignore) a certain number of data values, in order to move the pointer to the desired location. Consider the following:

```
100 DIM X(15)
105 FOR I = 1 TO 15
110     READ X(I)
115 NEXT I
130 RESTORE
135 DIM Y(15)
140 FOR I = 1 TO 15
150     READ Y(I)
160 NEXT I
170 DATA 3,2,1,6,9,15,10,8,7,9,12,13,8,7,9
```

This program loads both arrays X and Y with the same data set. Without the **RESTORE** statement we would get an **OUT OF DATA** error at our first attempt to execute statement 150. Of course, there is a simpler way to load Y than that shown above.

7.9 TWO-DIMENSIONAL ARRAYS

In many problems we deal with two-dimensional displays of data such as the percentage of car sales by car size by region, which is displayed in Table 7.1. It is important that we be able to retain this two-dimensional format when we read information into the computer. The two-dimensional array is designed for that purpose. The term matrix is frequently applied to such an array, particularly when it is used to manipulate data.

Table 7.1
Percentage of Sales by Car Size by Region

Region	Size		
	Small	Medium	Large
I	75	15	10
II	40	50	10
III	60	25	15
IV	47	46	7

We need some additional terminology to understand the two-dimensional array. Each vertical alignment of data is called a *column* (columns stand upright) while each horizontal alignment is called a *row*. If our array has more than ten rows or columns it must be explicitly dimensioned. We recommend **dimensioning** in any case. It is necessary in the dimension statement to distinguish between rows and columns. The table above has dimensions of four rows by three columns. An appropriate dimension statement for this table would be:

100 DIM A(4,3)

Rows always come before columns in referring to dimensions. An 11 by 2 array would have eleven rows and two columns.

Suppose we wish to read the data above into an array and preserve its natural order. We need an array such as follows:

```
A(1,1)    A(1,2)    A(1,3)
A(2,1)    A(2,2)    A(2,3)
A(3,1)    A(3,2)    A(3,3)
A(4,1)    A(4,2)    A(4,3)
```

Each piece of data has a double subscript to identify its place in the table. We need to get the data values into the array. Twelve assignment statements would do the job. Or, we might consider three loops of four repetitions. Both these methods are cumbersome and fail to take advantage of the combination of **FOR-NEXT** loops and subscript notation.

A better solution is to use a pair of nested loops. We may write:

```
100  FOR I = 1 TO 4
110      FOR J = 1 TO 3
120          READ A(I,J)
130      NEXT J
140  NEXT I
```

We might try hand-tracing this fragment that loads the matrix. On the first pass **I=1** and upon entry of the **J** loop **J=1**. Line 120 then means **READ A(1,1)**. We encounter **NEXT J** which increments **J** to **2** and statement 120 then means **READ A(1,2)**. Next we read **A(1,3)**, leave the **J** loop, encounter **NEXT I** and increase **I** to **2**. We then enter the **J** loop again and read the second row of the array. This process continues until all four rows are read.

We emphasize this detail because it is important to know the order in which the data must appear in the data statements. The order is obviously all first row data, then all second row data, and so forth. An appropriate data statement would be:

150 DATA 75,15,10,40,50,10,60,25,15,47,46,7

If we put the above program fragments together (statements 100 through 150) and run the program we should load matrix *A*. Suppose we wish to reproduce the table. The following nested loop structure will accomplish this:

```
200  FOR I = 1 TO 4
210     FOR J = 1 TO 3
230        PRINT A(I,J);" ";     (blank space is needed only for the
240     NEXT J                   Apple)
250     PRINT
260  NEXT I
```

Or, we could simply insert the following statements in the loop structure that loads *A*:

```
125  PRINT A(I,J);" ";
135  PRINT
```

Our output is:

```
75 15 10
40 50 10
60 25 15
47 46  7
```

The blank following the array reference in statements 230 and 125 cause a single space to be printed between the columns on a line. If you are not using an Apple, you can probably omit this blank. The semicolon in the same statements keeps the printer on the same line as a row is printed. Statements 135 and 250 move the printing head to the next line, cancelling the effect of the semicolon as the printing of a row is completed.

We include here a general program for loading an *M* by *N* array:

```
100  FOR I = 1 TO M          →  Moves row pointer
110     FOR J = 1 TO N       →  Moves column pointer
120        READ A(I,J)       →  Read data item
130     NEXT J
140  NEXT I
150  DATA                    →  Enter in normal reading order—
                                 left to right by rows.
```

EXERCISE SET 7.3

1. Load the following tables:

   (a) Load into array *B*:

   ```
   1.5    2.6    1.1
   3.2    2.4    1.5
   ```

(b) Load into array C:

23	15	37	41	62
14	19	21	35	15
22	34	11	29	12

2. Load an *identity matrix* of dimension four by four. An identity matrix has the number 1 everywhere on the left-top to bottom-right diagonal and zeros every place else. You should be able to load this array without using data lines.

3. Print out the arrays in problems 1 and 2.

7.10 MATRIX OPERATIONS

There are several important operations involving arrays which we will discuss here. These are:
1. Matrix addition (including subtraction),
2. Matrix multiplication, and
3. Matrix inversion.

These operations will be defined in the usual mathematical sense. Later in this chapter we will illustrate the use of two of these operations in solving practical problems. The use of matrix inversion will be discussed in Chapter 12.

Matrix addition is defined as an element by element addition of two matrices of the same dimensions. Addition of two simple matrices is indicated below:

$$\begin{bmatrix} 3 & 2 \\ 0 & 1 \\ -1 & 0 \end{bmatrix} + \begin{bmatrix} 1 & 0 \\ 2 & -1 \\ 0 & 3 \end{bmatrix} = \begin{bmatrix} 4 & 2 \\ 2 & 0 \\ -1 & 3 \end{bmatrix}$$

We could write a general program for this operation of addition as follows:

```
100 FOR I = 1 TO M
110     FOR J = 1 TO N
120         LET C(I,J) = A(I,J) + B(I,J)
130     NEXT J
140 NEXT I
```

A, *B*, and *C* matrices all have the same dimensions. Subtraction is accomplished by using a minus sign in place of the plus sign.

Matrix multiplication is a more complicated process. Two matrices may be multiplied only if the number of columns of the left matrix equals the number of rows in the right matrix. For example, we can multiply the following two matrices together:

$$[2 \quad 1 \quad -1] \begin{bmatrix} 3 & 2 \\ 0 & 4 \\ 1 & -1 \end{bmatrix}$$

However, if we were to reverse their order so that we attempted to multiply in the following manner:

$$\begin{bmatrix} 3 & 2 \\ 0 & 4 \\ 1 & -1 \end{bmatrix} [2 \quad 1 \quad -1]$$

the multiplication could not be completed since the left matrix has two columns while the right matrix has one row. This rule arises because of the manner in which matrix multiplication is performed. Each element of the product matrix is obtained by applying the entire row of the left matrix to a column of the right matrix. Let us perform the multiplication:

$$[2 \quad 1 \quad -1] \begin{bmatrix} 3 & 2 \\ 0 & 4 \\ 1 & -1 \end{bmatrix}$$

We start by applying the first row of the left matrix to the first column of the right in the following manner:

$$[2 \quad 1 \quad -1] \begin{bmatrix} 3 \\ 0 \\ 1 \end{bmatrix} = 2*3 + 1*0 + (-1)*1$$
$$= 6 + 0 - 1$$
$$= 5$$

Five is the value of the 1,1th element of the product matrix. Next, we apply the first row to the remaining columns of the right matrix. We obtain:

$$[2 \quad 1 \quad -1] \begin{bmatrix} 2 \\ 4 \\ -1 \end{bmatrix} = 2*2 + 1*4 + (-1)*(-1)$$
$$= 4 + 4 + 1$$
$$= 9$$

Nine is the 1,2th element of the product matrix. There are no more columns in the second matrix so we have generated the entire first row of the product matrix. The second row is obtained by applying the second row of the left matrix in the same manner. But the left matrix has no second row so the entire product is

$$[5 \quad 9]$$

Note that the number of rows in the product agrees with the number of rows in the left matrix. The number of columns of the product agrees with the number of columns of the right matrix.

Programming the matrix multiplication is more complex. We present a program fragment which accomplishes this multiplication. This procedure is documented in the Library of Subroutines. (Appendix B., p. B15).

```
100  FOR I = 1 TO M
110     FOR J = 1 TO L
120        FOR K = 1 TO N
130           LET C(I,J) = C(I,J) + A(I,K) * B(K,J)
140        NEXT K
150     NEXT J
160  NEXT I
```

Note the use of the triple nested loops. **M** is the number of rows in the left matrix, **L** is the number of columns in the right matrix, and **N** is the number of columns in the left matrix.

The third important matrix operation is *inversion*. Inversion of a matrix means finding another matrix, which, when multiplied by the given matrix, yields an identity matrix. In discussing inversion we will only consider matrices that have the same number of rows as columns (called square matrices). The identity matrix is a square matrix such as that shown below:

$$\begin{bmatrix} 1 & 0 & 0 \\ 0 & 1 & 0 \\ 0 & 0 & 1 \end{bmatrix}$$

Note: The diagonal from top left to bottom right is filled with ones. All other elements are zero. This is a three by three identity matrix. One can be written for any dimension. A subroutine for inversion is contained in the Library of Subroutines. (Appendix B, p. B17) Its use will be discussed in Chapter 12.

7.11 ORDER EXPLODING USING ARRAYS

Consider a very simple fabrication operation. A skateboard manufacturer produces three models of skateboards—

Model A(1)—Standard,

Model A(2)—Deluxe, and

Model A(3)—Super.

These boards are fabricated from some combination of the following five components—standard wheel set, heavy duty wheel set, reinforced board, laminated board, and a plastic guard.

The standard model is fabricated from two standard wheel pairs and a reinforced board. The deluxe model is fabricated from two standard wheel pairs, a laminated board and a plastic guard. Finally, the super model has two heavy duty wheel sets, a laminated board and two plastic guards. This information could be collected in a two-dimensional array as in Table 7.2.

Table 7.2

Skateboard Models and Their Components

Model	Std. Wheels	Heavy Duty Wheels	Reinf. Board	Lamin. Board	Guard
A(1)—Standard	2	0	1	0	0
A(2)—Deluxe	2	0	0	1	1
A(3)—Super	0	2	0	1	2

Suppose the manufacturer is to fabricate an order for 100 standard models, 150 deluxe models, and 75 super models. To find the number of each component needed to fill this order we could do the necessary arithmetic. This would yield:

500 standard wheel sets

150 heavy duty wheel sets

100 reinforced boards

225 laminated boards

300 plastic guards

Now perform a matrix multiplication. Multiply the order, written as a one by three matrix, by the component array above.

$$[100 \quad 150 \quad 75] \begin{bmatrix} 2 & 0 & 1 & 0 & 0 \\ 2 & 0 & 0 & 1 & 1 \\ 0 & 2 & 0 & 1 & 2 \end{bmatrix}$$

The result is the array

$$[500 \quad 150 \quad 100 \quad 225 \quad 300]$$

which is the number of components needed. This process in which an order for assemblies is converted into a corresponding set of components is called *order exploding*. We would quickly see the advantage of the matrix multiplication over the hand calculation if we were dealing with more complex fabrications where the number of components may run into the hundreds.

The matrix multiplication for order exploding may be simplified somewhat from that shown in Section 7.10, since we are dealing with a one row matrix on the left. We write:

```
100 FOR J = 1 TO L
110     FOR K = 1 TO N
120         LET C(J) = C(J) + A(K) * B(K,J)
130     NEXT K
140 NEXT J
```

The matrix *C* will have the number of each component needed to fill order *A*.

We write here a general program that will allow the user to read the component matrix from data lines, to enter the order matrix from the keyboard, and to calculate needed components.

```
100 REM -- EXPLODE
105 REM     PROGRAM TO EXPLODE AN ORDER
110 REM -- INPUT VARIABLES: B(N,L),A(N)
115 REM -- LOCAL VARIABLES: J,K,N,L
120 REM -- OUTPUT VARIABLES: I,C(N)
125 LET N = 3 : LET L = 5
130 REM -- LOAD COMPONENT MATRIX
135 FOR I = 1 TO N
140     FOR J = 1 TO L
145         READ B(I,J)
150     NEXT J
155 NEXT I
160 REM -- INPUT ORDER
165 FOR I = 1 TO N
170     PRINT "ENTER QUANTITY OF MODEL A(";I;").";
175     INPUT A(I)
```

```
180 NEXT I
185 REM -- MATRIX MULTIPLICATION
190 FOR J = 1 TO L
195     FOR K = 1 TO N
200         LET C(J) = C(J) + A(K) * B(K,J)
205     NEXT K
210 NEXT J
215 PRINT
220 REM -- PRINT COMPONENT LIST
225 PRINT "HERE ARE COMPONENTS NEEDED"
230 PRINT
235 PRINT "COMPONENT #","QUANTITY"
240 FOR I = 1 TO L
245     PRINT I,C(I)
250 NEXT I
255 DATA 2,0,1,0,0,2,0,0,1,1,0,2,0,1,2
260 END
```

Here is a run of this program for the skateboard fabrication problem:

ENTER QUANTITY OF MODEL A(1).? 100
ENTER QUANTITY OF MODEL A(2).? 150
ENTER QUANTITY OF MODEL A(3).? 75

HERE ARE THE COMPONENTS NEEDED

COMPONENT #	QUANTITY
1	500
2	150
3	100
4	225
5	300

Note that at this point, if one had the inventory of components in array I, subtraction of array C from array I would provide an adjusted inventory or indicate where deficiencies of components exist.

EXERCISE SET 7.4

1. Use the general program on order exploding to solve the following problem. The array of assemblies versus components for a manufacturer of heaters is displayed on the following page.

	Components													
Heater	1	2	3	4	5	6	7	8	9	10	11	12	13	14
H(1)	0	2	1	5	3	1	0	0	0	2	4	1	2	3
H(2)	1	0	1	5	3	1	1	1	1	2	4	1	0	1
H(3)	1	0	0	0	0	0	0	1	1	2	4	1	2	1
H(4)	1	0	0	2	2	0	0	1	1	2	4	1	1	1
H(5)	2	2	1	5	3	1	1	1	1	2	4	1	2	2

(a) Construct data lines from which this array may be read into array B in proper order.

(b) The following order has been received from a department store chain:

Heater H(1) 475

Heater H(2) 200

Heater H(3) 750

Heater H(4) 275

Heater H(5) 100

Enter this order at the keyboard and determine the components needed to fill the order.

2. Write a program that will generate 200 random integers in the range from five to fourteen. Tabulate and print out the number of each integer obtained. How many of each integer would you expect to find when a total of 200 is generated?

3. Assume an inventory matrix for problem 1 as follows:

i(1) i(2) i(3) i(4) i(5) i(6) i(7)
1350 750 650 6000 6000 2000 900

i(8) i(9) i(10) i(11) i(12) i(13) i(14)
1400 2100 3300 7500 2500 2500 4000

Write a program to subtract the component matrix developed in problem 1 from this inventory matrix. What do negative entries in the difference matrix represent?

Review

The addition of arrays and their combination with **FOR-NEXT** loops introduce the real power of the computer in performing repetitive processes on large data sets. We summarize the new terms and the BASIC syntax introduced in this chapter.

ONE-DIMENSIONAL ARRAY   a set of memory locations addressed with a BASIC variable name plus a number called a subscript, for example, **A1(8)** references the eighth location in array A1. One-dimensional arrays are suitable for storing lists. (Section 7.4)

TWO-DIMENSIONAL ARRAYS   a set of memory locations addressed with a BASIC variable name plus a pair of numbers called subscripts, for example, **B(2,3)** references the element of B which is in the second row and the third column. (Section 7.4)

DIMENSIONING   the process of fixing the size of an array. (Section 7.4)

MATRIX   a mathematical term frequently used to describe an array. The mathematical notation used with arrays and the manipulation of arrays predates computers. (Section 7.4)

NESTING   the process of enclosing one structure entirely within another. We considered the nesting of loops which requires distinct loop indices. (Section 7.6)

BASIC SYNTAX

DIM   a BASIC keyword used to indicate that a dimension assignment follows. For example, **DIM A9(23)** saves twenty-three locations for the one-dimensional array A9. (Section 7.4)

RESTORE   BASIC syntax that moves the internal data set pointer to the first data value in the program. Some dialects of BASIC require the use of **RESET** instead of **RESTORE**. (Section 7.8)

8 STRINGS AND STRING FUNCTIONS

8.1 INTRODUCTION TO STRINGS AND STRING FUNCTIONS

In this chapter, we will introduce methods of processing character data. These methods allow us to solve such practical problems as alphabetizing, answer screening, searching, and formatting of both numeric and character information. These string-handling facilities of BASIC expand our capability to use the computer for other than the processing of numerical data.

8.2 CHARACTER DATA AND THE ASCII CODING SYSTEM

So far, we have been primarily concerned with processing numeric data. However, most versions of BASIC include powerful facilities that make it easy for us to process character data. Strictly speaking, any symbol on the keyboard is a *character*. Each character is stored internally by the computer using a numeric coding scheme. The most common internal coding schemes are EBCDIC and ASCII. The latter, an acronym representing American Standard Code for Information Interchange is used by the Apple, the PET, and the TRS-80 and most other microcomputers and minicomputers.

Table 8.1
ASCII Character Set

	Range
Letters (A-Z)	65-90
Digits (0-9)	48-57
Special Characters	33-47
	58-64

In the ASCII coding system—pronounced "askey"—alphabetic characters, commonly called letters, have codes beginning with 65 for the letter A and ending with 90 for the character Z. Numeric symbols, digits, have codes beginning with 48 for zero and ending with 57 for nine. In addition to letters and digits, you have a variety of other characters on the keyboard, including the following: $ # " % & * ? / ( ) +. All these symbols—usually called special characters—have ASCII codes also. In addition, ASCII codes are assigned to a series of nonprinting characters, which are used to control the operation of the computer. For example, a carriage return has a code of 13, the bell has a code of 7, and the space or blank character is represented by the ASCII code of 32. The codes are summarized in Table 8.1.

8.3 STRING VARIABLES

Generally speaking, we do not need to concern ourselves with the computer's internal coding system, but for certain string processing applications, a basic knowledge of the internal coding system is desirable. A *string* is a sequence of characters or symbols enclosed within quotation marks. Just as BASIC provides for numeric constants and variables, it also provides for string constants and variables. Let us consider the following:

    100 LET A$ = "ABCDEF"

In this statement, **A$** is the name of a string variable. While the rules for naming string variables are basically the same as for numeric variables, the dollar sign **"$"** must always be the last character in string variable names in order to distinguish string variables from numeric variables. The character sequence **ABCDEF** contained within quotation marks in statement 100 is a *string constant*. This is a string assignment statement that assigns the value of the constant to the string variable in a manner similar to arithmetic assignment statements. Only string variables may be assigned string values.

8.4 TRANSLATING FROM ASCII CODE TO CHARACTER AND BACK

Most versions of BASIC provide a series of string functions for use in processing character data. During the course of this chapter, you will be introduced to ten string functions, most of which are available on the Apple, the TRS-80 and the PET. The reader should be forewarned that there is considerable variation among computers on string handling functions. We will demonstrate the most common syntax and also point out some common variations.*

The first two functions to be introduced are complements of each other. One function translates a single numeric ASCII code into a character and the other translates a single character into its equivalent ASCII code. Let us examine the following:

```
100 LET A$ = CHR$(42)
110 PRINT A$
```

In statement 100, a string assignment statement, the string variable **A$** receives a string value from the **CHR$ function**. Like arithmetic functions, we can think of string functions as *black boxes* that receive something, transform it, and produce output.

$$A\$ = \boxed{*} \leftarrow \boxed{CHR\$} \leftarrow \boxed{42}$$

Output ← Function ← Input

In this case, we give the function the number **42** by enclosing it within parentheses, after which **CHR$** transforms the number into an asterisk or star, which it passes to the string variable **A$**. The rules of BASIC permit an even more simple application that can be done in immediate mode as well as in program mode:

PRINT CHR$(42)

The computer will respond by printing a star.
Let us pause here to take note of two technical points. (1) The value passed to the function is called an *argument*. **CHR$** accepts only a single argument, but some functions require more than one argument. (2) Note how the name of the **CHR$** function includes a dollar sign **($)** at the end just as in string variable names. Some

---

*If you are using some other microcomputer, we suggest that you consult the following book for information about your computer: David A. Lien, *The BASIC Handbook,* 2nd. ed., San Diego: Compusoft Publishing, 1981.

string functions have the dollar sign at the end of their name and some do not. The rule is that those string functions that yield string results must include the dollar sign in their name. Those string functions that return numeric results may not have a dollar sign in their name. All versions of BASIC impose a limit on the range of values that can be used as arguments for **CHR$**. Such limits actually specify the limits of the ASCII coding system for a given computer. Generally speaking, you can be safe if you limit the argument passed to the **CHR$** to the range from zero to 127. The Apple, the TRS-80, and the PET all accept values in the range from zero to 255. Digital's MUBASIC will accept any positive numeric value but it will divide by 127 any value greater than 127 to obtain the actual argument. With some systems, values exceeding 127 are used for graphic characters and lower case characters. The PET is an example. Values outside the range for a given machine may cause error messages if used.

Just as BASIC allows one to input an ASCII code to the **CHR$** function and receive a character in return, it also allows one to give a single character to a function known as **ASC** and receive the corresponding ASCII code in return. Here are three examples of its use:

1   100 LET J = ASC("$")
    110 PRINT J
2   100 LET A$ = "$"
    110 LET J = ASC(A$)
    120 PRINT J
3   PRINT ASC("$")

All three of the preceding program fragments are functional equivalents and will produce the same results—the number 36 will print on the screen. It is also legal for one to write the following:

110 PRINT ASC("ABCDEF")

However, BASIC will only return the ASCII code for the leftmost character in the string.

Using the **CHR$** function in a loop will allow us to display the entire character set on the screen. Enter and run the following program:

100 FOR I = 0 TO 255
110 PRINT CHR$(I);
120 NEXT I

You may note some erratic behavior on the screen because some of the ASCII characters have no graphic representation but do cause the computer to perform certain functions including carriage return, line feed, and clear screen, to name only three. PET output will be particularly erratic. If you experiment with this program using the PET you will find that much of the output—roughly the first half that contains the letters and numbers—prints as black on white. This is because on the PET, ASCII code 18 instructs the computer to reverse the screen image and print black on white. You can eliminate this annoyance by beginning the loop index at 32.

If you try this little program on the Apple, you will find that it produces two copies of the same thing, suggesting that the Apple cannot distinguish upper from lower case. The fact is, that the Apple can tell upper from lower case as could be demonstrated if program output were directed to a printer. However, the character generator that converts ASCII codes to characters for screen display does not contain the necessary information to produce lower case characters and thus produces upper case characters instead. Several kits are available to remedy this situation.

The character set for the TRS-80 contains lower case characters and graphic characters in the interval between 96 and 191. On other computers, ASCII codes above 127 may include lower case letters.

If you are using the PET, you will also notice that the screen becomes completely dark at one point. This is because **CHR$(147)** instructs the machine to clear the screen. We obtain the same results with the Apple by coding the keyword **HOME**. TRS-80 users can obtain the same results with the keyword **CLS**.

Clearing the Screen

PET:	**100 PRINT CHR$(147)**
Apple:	**100 HOME**
TRS-80:	**100 CLS**

Note that clearing the screen does not destroy the copy of your program in the computer's memory; it just clears the copy on the screen. You may wish to satisfy yourself by trying to list your program after clearing the screen.

8.5 BASIC STRING OPERATIONS

There are six basic string operations to be discussed in this chapter. They are:

1. String assignment,
2. String comparison,
3. String concatenation,
4. String length determination,
5. Substring selection, and
6. Substring indexing.

These six operations are basic to string manipulation. In addition, the use of several other functions will be discussed and illustrated. Because string assignments have been illustrated in detail in the process of treating the **CHR$** and **ASC** functions, they will not receive additional treatment here.

8.6 STRING COMPARISON

Strings can be compared in **IF-THEN** statements in a manner similar to numeric quantities. For example, if a particular program wishes to give the user the option of performing a certain activity or not, the program might solicit user choice in a sequence of statements like the following:

```
100 PRINT "YOU MAY CHOOSE TO PERFORM EXPERIMENT FIVE OR NOT"
110 PRINT "INDICATE YOUR CHOICE (YES OR NO)"
120 INPUT R$
130 IF R$ <> "YES" THEN 200
```

. . . the BASIC code for experiment five would go here . . .

```
200 REM
```

Here statement 120 inputs the user's response as a string. In statement 130 the response in **R$** is compared with the string constant **YES**. If the two are not exactly the same, the expression is evaluated as false and the program continues with statement 200. Only if the string variable and the constant are exactly the same will the block of statements associated with experiment five be executed. The following strings will not be found equal to **YES**:

1. "YES OR NO"
2. " YES"
3. "Y ES"

While leading blanks will cause strings to be unequal, for example in comparing **"YES"** with **" YES"**, trailing blanks may not. This is because some computers automatically trim trailing blanks from input strings.

Thus far, we have been comparing strings for equality or the absence of equality. But, it is also possible to determine whether one string is greater than or smaller than another string. Such comparisons are the basis of sorting names into alphabetical order. Consider the following:

```
170 IF "ABC" < "DEF" THEN PRINT "TRUE"
```

When this statement is executed, the word **"TRUE"** will be printed because the computer will determine which is greater in the same way we would if we were sorting the strings into ascending alphabetical order. Care should be taken, however, when using less than or greater than comparisons for strings, if one or both strings contain either special characters or digits. When either case prevails, the same program may produce different results on different computers. This is particularly important in programs which sort character strings. The Apple, the TRS-80, and the PET all will produce the same results only when upper case letters and numbers are present in strings.

8.7 STRING CONCATENATION

Another basic string operation is concatenation—the process of joining one string to another. The concatenation operator is the plus sign "+". Some computers allow or even require the use of the ampersand "&" instead. The Apple, the PET, and the TRS-80 all require the plus sign. Here is an example:

100 LET A$ = B$ + C$

Since the plus sign is also used in arithmetic assignment statements to indicate addition, we must be careful to avoid confusion. In arithmetic assignment statements, the plus sign is an arithmetic operator causing addition to occur; but in string operations, it is a concatenation operator causing two or more strings to be joined. The following program fragment will distinguish the two operations:

10 PRINT 1 + 1
20 PRINT "1" + "1"
90 END

Statement 10 will cause the value **2** to be printed—the result of addition. In contrast, statement 20 will cause the string **"11"** to be printed—the result of concatenation. Thus, we can see that concatenation merely joins two strings together in the same way that two box cars might be coupled in a train. More than two strings can be concatenated in the same statement. The following examples will illustrate. Attempt to determine what each fragment will do before you run them.

1   **100 PRINT "MERRY CHRISTMAS" + CHR$(38) + "A HAPPY NEW YEAR"**
2   **190 LET S$ = ""**
       200 FOR I = 1 TO 25
       210 LET S$ = S$ + CHR$(42)
       220 NEXT I
       230 PRINT S$

Statement 190 might be confusing. It simply initializes the string **S$** to a null or empty string.

8.8 STRING LENGTH DETERMINATION

In certain cases, we need to know how many characters a particular string contains; that is, we need to know the length of a particular string. BASIC itself imposes a maximum string length, which differs from one computer to another. The Apple, the

PET, and the TRS-80 all have a maximum string size of 255—as do most other versions of BASIC. We should point out that it may not be possible to enter a single string of length 255 all at one time because of a buffer size limitation. Under such circumstances, it will be necessary to enter a long string in sections and concatenate the sections in the program.

The TRS-80 reserves a rather small area for string storage under ordinary circumstances. As a result, there is only enough room for fifty characters of string storage. Programs attempting to use more than that amount will terminate with an **"OS"**, or operating system error. The following program will serve as an example:

```
1  X = 255
2  S$ = " "
3  FOR I = 1 TO X
4     S$ = S$ + "#"
5  NEXT I
6  PRINT S$
7  PRINT LEN(S$)
```

This program merely builds a string of 255 "#" characters, one at a time, and then prints the string and its length. In order to avoid the error message mentioned above, type the following before you run the program:

CLEAR 510

This command initializes all storage locations, resets pointers, and sets the string storage area at 510 bytes. Experimentation suggests that the value specified in the **CLEAR** command should be twice the string space required by the program.

In order to determine the length of a string, BASIC provides a length function called **LEN.** The function accepts a single argument that must be a string variable name, a string expression, or a string constant. **LEN** returns a numeric value indicating the number of characters in the string argument. Here is an example:

```
100  LET S$ = "ABCDEF"
110  PRINT LEN (S$)
```

or simply:

```
100  PRINT LEN("ABCDEF")
```

Both these fragments will cause the number **6** to be printed. We can use the **LEN** function or its output anywhere that it is legal to use a number. The following statement will produce the value zero on most computers:

```
300  PRINT LEN(" ")
```

The length of a null string is zero.

8.9 SUBSTRING SELECTION

A substring is a contiguous segment of a string. A substring is bound by the length restrictions imposed upon strings by a particular dialect of BASIC. Furthermore, since a substring is selected from a string, the substring cannot be longer than the string from which it is selected. Many versions of BASIC, including the Apple, the PET, and the TRS-80, provide three substring selection functions—two of which are actually specialized versions of the third. The functions summarized in Table 8.2 are: **LEFT$**, to select a specified number of characters from the left end of the string; **RIGHT$**, to select a specified number of characters from the right end of the string; and **MID$**, to select a specified number of characters from a point specified within the string. The following fragment will illustrate:

```
200  S$ = "TRUMAN HARRY S"
210  L$ = LEFT$(S$,6)
220  M$ = RIGHT$(S$,1)
230  F$ = MID$(S$,8,5)
```

Statement 200 begins by assigning the string constant **"TRUMAN HARRY S"** to **S$**. Statement 210 selects the leftmost six characters from **S$** and passes them to **L$**. Similarly, statement 220 selects the rightmost character from **S$** and assigns it to **M$**. Finally, **F$** selects a substring from **S$** beginning at character eight and having a length of five characters. By adding the following statements we can see the results of the process:

```
240  PRINT S$
250  PRINT L$
260  PRINT M$
280  PRINT F$
290  PRINT F$;" ";M$;" ";L$
```

Try to predict what statement 290 will do before testing your program. If you use an Apple, you may have noticed that you can omit the semicolons without ill effect. This process of implied concatenation is not common, and, as a rule, should be avoided.

Table 8.2
Substring Functions

Function	Arguments
LEFT$	(string name, substring length)
RIGHT$	(string name, substring length)
MID$	(string name, location of first character of substring, substring length)

Some versions of BASIC, for example, Digital's MUBASIC, provide a function called **SEG$**. It is quite similar to the **MID$** function with the single important exception of the third argument. With **MID$**, the third argument is the length of the substring to be selected, while with **SEG$**, the third argument is the location of the last character in the substring to be selected. The following program fragments will illustrate:

```
100 REM--FRAGMENT #1
110 Z$ = "SUBSTRING SELECTION"
120 PRINT MID$(Z$,6,4)


100 REM--FRAGMENT #2
110 Z$ = "SUBSTRING SELECTION"
120 PRINT SEG$(Z$,6,9)
```

Both program fragments will cause the string "**RING**" to be printed. It is likely that any computer you may be using will support one of these functions, but not both. Also, remember the difference in the third argument.

As suggested above, the **LEFT$** and **RIGHT$** functions are merely specialized versions of the **MID$** function. The following pairs of statements are equivalents:

```
A$=LEFT$(B$,5)       A$=MID$(B$,1,5)

A$=RIGHT$(B$,5)      A$=MID$(B$,LEN(B$)-5+1,5)
```

Some dialects of BASIC permit a statement like the following:

```
110 CHANGE A$ TO A
```

Such a statement instructs the computer to translate each character of the string **A$** into its equivalent ASCII code and store the codes in successive elements of the array A, so that the ASCII code for the first character of **A$** is in A(1), and the second in A(2) and so forth. We can simulate such a function using the **ASC** and **MID$** functions in a loop as the following program fragment illustrates:

```
100 REM--CHANGE
110 DIM A(25)
120 PRINT "ENTER STRING--NO MORE THAN 25 CHARACTERS"
130 INPUT A$
140 FOR I = 1 TO LEN(A$)
150 LET A(I) = ASC(MID$(A$,I,1))
160 PRINT A(I);" ";
170 NEXT I
180 END
```

```
RUN
ENTER STRING--NO MORE THAN 25 CHARACTERS
? HELLO
72 69 76 76 79
```

The numbers printed are the ASCII codes for the characters entered. If you are *not* using an Apple computer, you can probably omit the single blank character printed in line 160.

The second and third arguments of **MID$** and **SEG$** and the last argument of **RIGHT$** and **LEFT$** can be either numeric constants, numeric variables, or arithmetic expressions as long as their values are not out of range. More specifically, these arguments should either be or evaluate to positive numeric values, no greater than the length of the string. Furthermore, the third argument of **SEG$** should not be less than the second argument. In addition, the sum of the second and third arguments of **MID$** should not exceed the string length. If your program violates these specifications, the results will be unpredictable. Some computers will print error messages and interrupt your program. Other computers will print error messages only when negative numeric values are used as arguments. In any case, you will want to be sure that your programs do not violate either the syntax requirements of the computer language or common sense.

8.10 SUBSTRING INDEXING

The final string operation to be demonstrated is the *substring indexing function*. It performs two tasks: (1) it determines whether a substring is present in a string, and (2) if the substring is present, it returns a numeric value indicating the location of the starting character of the substring in the string.

Because neither the PET, the Apple, nor the TRS-80 provide a substring index function, we are forced to write our own. Fortunately, this is not a very complicated task. Let us consider the following fragment:

```
100  LET A$ = "TIPPECANOE AND TYLER TOO"
110  LET B$ = "TYLER"
500  FOR P = 1 TO LEN(A$)−LEN(B$)+1
510  IF B$ = MID$(A$,P,LEN(B$)) THEN 540
520  NEXT P
530  LET P = 0
540  PRINT P
```

This program makes successive comparisons of five character segments of **A$**, beginning with the leftmost five characters until a match occurs. In order to *watch* the program work, insert the following statement:

505 PRINT B$;" ";MID$(A$,P,LEN(B$));" ";P

The following should appear on your screen:

```
TYLER TIPPE 1
TYLER IPPEC 2
TYLER PPECA 3
TYLER PECAN 4
TYLER ECANO 5
TYLER CANOE 6
TYLER ANOE  7
TYLER NOE A 8
TYLER OE AN 9
TYLER E AND 10
TYLER  AND  11
TYLER AND T 12
TYLER ND TY 13
TYLER D TYL 14
TYLER  TYLE 15
TYLER TYLER 16
16
```

Examine the output carefully until you are confident you understand how the program works. Apple, PET, and TRS-80 users will want to take special note of this program fragment for future use. It can be a valuable part of your library of programming tools.

Suppose you were given the assignment of writing a small program intended to test a student's knowledge of geography. More specifically, suppose the program were to print the name of one of the fifty states and ask the student to type in the part of the country where that state was located. Such questions will probably have more than one correct answer and the program will need to check the student's response against each of the acceptable answers. You can accomplish this task using strings and the substring index operation. In such a program, the answer string must be searched in order to determine whether the response string is present in it. Consider the following:

```
100 REM -- GEOGRAPHY QUIZ
110 LET A$ = "EAST NORTHEAST NEW ENGLAND"
120 PRINT "IN WHAT PART OF THE COUNTRY IS CONNECTICUT"
130 INPUT B$
140 FOR P = 1 TO LEN(A$) − LEN(B$) + 1
150    IF B$ = MID$(A$,P,LEN(B$)) THEN 200
160 NEXT P
```

170 PRINT "SORRY, YOUR ANSWER IS WRONG"
180 GOTO 999
200 PRINT "CORRECT"
999 END

At this point, we recommend that you type in this program and run it in order to satisfy yourself that it works correctly. In addition to the correct answers, try each of the following:

NORTH	ENGLAND	E
NEW	LAND	W E
THE		

Your program should accept all of the obviously incorrect answers and print a congratulatory message. Clearly, this program needs some more work. Read over the results and try to diagnose the problem before you proceed to the next paragraph.

The problem, as you have probably deduced by now, is that humans make certain assumptions about the answer string that are unknown to the computer. When we look at statement 110, we see four words in the answer string constituting three correct answers. They are: **EAST**, **NORTHEAST** and **NEW ENGLAND**. We read the answer string in this manner because we recognize the words in it. We know that NEW ENGLAND is one answer because the words refer to a part of the country. Also, very importantly, we interpret the blank character, or space, as a word delimiter—that is, as separating words from each other. Computers make no such assumption. The blank is just as much a character to the computer as the "T". It is also clear that the blank between NEW and ENGLAND is different in its meaning from the blank which follows EAST. The blank that follows EAST separates one correct answer from another while the blank between NEW and ENGLAND only separates two words in the same correct answer. We must make several minor changes in our program in order to insure that it interprets answers the way we do. More specifically, we need to distinguish between those spaces that delimit correct answers and those that separate words in the same answer. Our objective is rather easily achieved by the modification of statement 110 and the addition of statement 135.

110 LET A$="$EAST$NORTHEAST$NEW ENGLAND$"
135 LET B$="$"+B$+"$"

Now rerun the program trying all the incorrect answers given above as well as the correct ones. Does the program now distinguish the correct answers from the incorrect ones?

Our technique here is a simple one. We merely insert dollar signs into the answer string so that each correct answer begins and ends with a dollar sign. Unknown to the student, the program also adds a dollar sign to the front and the end of the student's answer string.

EXERCISE SET 8.1

1. Read the following program fragments carefully and determine what the computer will print when you run the fragments. After doing so, enter and run them and check your answers.

    (a) 100 LET A$ = "HAPPY BASTILLE DAY"
         110 FOR I = 1 TO LEN(A$)
         120 PRINT MID$(A$,I,1)
         130 NEXT I

    (b) 100 LET A$ = "HAPPY BASTILLE DAY"
         110 FOR I = LEN(A$) TO 1 STEP −1
         120 PRINT MID$(A$,I,1)
         130 NEXT I

    (c) 100 LET A$ = "YOUR NAME"
         110 LET B$ = " "
         120 LET K = LEN(A$)
         130 FOR I = 1 TO LEN(A$)
         140 LET B$ = B$ + MID$(A$,K,1)
         150 LET K = K−1
         160 NEXT I
         170 PRINT A$
         180 PRINT B$

2. A sentence is entered as a single string on a data line. Write a program that determines the length of the first word in this sentence. Assume that the sentence has no internal punctuation and ends with a period.

3. Consider problem 2 above again. Write a program that counts and prints the total number of words in the sentence.

4. Assume that the computer you are using does not support the **RIGHT$** and **LEFT$** functions. Rewrite the following statements using the **MID$** function. If you are using a computer that supports another substring function, convert these statements to use the available function.

    PRINT LEFT$(S$,5)
    PRINT RIGHT$(S$,2)
    PRINT RIGHT$(S$,10)
    PRINT LEFT$(S$,12)

    Note: We have not specified the length of **S$** and you should not assume any particular length except that the string is at least as long as the substring we are attempting to select.

5. Rewrite the following statements to use the **MID$** function.

   X$ = SEG$(B$,9,11)
   PJ$ = SEG$(X$,9,9)
   A3$ = SEG$(Z$,10,14)

6. If your machine does not support the **MID$** function, rewrite the following statements to use whatever substring function you have available.

   X$ = MID$(A$,5,7)
   D$ = MID$(NAME$,2,2)
   SS$ = MID$(ST$,I,1)

8.11 STRING APPLICATIONS: DECIMAL POINT ALIGNMENT

Let us now look at several small programs that apply the functions, operations, and techniques we have demonstrated. Many dialects of BASIC, including TRS-80 Level II BASIC, support some syntax that allows the programmer to prescribe the format under which values will be printed. For example, one could decide that the value of a given variable will be rounded to the second decimal place and printed in a field eight characters wide beginning at column 21 on the screen. This gives us the ability to make the decimal points line up vertically in a column of figures. Neither the Apple nor the PET provides such a formatting facility. Fortunately, this is not a difficult application to program. First, consider the following program and its output as an illustration of the problem we wish to solve:

```
100 REM-----NOFORMAT 11-24-78
105 FOR I = 1 TO 6
110 READ V
120 PRINT V
130 NEXT I
200 DATA 1.23, 231.44, .45, 2.98, 179.99
202 DATA 12.21

RUN
1.23
231.44
.45
2.98
179.99
12.21
```

Notice how each number printed begins in the same column. This makes it difficult for one to read such a column of figures. It is not easy to find the largest or smallest number. In contrast, consider the following program and output listing. All the decimal points line up over one another and the column is relatively easy to read.

```
100 REM -- WITHFORMAT 11-24-78
105 FOR I = 1 TO 6
110 READ V
120 LET V$ = STR$(V)
130 FOR J = 1 TO LEN(V$)
140    IF MID$(V$,J,1) = "." THEN O = J - 1 : GOTO 170
150 NEXT J
160 LET O = LEN(V$)
170 PRINT TAB(10 - O)V
180 NEXT I
200 DATA 1.23, 231.44, .45, 2.98, 179.99
202 DATA 12.21

RUN
   1.23
 231.44
    .45
   2.98
 179.99
  12.21
```

This program and the one to be used in Section 8.14 introduce two new functions, which are available in most dialects of BASIC. The two functions are complements of each other. One changes a string value into a numeric value and the other changes a numeric value into a string. **STR$** accepts a single numeric argument and produces a string representation of that value as output. For example:

```
200 LET X = 129
210 LET X$ = STR$(X)
220 PRINT X$
```

This fragment will change the numeric value 129 into a three character string if you use an Apple. If you use a PET, a four character string will be printed, which consists of a single blank followed by "**129**". MUBASIC behaves like the Apple. The TRS-80 behaves just like the PET in this regard. You can test the behavior of your computer by adding one additional statement as follows:

```
230 PRINT LEN(X$)
```

If the value assigned to **X** in statement 200 is changed to -129 all dialects of BASIC mentioned above will produce strings four characters long each beginning with a minus sign.

The **VAL** function translates a string into its numeric representation. As you might expect, **VAL** will not work correctly (or at all) if the string to be translated contains nonnumeric characters. The following will illustrate:

```
100  LET S$ = "$225.98"
110  LET S = VAL(RIGHT$(S$,6))
120  PRINT S
```

This fragment will cause the second through seventh characters to be segmented and then translated by **VAL** into a numeric value. For that reason, the dollar sign was omitted from the substring passed to **VAL**. Had we not done so, an error message would have resulted. The Apple, the PET, and the TRS-80 are a little more tolerant of illegal characters in the **VAL** statement argument. The following program will run correctly on the microcomputers named above but not in many dialects of BASIC.

```
200  LET X$ = "123XX"
210  LET X = VAL(X$)
220  PRINT X
```

Assuming that the **"XX"** represents junk in which you are not interested, the Apple, the PET, and the TRS-80 will return a correct result of 123.

8.12 STRING APPLICATIONS: RANDOM WORDS

In Chapter 6, you were introduced to random numbers and some of their applications. Since alphabetic characters are represented internally in the computer as numeric codes, we can use the random number generator to produce random words. In this case, we use the random number generator to produce values, which our program scales so that they all fall in the range from sixty-five to ninety, the range of ASCII codes for alphabetic characters. The following program produces 160 randomly created four-letter words. You will note that the program produces a different set of random words on each execution. On the basis of extensive testing, we are satisfied that the program behaves itself and confines its creativity to four-letter words that are socially acceptable. You will have to be patient with your computer, because if it is like ours, it is a bit inarticulate and produces few if any recognizable words in each execution. Here is a version that will run on the Apple:

================================ APPLE ================================

```
100 REM -- RANDOM WORDS
105 REM     APPLE VERSION
110 HOME
120 FOR I = 1 TO 20
130    FOR J = 1 TO 8
140       FOR K = 1 TO 4
150          LET L = RND(1)
160          LET L = INT(L *(90-65+1)+65)
170          PRINT CHR$(L);
180       NEXT K
190       PRINT " ";
200    NEXT J
220 NEXT I

RUN

SIAW EBUN YMFV JSON VLST PWYI OLHL NIXU
NHHZ JNSM APMM GPKK TYRH PCVT FVJM OSUJ
WTJM SMKF SBPE LOWV SIJW STUD MPHO JVZE
XUQN HMAX SXUE EXED RVPG DXSQ ZCTY XRLZ
HHLE XOTY RZIH UTAL YSRT WXOS TSLQ TOZU
EVUE XVPD IRHQ YNTR GGHL GPLL SUNK CXJR
OFUO NONT UGVJ HZLU IGEZ YSSU GLUC LQPH
CKMT CBHV QODJ UJOT FECT QJIX XDOZ PEOI
YPVT GXZI KIQL HWYJ KMUS GWRE TITW ARUA
EIIC CBAB KUJK WHCV NUSC COAU YYQW PHLO
KGSK IOYC OKBI LJXV YHKC ZQNF VMID EYGL
KREW ABVW KWIQ PVVD GAQD GEHJ HERQ LAGA
QSVO AMRO AXUB BGBD XLJP SOMG SCOR ZCPO
PPTH XHDS QEBH SVIC VRMI EUKA TRFG EUPI
SRJC GRDE VARW TWBG VVGA WGJQ YSNU JOZQ
KWGO YTTY JAEX WKMW RNAD BRRV BFKJ VHXF
VECE CRPB LYAX TXZL VAZU GSHH XSGZ GEGT
KYWX UHLF OYPC XPFC QYKY RTQM RGQX LVAL
NHYM OFDL YXJG JLXM LAPW WGBH KGYD LKBB
URMS ILGP IYHO UOFO WVID KYSD ZZHF WNJF
```

If you wish to run this program on the PET you should replace statement 110 and insert statement 115 as indicated in the boxed PET program:

Sec. 8.12 String Applications: Random Words

PET

```
100 REM -- RANDOM WORDS
105 REM     PET VERSION
110 PRINT CHR$(147)
115 LET D = RND(-TI)
120 FOR I = 1 TO 20
130    FOR J = 1 TO 8
140       FOR K = 1 TO 4
150          LET L = RND(1)
160          LET L = INT(L *(90-65+1)+65)
170          PRINT CHR$(L);
180       NEXT K
190       PRINT " ";
200    NEXT J
220 NEXT I
```

Statement 115 is intended to help the PET produce a more acceptable series of random numbers by passing a more or less random seed to the random number generator. The value returned to **D** is not intended for any use. **TI** is a PET special variable that retains the count of the number of ticks (60ths of a second) that have passed since the machine was turned on or the time was reset. **TI** and its companion **TI$** will be discussed further in section 10.13.*

The TRS-80 version, which is quite similar to the Apple version, is presented below.

TRS-80

```
100 REM -- RANDOM WORDS
105 REM     TRS-80 VERSION
110 CLS
120 FOR I = 1 TO 20
130    FOR J = 1 TO 8
140       FOR K = 1 TO 4
150          LET L = RND(0)
160          LET L = INT(L *(90-65+1) +65)
```

*Our usage here follows the manufacturer's recommendation. See *PET 2001-8 PERSONAL COMPUTER USER MANUAL*. First Edition (Palo Alto: Commodore Business Machines, 1978), p. 30.

```
170        PRINT CHR$(L);
180     NEXT K
190     PRINT " ";
200  NEXT J
210  PRINT
220 NEXT I
```

8.13 STRING APPLICATIONS: SORTING STRINGS

A common data processing task for business and research is sorting. Sorting is made possible by the order in the ASCII (or EBCDIC) coding system. Following is a short progam that sorts the last names of some of your favorite composers of classical music. The algorithm used here is the simple bubble sort demonstrated in Section 6.4 with numeric data.

```
100  REM---STRING SORT
101  REM
110  DIM N$(15)
115  LET N = 15
117  REM
118  REM---READ UNSORTED LIST
119  REM
120  FOR I = 1 TO N
125     READ N$(I)
130  NEXT I
189  REM
190  REM---SORT ROUTINE
191  REM
200  FOR I = N TO 2 STEP −1
210     FOR J = 1 TO I−1
220        IF N$(J) <= N$(J+1) THEN 250
225        LET S$ = N$(J)
230        LET N$(J) = N$(J+1)
235        LET N$(J+1) = S$
250     NEXT J
260  NEXT I
269  REM
```

```
270  REM---PRINT SORTED LIST
271  REM
275  FOR I = 1 TO N
280     PRINT N$(I)
285  NEXT I
299  REM
300  DATA BEETHOVEN,VAUGHAN WILLIAMS,MOZART
301  DATA BRAHMS,RESPIGHI,ELGAR,DELIUS
302  DATA VIVALDI,PURCELL,POULENC,FRANK
303  DATA PROKOFIEV,BORODIN,GLINKA,FAURE

RUN
BEETHOVEN
BORODIN
BRAHMS
DELIUS
ELGAR
FAURE
GLINKA
MOZART
POULENC
PROKOFIEV
PURCELL
RESPIGHI
VAUGHAN WILLIAMS
VIVALDI
```

8.14 STRING APPLICATIONS: INPUT VALIDATION

A common type of user error that can occur with any computer language is the accidental entry of nonnumeric data when a number is required. Depending upon the language, this error causes at least the generation of an error message and often causes abnormal termination of the program. To cope with this problem, all serious programmers write code to check all input for illegal characters. This process is called *validation of input* or *laundering of input*. For example, if a program requires its user to enter a number, whatever is actually entered must be checked for illegal characters before the program proceeds any further. We can accomplish this goal by first reading the response as a string and then proceeding to validate the input.

156 *Strings and String Functions* Ch. 8

Consider this problem: If a novice user incorrectly enters the letter "O" in place of the number "0", the computer will respond with an error message. We can include within our programs a test that traps such errors and reports them to the user. The prototype program below uses several string manipulation techniques which were discussed earlier in this chapter. Notice how the user response is converted to a numeric value only after it is found to contain only numeric characters. Examine the program closely. After you think you understand it, make a list of the assumptions that the program makes about what is and what is not a numeric value. Also, note the use of the **CHR$** function in line 300. With many dialects of BASIC, this is the only way a program can print a quotation mark.

```
100 REM---BAD DATA CHECK
105 REM
200 PRINT "ENTER A NUMBER"
210 INPUT R$
220 FOR I = 1 TO LEN(R$)
230    IF MID$(R$,I,1) < "0" THEN 290
240    IF MID$(R$,I,1) > "9" THEN 290
250 NEXT I
260 LET K = VAL(R$)
270 PRINT "THE NUMBER ENTERED IS ";K
280 GOTO 999
290 PRINT "A NON-NUMERIC CHARACTER HAS BEEN ENTERED"
300 PRINT CHR$(34); MID$(R$,I,1); CHR$(34); " IS NON-NUMERIC"
999 END

RUN
ENTER A NUMBER
?12W
A NON-NUMERIC CHARACTER HAS BEEN ENTERED
"W" IS NON-NUMERIC
RUN
ENTER A NUMBER
?123
THE NUMBER ENTERED IS 123
```

On many computers—including the Apple, the PET and the TRS-80—it is possible to combine the logical tests in statements 230 and 240 into a single statement as follows:

230 IF MID$(R$,I,1) < "0" OR MID$(R$,I,1) > "9" THEN 290

Other computers may not allow this syntax.

8.15 STRING APPLICATIONS: LOWER CASE

Some dialects of BASIC permit the printing of lower case letters. Under some circumstances, we may wish to translate characters from upper to lower case. We can do this by using different string manipulation techniques discussed in earlier sections of this chapter. First, we must translate each character in the string into its respective ASCII code using the **ASC** function and store these codes in an array as illustrated in Section 8.9. Then, we add thirty-two to each alphabetic code in the array; that is, to each ASCII code in the range of sixty-five to ninety. Finally, we translate the array of ASCII codes back to characters using the **CHR$** function. Here is the program. It is written in the MUBASIC dialect and will not run on the Apple, the PET, or the TRS-80.

```
100 REM---LOWER CASE
101 REM    MUBASIC VERSION
102 REM
110 DIM A(25)
120 PRINT "ENTER A STRING"
125 INPUT A$
126 REM
127 REM---CHANGE TO ASCII CODES
128 REM
130 FOR I = 1 TO LEN(A$)
135     LET A(I) = ASC(SEG$(A$,I,I))
140 NEXT I
144 REM
145 REM---CHANGE TO LOWER CASE
146 REM
150 FOR I = 1 TO LEN(A$)
160     IF A(I) < 65 THEN 190
170     IF A(I) > 90 THEN 190
180     LET A(I) = A(I) + 32
190 NEXT I
194 REM
195 REM---PRINT LOWER CASE
196 REM
200 FOR I = 1 TO LEN(A$)
210     PRINT CHR$(A(I));
220 NEXT I
230 END
```

Here is a run:

RUN
ENTER STRING? MICKEY MOUSE
mickey mouse

Statements 160 and 170 together prevent ASCII codes from being modified if the original symbol was not an upper case letter. Without these statements, our program would produce strange results for numbers, special characters, and blanks. By using these statements, such characters are left alone.

Next, we will present a version of the same program that will run on the PET. It is quite similar to the MUBASIC version. The PET actually has two character sets, the standard character set that contains the symbols found on the keyboard and a second character set that does not contain the graphic symbols seen on the keyboard but substitutes lower case characters instead. The standard character set is always used by the PET unless we direct otherwise. One memory location in the PET is used to take note of which character set is currently in use. When we wish to change character sets we must insert a numeric value into that memory location, something we do with the **POKE** command. (For the record, **POKE** is really a function, but it is often used as if it were a command. **POKE** inserts a numeric value into a memory location specified by its address.) To instruct the PET to use its second character set, we use the following statement:

POKE 59468,14

This statement causes the decimal value fourteen to be inserted or POKEd into memory location 59468. Such a statement can be included in any BASIC program and can also be used in immediate mode. To change back to the standard character set, we merely **POKE** the value twelve into the same location. Whenever the PET is turned on, the value twelve is POKEd into location 59468 to assure that the standard character set will be used. The PET version of the program is reproduced here:

================================ PET ================================

```
100  REM---PET VERSION OF
101  REM    LOWER CASE
110  DIM A(25)
120  PRINT "ENTER A STRING";
125  INPUT A$
130  REM---CHANGE TO ASCII CODES
135  FOR I = 1 TO LEN(A$)
140  LET A(I) = ASC(MID$(A$,I,1))
145  NEXT I
150  REM---CHANGE TO LOWER CASE
```

```
155 FOR I = 1 TO LEN(A$)
160 LET A(I) = A(I) + 128
170 NEXT I
175 PRINT
178 REM---PRINT LOWER CASE
180 FOR I = 1 TO LEN(A$)
185 PRINT CHR$(A(I));
190 NEXT I
195 REM---DELAY
200 FOR I = 1 TO 3000
210 NEXT I
220 POKE 59468,12
230 END
```

The FOR-NEXT loop beginning at statement 200 is a delay loop that eats up time before statement 220 is executed. Statement 220 will have the effect of changing all the lower case characters on the screen to graphic characters. (You can delete this statement if you wish to continue with lower case.) Because the PET continually refreshes the screen image from an internal buffer (sixty times a second), changing the character set with the **POKE** command changes all characters on the screen. To enter lower case characters from the keyboard (assuming the PET is already instructed to use the second character set), first depress the shift key, and then type the key with the desired character on it. This sequence is opposite to the way typewriters work. Note that in statement 160, the ASCII codes are incremented by 128 rather than 32 as in the earlier example.

EXERCISE SET 8.2

1. Enter the **FORMAT** program discussed in Section 8.11. Change the contents of the **DATA** statements so that there is one negative value in the program. Then run the program. Do the decimal points still line up correctly? On some computers, the negative value will be misaligned. If this problem occurs, modify the program to handle negative values correctly.

2. Using the random word generator discussed in Section 8.12 as a model, write a program to accept a word from the keyboard and then attempt to generate the same word randomly. The program should keep track of how many tries are necessary before the desired word is generated. A word of warning: if you attempt to get the computer to generate a word with more than three characters, be prepared for a long wait.

3. Modify the bad data check program in Section 8.14 so that it accepts decimal values. Be sure that only one decimal point is accepted. Test your program.

4. If your computer is not one of those we discussed when we treated lower case, consult the documentation for your computer or ask your instructor if your computer can produce lower case characters. If it can, write your own program to translate upper case to lower case using our sample programs as models.

Review

Here we list the new BASIC syntax introduced in this chapter.

BASIC SYNTAX

CHR$ () a string function that returns the character corresponding to the ASCII code argument. (Section 8.4)

ASC () a string function (the complement of **CHR$**) that returns the ASCII code for a single character string argument. (Section 8.4)

SEG$ (, ,) a substring selection function that returns a specified segment of a string. The arguments are the string, the starting character of the substring to be selected, and the last character of the substring to be selected. (Section 8.9)

MID$ (, ,) another substring selection function very similar to **SEG$**. The only difference is the third argument which, in the case of **MID$**, is the length of the substring to be selected. (Section 8.9)

LEN ( ) a string function that returns the length of its string argument. (Section 8.8)

STR$ ( ) a string function that returns a character representation of its numeric argument. (Section 8.11)

VAL ( ) a string function that returns a numeric representation of its string argument. This function is the complement of **STR$**. The argument should contain a character representation of a number. (Section 8.11)

LEFT$ (,) a substring selection function that returns a substring of specified length from the left end of a string. The first argument is the string name or a string constant and the second argument is the length of the substring to be selected. (Section 8.9)

RIGHT$ (,) a substring selection function that returns a substring of specified length from the right end of the string. The first argument is the string name or a string constant and the second argument is the length of the substring to be selected. (Section 8.9)

9
PROGRAM STRUCTURE AND DEBUGGING

9.1 INTRODUCTION TO PROGRAM STRUCTURE AND DEBUGGING

People who use computers frequently refer to program errors as **bugs** and the process of removing errors from programs as **debugging**. The detection and correction of errors is a normal everyday part of the process of using a computer as a problem-solving tool. Some errors are obvious and easy to detect while others are subtle and may exist in a program for months without detection. Serious programmers (those who program for a living) devote a substantial amount of time to the testing of their programs in order to find and eliminate the bugs. We can classify errors as follows:

Typology of Programming Errors

1. Program is interrupted prematurely with an error message.
2. Program runs (or seems to run) but does not produce any results.
3. Program runs and produces obviously incorrect results.
4. Program runs and produces plausible but incorrect results.

While type 1 errors often seem to overwhelm the novice programmer, they are detected by the computer and are relatively easy to handle. In contrast, type 4 errors may go undetected indefinitely.

In this chapter we will be concerned with the detection and correction of errors. But we must begin with the programming development process because many errors originate here.

9.2 PREVENTING ERRORS

While we do not wish to imply that all errors can be prevented, we are convinced that programs that are well developed from the beginning are less subject to errors. Furthermore, in such programs, errors are easier to detect and to correct. We recognize that there is an experimental aspect to programming which implies that trial and error methods will often be used.

In Chapter 3 we introduced an algorithmic language, which we recommended that you use in the process of program development for all but the most trivial tasks. The use of algorithmic language prior to coding in BASIC helps us to detect logical inconsistencies early in the design process. This reduces the need for *quick fixes* in programs, which tend to obscure program meaning. The algorithmic representation of our problem solution will be an important reference document as we attempt to find and correct errors. Other valuable documents will be cross reference tables and variable lists.

9.3 PROGRAM STRUCTURE

Up to this point, we have emphasized the construction of short rather simple programs. The most complicated task attempted was in Section 7.11 where we developed a program for exploding orders. That program was nearly thirty lines long. As we begin to solve more complex problems our algorithms and programs become longer and potentially more difficult to understand.

All but the simplest programs have component parts or can be segmented into components. These components constitute a kind of *natural program structure*. If we are able to recognize this natural structure or even enhance it, we can make our programs easier to read and understand. Kernighan and Plauger have written, "in our experience, readability is the single best criterion of program quality: if a program is easy to read, it is probably a good program, if it is hard to read, it probably isn't good."* Implicit in this statement is the proposition that programs are intended to be read by persons (including their original authors) as well as by machines. We should hasten to add that readable programs are easier to debug.

---

*Kernighan and Plauger, *Software Tools*, p. 28.

Some dialects of BASIC make it easy to improve the readability of our programs while other dialects offer little help. Consider the following two examples. Which line is easier to understand?

    200 FORKS=1TOAD

or

    200 FOR KS = 1 TO AD

While the computer will execute both statements correctly, we think you will agree that the second statement is more comprehensible to humans. Were we to enter the first version, the Apple would automatically produce the second version upon being given a list command. In contrast, the PET will retain the earlier version if you use it. Thus, more care must be taken with the PET. In fairness, we must admit that the first example does save some memory. With a microcomputer with limited memory this is a consideration. But conservation of memory may be achieved at a high price.

Some BASIC dialects permit empty lines—that is, with nothing following the statement number—and some allow one to indent in order to set off blocks of statements. Unfortunately, most microcomputers, the Apple and the PET included, do not provide such facilities and we are forced to improvise. The TRS-80 is the exception, permitting both blank lines and statement indentation. Loop indentation can be achieved on any computer by using the colon to force indentation as follows:

    200   FOR I = 1 TO LAST
    210 : READ X(I)
    220 : PRINT X(I)
    230   NEXT I

This may not be as satisfactory as the following:

    200 FOR I = 1 TO LAST
    210   READ X(I)
    220   PRINT X(I)
    230 NEXT I

We like the latter approach and have written an editor program which will print hard copies of your programs with such indentation. This program is described in Appendix D, page D1.

Careful use of comment statements can also help improve the readability of programs by marking off blocks of statements vertically. Generally speaking, we recommend that you avoid excessive comments and comments that echo the code. For example, in both the following fragments, the comments do not add to our understanding of what the program is doing:

    200 REM---ADD A TO B GIVING C
    210 C = A + B

```
200 REM---ADD C TO B GIVING A
210 C = A + B
```

In the second case, the comment actually misleads. Since comment statements look more like English than BASIC statements do, we are more likely to read and trust the comment than the code.*

We have been using **REM** statements to separate blocks of statements vertically without comment but now we need to make this approach more explicit. Here we present the same program to explode an order with a more fully developed use of **REM** statements.

```
100 REM -- EXPLODE
101 REM     PROGRAM TO EXPLODE AN ORDER
103 REM
105 LET N = 3 : LET L = 5
107 REM---------------------------
108 REM          LOAD COMPONENT MATRIX
109 REM---------------------------
110 FOR I = 1 TO N
115     FOR J = 1 TO L
120         READ B(I,J)
130     NEXT J
140 NEXT I
144 REM---------------------------
145 REM    INPUT ORDER FROM KEYBOARD
146 REM---------------------------
150 FOR I = 1 TO N
160     PRINT "ENTER QUANTITY OF MODEL A(";I;"). ";
170     INPUT A(I)
180 NEXT I
184 REM---------------------------
185 REM          EXPLODE THE ORDER
186 REM---------------------------
190 FOR J = 1 TO L
200     FOR K = 1 TO N
210         LET C(J) = C(J) + A(K) * B(K,J)
220     NEXT K
230 NEXT J
232 PRINT
```

---

*Kernighan and Plauger, *The Elements of Programming Style,* Second Edition (New York: McGraw-Hill, 1978,) p. 142.

```
233 REM---------------------------
234 REM      DISPLAY COMPONENT LIST
236 REM---------------------------
236 PRINT "HERE ARE COMPONENTS NEEDED"
238 PRINT
240 PRINT "COMPONENT #","QUANTITY"
250 FOR I = 1 TO L
260     PRINT I,C(I)" ";
270 NEXT I
277 REM---------------------------
279 REM DATA SET: COMPONENT MATRIX
280 REM---------------------------
280 DATA 2,0,1,0,0,2,0,0,1,1,0,2,0,1,2
290 END
```

Our use of **REM** statements here is merely an illustration of an approach to improving the readability of programs. We recommend the approach to you, but not necessarily our implementation of it. Let us summarize the major components:

1   We use the dash to create vertical segments. The lines of dashes are of uniform length.

2   We mark off major blocks of the program using **REM** statements to indicate the function of the blocks.

3   We use three-digit line numbers to achieve left justification.

4   The first statement in our programs is always numbered 100 and always contains the name of the program. The program is saved on disk under this name. When it is time to save a program and we forget its name, we merely have to list statement 100 in order to prevent accidental overwriting of the wrong file.

5   We indent the contents of each **FOR-NEXT** loop.

As we indicated above, there are many possible variations on our approach and we advise you to adopt your own approach and use it consistently. Among the important considerations in selecting a style are the following:

1   How much memory is available? If you have a small amount of memory, you may have to reduce the length of the **REM** statements as well as their number.

2   Is a printer available? If one is available, you may not be concerned about line wrap-around because on the printer, it comes out as a single line. If a printer is not readily available, you might want to limit statement length to facilitate reading BASIC code on a screen.

3   How wide is your screen? If the dialect of BASIC available to you permits

seventy-two or eighty characters to be displayed per line, you may take a different approach than you would take if you have a forty column display limit.

The key is to adopt a style and use it consistently.

9.4 STRUCTURED PROGRAMMING

The term **structured programming** has obtained common usage in the field of computing in recent years, but there seems to be no consensus on its meaning. Here we will follow a definition by Kernighan and Plauger who have written that "structured programming in a very narrow sense implies programming with a limited set of control flow statements, and avoiding gotos."* Some have argued for the complete elimination of **GOTO** statements. However, this is an extreme remedy, one not feasible in BASIC. Yet, we can greatly improve the structure of our programs by carefully scrutinizing every **GOTO** statement and eliminating those that do not implement fundamental structures; and, by modularizing our programs through the use of **subroutines**, which are discrete program segments that perform specific tasks. For those who wonder what is wrong with using **GOTO** statements, Professor Weinberg answers:

> Experiments with problem solving in programming-like situations indicate that a series of decisions arranged in a strictly linear sequence is typically easier to handle than a branching or looping sequence. Experience with programming languages seems to bear this out, for programs with numerous GO TO statements or other branches are notoriously difficult to understand or debug.†

Each **GOTO** or branching statement "breaks our normal sequential mode of scanning the program or thinking about it."‡ There is also evidence that "unrestrained branching via GOTO, produces structures that lend themselves to logical errors."§ Following is a program fragment that contains a classic example of the incorrect use of the **GOTO** statement:

```
200  BIG = A(1)
210  FOR I = 2 TO 10
220     IF A(I) > BIG THEN 240
230     GOTO 250
```

---

*Kernighan and Plauger, *Software Tools*, p. 2.
†Weinberg, *The Psychology of Computer Programming*, pp. 231-2.
‡Weinberg, *The Psychology of Computer Programming*, pp. 231-2.
§Frederick P. Brooks, *The Mythical Man-Month: Essays on Software Engineering*, (Reading, Mass.: Addison-Wesley Co., 1975,) p. 144.

```
240     BIG = A(I)
250 NEXT I
```

This fragment really contains two branching statements—lines 220 and 230. The combined effect is to complicate what would otherwise be a straightforward algorithm. Indeed, we are never quite sure we understand what the algorithm is doing. This illustrates a very common error often made both by those learning to program and by experienced programmers who should know better. This fragment merely finds the largest value in the array *A*—a procedure we have seen before. But the fragment is complicated by one statement branching around another branching statement. Following is a simple and clear version of the same procedure.

```
200  BIG = A(1)
210  FOR I = 2 TO 10
220      IF A(I) > BIG THEN BIG = A(I)
230  NEXT I
```

Not only is the second version easier for us to understand, it also is shorter by two statements.*

9.5 PROGRAM BLOCKS

It is possible to achieve the linearity that Weinberg writes about by organizing our program in **blocks**; that is, major sections of the program that are devoted to a specific task, that are linked sequentially. We present a general system for organizing a program that can be followed. It is intended as an illustration of an approach not as the only way to do it. Depending upon your program, certain blocks might be omitted. The basic approach we advocate here is not the segmentation of certain specific blocks in every program, but the segmentation of major blocks in each program. You will note that we do not follow the block segmentation technique rigidly but rather take a flexible approach that is intended to set off and label each significant program block. We recommend this flexible approach to you.

A Possible Approach to Segmenting
A Program into Major Blocks

1 Program Identification & Initialization
2 Main Program Loop
3 Data Set Block (if any)

*We owe this example to Kernighan and Plauger, *Elements of Programming Style*, p. 18.

4   Subroutine 1

5   Subroutine 2

6   Subroutine n

In order to illustrate this approach of block segmentation we will use as an example a program that finds the mean, the standard deviation, and the median of a data set. We will discuss the program as it corresponds to our model for segmenting a program into blocks.

1   Program Identification and Initialization

This block always begins with statement 100 which is a **REM** statement containing the name of the program (this is the name under which it is stored on disk or tape) and the date on which the program was written. In some cases where it matters, we also add another **REM** statement indicating a revision date. Immediately following statement 100 come a series of **REM** statements that indicate the purpose of the program and contain any warnings deemed necessary. Next, come initialization statements that declare arrays, and initialize variables or arrays. Here is this block of our program:

```
100 REM -- SIGMA     8-9-79
101 REM
102 REM      REVISED   1-1-80
103 REM
104 REM      THIS PROGRAM EVALUATES THE MEAN
105 REM      STANDARD DEVIATION AND MEDIAN
106 REM      OF A DATA SET.
107 REM
108 REM      WARNING: IN COMPUTING STANDARD DEVIATION
109 REM      WE HAVE ASSUMED SAMPLE DATA,
110 REM      NOT A POPULATION.
111 REM
210 REM
220 DIM X(15)
230 LET S = 0
301 REM
310 REM
320 PRINT "HOW MANY PIECES OF DATA WILL BE ANALYZED? (MAXIMUM OF 15)"
330 INPUT N
335 FOR I = 1 TO N
340    READ X(I)
345 NEXT I
```

2. Main Program Loop

Next, we have the main program loop. It controls the flow of the program through the computational and output steps.

```
400 REM =========MAIN PROGRAM ================
401 REM
402 REM----------------------EVALUATE THE MEAN
403 REM
430 FOR I = 1 TO N
440     LET S = S + X(I)
450 NEXT I
460 LET M = S / N
470 REM
480 REM--------CALL STANDARD DEVIATION ROUTINE
490 REM
500 GOSUB 9100
520 REM
530 REM----------------------CALL SORT ROUTINE
540 REM
550 GOSUB 8900
560 REM
570 REM--------------------CALL MEDIAN ROUTINE
580 REM
590 GOSUB 9200
600 REM
610 REM--------------------DISPLAY THE RESULTS
620 REM
630 PRINT "HERE IS THE SORTED DATA SET"
640 PRINT
650 FOR I = 1 TO N : PRINT X(I) : NEXT I
660 PRINT : PRINT
670 PRINT "THE MEAN OF THE DATA SET IS "; M
680 PRINT
690 PRINT "THE STANDARD DEVIATION IS ";S8
700 PRINT
710 PRINT "THE MEDIAN IS ";M9
```

3. Data Set

In this block, we find the data lines from which the program reads the data set. If the data set were to be entered from the keyboard or read from a file, this block would not be present.

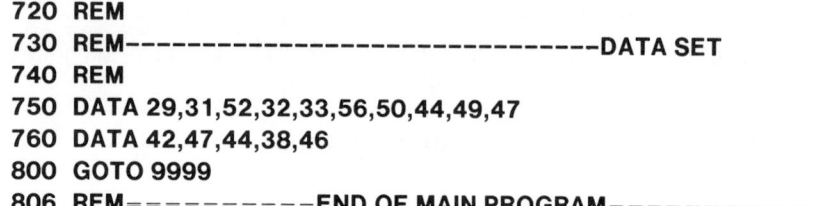

4   Subroutines

The remaining blocks in the program (4, 5, and 6) are subroutine blocks. Programs may have one or more subroutines as required. We should mention that our placement of subroutines at the end, that is, the bottom of the program, may be questioned. When a program has one or more subroutines that are executed many times, one might consider moving such subroutines to the top of the program—before the main program loop—to improve program execution speed. In most cases, little or nothing will be gained by doing so, and therefore, we prefer to place subroutines at the bottom. The subroutines called here can all be found in the Subroutine Library in Appendix B.

9.6 SUBROUTINES

The syntax associated with the use of subroutines—both in pseudocode and in BASIC—is quite similar to that used on the main program segment. In pseudocode, all subroutines begin with their name followed by a colon and end with *end.*, in the same way as main program segments. In addition, the *return* statement must appear somewhere in the subroutine in order to transfer control back to the main program. A subroutine procedure can be invoked anywhere in the main program or in another subroutine by the word *call* followed by the name of the subroutine to be invoked. In both our pseudocode and in BASIC, we assume all variables to be global variables no matter where they occur: only in the main program, only in the subroutine, or in both. A global variable is known to all program segments and has the same value in all program segments. The following visual depicts the relationship between the main program and the subroutines in the program presented in Section 9.5.

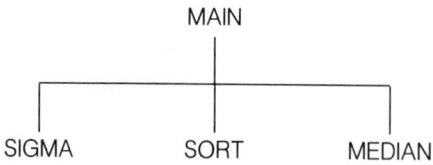

Using pseudocode, we can represent that program as follows:

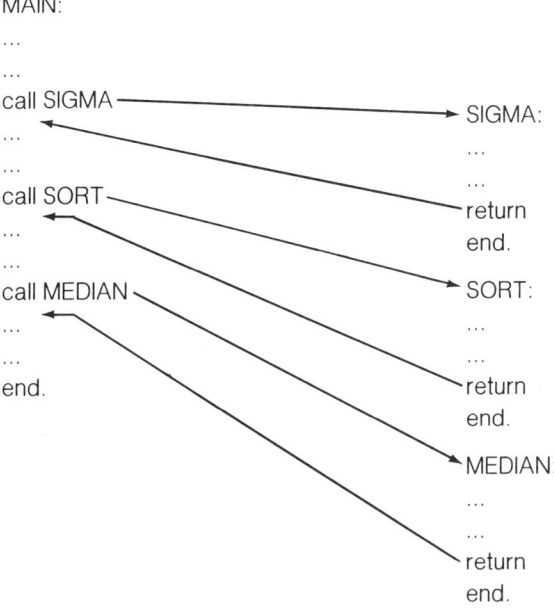

Many computer languages provide subroutine facilities. However, there is a good deal of difference among them in the manner of doing so. Even among dialects of BASIC there are differences. Readers familiar with a language like FORTRAN know that it supports subroutines that are complete and separate program units, so much so, that the main program and subroutines can reuse the same variable names and statement numbers without conflict. While some dialects of BASIC provide similar subroutine support, most do not. We will, therefore, describe subroutine syntax—as supported on the Apple, the PET, and the TRS-80—which is similar, if not identical, to many other dialects. We define a subroutine as a discrete program segment that performs a specific task. There are various advantages in using subroutines, the chief advantage is that they help us modularize our programs, which makes them easier to understand and debug. Subroutines also make it possible to eliminate redundant code when a particular task must be performed at more than one place in a program. Finally, use of subroutines makes it possible to build a library of subroutines which are tools to be used as needed in various programs. For example, see Appendix B.

Some dialects of BASIC make it easy to append subroutines to a main program with an **APPEND** command. Unfortunately, neither the Apple, the PET, nor the TRS-80 have the **APPEND** command.* Therefore, we are forced to keep our library as a single

---

*Apple users who have access to the **RENUMBER** routine can use it to append files.

file that we load first when writing a program. Next, we add other statements as required and use the **DEL** command to eliminate unneeded subroutine modules. We should point out that all modules in our subroutine library have distinct statement number ranges, in order to faciliate this use. In our program above we used three subroutines—one each to compute the standard deviation, to sort the data set, and to compute the median. In this case, our chief motive was to increase the readability of the program by placing discrete modules in separate program units.

In our program, we introduced two new syntax items that are necessary for the use of subroutines. We used the **GOSUB** syntax to call a subroutine, that is, to transfer program control to it. A **RETURN** statement was used to mark the end of the subroutine. The **GOSUB** statement means: **GOTO** statement number *nnn* and continue executing statements until you encounter a **RETURN** statement whereupon you return to the statement following the calling statement. Figure 9.1 may help illustrate:

Figure 9.1
Use of GOSUB and RETURN
Statements in Subroutines

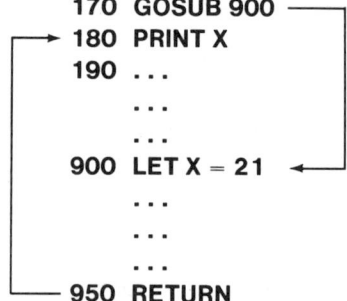

Statement 170 transfers control to a block of statements beginning at line 900. There, execution continues until statement 950 containing the **RETURN** instruction is encountered. Then, control returns to statement 180—the next statement following the one that transferred control to the subroutine.

Two important caveats must be borne in mind when using subroutines. First, we must avoid accidental entrance into a subroutine. Accidental entry will eventually produce an error message not to mention any erroneous results. The best solution to this problem is to enter a **GOTO 9999** statement before the first statement of the first subroutine as we did in statement 800. (Make sure that statement **9999** is an **END** statement.) If you are using one of the three microcomputers to which we are orienting our presentation, you may as an alternative use an **END** statement in the same place. Second, bear in mind that all variables available to the main program are also available to all subroutines. Thus, while we think of subroutines as discrete units, they still share data with each other and the main program. Therefore, we should take care to see to it that one module does not inadvertently modify a variable used by another module. In the Subroutine Library we are careful not to reuse the same variable name except deliberately. Furthermore, we choose unusual variable names, such as **X8** and **Z9** rather than just **X** or **Z** that might also be used by a main routine. Following we present a simple demonstration program to illustrate subroutine usage.

```
100  REM -- DEMO99
110  LET A$ = "USING SUBROUTINES"
120  PRINT A$
130  GOSUB 500
140  PRINT A$
150  GOSUB 600
160  PRINT A$
170  GOTO 999
500  LET A$ = A$ + " HELPS ORGANIZE"
510  RETURN
600  LET A$ = A$ + " YOUR PROGRAM"
610  RETURN
999  END
```

When we run the program we get the following results. Try it.

USING SUBROUTINES
USING SUBROUTINES HELPS ORGANIZE
USING SUBROUTINES HELPS ORGANIZE YOUR PROGRAM

===================== PSEUDOCODE RULE 13 =====================

Subroutines are expressed in pseudocode in the following manner.

A subroutine is invoked by a main program with a call statement that contains the subroutine name:

call SORT

The subroutine itself is written in a format similar to that used for main programs. It must begin with its name, terminate with an *end.* statement and contain at least one return statement.

SORT:
...
...
...
return
end.

9.7 THE CASE STRUCTURE

Now that you are familiar with subroutine usage, it is an appropriate time to introduce the **CASE** or **multiple alternative decision structure**. Sometimes in solving a problem we wish to select one procedure from a series of options. BASIC provides two alternative solutions to such a problem. Before looking at BASIC syntax, however, we will present a sample problem and attack it in terms of our algorithmic language.

Let us assume that we are to write a program to calculate property tax bills given an assessment and a tax classification. Some tax classifications have different tax rates and some have a homestead exemption. We can set up the problem in Table 9.1.

Table 9.1
Calculation of Property Tax Bills
Using an Assessment and Tax Classification

Tax Class	Exemption	Tax Rate
1	first $5000	.025
2	first $10,000	.037
3	none	.055
4	none	.077
5	none	.089
6	none	.089
7	none	.089
8	none	.089

In Table 9.1, the first two classifications are for residential property and the last six classifications are for commercial property. Such a problem is amenable to solution using the CASE structure because it has more than two alternatives. Here we have basically five tax calculation blocks, one of which will be selected on the basis of the tax classification number. The first four tax classes constitute individual cases and the last four tax classes constitute the fifth case. The last four classes can be treated as a group because they have the same tax rate and none allow the homestead exemption. They only differ on tax classification code. In utilizing the CASE structure we have a default block that is executed if the value of the switch, CLASS in this case, is not specified as an individual case. This permits us to treat tax classes five through eight as a group. Now let us look at the CASE structure and our problem in pseudocode:

```
PROPERTYTAX:
declare numeric: CLASS, ASSESSMENT, ADJUSTED, TAX
put("ENTER TAX CLASS")
get(CLASS)
```

```
IF(CLASS < 1 or CLASS > 8 or CLASS <> INT(CLASS))
        [ put("BAD TAX CLASS ",CLASS)
          STOP ]
put("ENTER ASSESSMENT")
get(ASSESSMENT)
select(CLASS)
   case 1: [ ADJUSTED ← ASSESSMENT − 5000
           if(ADJUSTED < 0) ADJUSTED ← 0
           TAX ← ADJUSTED * .025 ]
   case 2: [ ADJUSTED ← ASSESSMENT − 10000
           if(ADJUSTED < 0) ADJUSTED ← 0
           TAX ← ADJUSTED * .037 ]
   case 3: [ ADJUSTED ← ASSESSMENT
           TAX ← ADJUSTED * .055 ]
   case 4: [ ADJUSTED ← ASSESSMENT
           TAX ← ADJUSTED * .077 ]
   default:[ ADJUSTED ← ASSESSMENT
           TAX ← ADJUSTED * .089 ]
put()
put("TAX CLASS IS ",CLASS)
put("ASSESSMENT IS ",ASSESSMENT)
put("ADJUSTED ASSESSMENT IS ",ADJUSTED)
put("TAX IS ",TAX)
end.
```

In this algorithmic representation of our program, the select statement transfers control to one of the CASE blocks depending upon the value of its argument CLASS. If CLASS has the value one, control shifts to the case 1 block. One and only one block is executed. If CLASS should have a value not specified in one of the case statements (values of five through eight) control passes to the default block. Since the value of CLASS is tested against the range of legitimate values immediately after it is input, we can be sure at this point in the program that CLASS will always have integer values in the range of one to eight.

Our algorithm can be implemented in BASIC in one of two ways:

ON CLASS GOTO
ON CLASS GOSUB

We will illustrate both methods even though we prefer the latter. In BASIC, control is transferred to a statement number depending upon the value of the argument which in our example is the variable CLASS. Thus, if we were to write:

300 ON CLASS GOTO 350,400,450,500

control would pass to statement **350** if **CLASS** had the value *one*, to statement **400** if **CLASS** had the value *two*, to statement **450** if **CLASS** had the value *three* and to statement **500** if **CLASS** had the value *four*. If **CLASS** had a value outside the range from one to four, control would pass to the statement that immediately follows statement **300**. Our BASIC program would look like the following:

```
100  REM -- PROPERTYTAX 2-1-81
101  REM
102  REM     VARIABLES:
103  REM        CLASS, ASSESSMENT
104  REM        ADJUSTMENT, TAX
105  REM
110  PRINT "ENTER TAX CLASS  ";
120  INPUT CLASS
130  IF CLASS => 1 AND CLASS <= 8 AND CLASS = INT(CLASS) THEN 145
135  PRINT "BAD TAX CLASS  ";CLASS
140  STOP
145  PRINT "ENTER ASSESSMENT  ";
150  INPUT ASSESSMENT
170  ON CLASS GOTO 180,220,260,290
173  GOTO 325
175  REM---------CLASS = 1-------
180  ADJUSTED = ASSESSMENT - 5000
190  IF ADJUSTED < 0 THEN ADJUSTED = 0
200  TAX = ADJUSTED * .025
210  GOTO 400
215  REM---------CLASS = 2-------
220  ADJUSTED = ASSESSMENT - 10000
230  IF ADJUSTED < 0 THEN ADJUSTED = 0
240  TAX = ADJUSTED * .037
250  GOTO 400
255  REM---------CLASS = 3-------
260  ADJUSTED = ASSESSMENT
270  TAX = ADJUSTED * .055
280  GOTO 400
285  REM---------CLASS = 4-------
290  ADJUSTED = ASSESSMENT
300  TAX = ADJUSTED * .077
310  GOTO 400
320  REM---------DEFAULT---------
325  ADJUSTED = ASSESSMENT
330  TAX = ADJUSTED * .089
390  REM
```

Sec. 9.7 The Case Structure 177

```
400 PRINT "TAX CLASS IS ";CLASS
410 PRINT "ASSESSMENT IS ";ASSESSMENT
420 PRINT "ADJUSTED ASSESSMENT IS "; ASSESSMENT
430 PRINT "TAX IS ";TAX
500 END
```

You will notice that statement 173 causes transfer to the default block.

We now present the second BASIC version which we prefer because it uses subroutines and thus avoids the multiple **GOTO** statements in the earlier version.

```
100 REM -- PROPERTYTAX2     2-1-81
101 REM
102 REM     VARIABLES
103 REM        CLASS, ASSESSMENT
104 REM        ADJUSTED, TAX
105 REM
110 PRINT "ENTER TAX CLASS";
115 INPUT CLASS
120 IF CLASS => 1 AND CLASS <= 8 AND CLASS = INT (CLASS) THEN 140
130 PRINT "BAD TAX CLASS ";CLASS
135 STOP
140 PRINT "ENTER ASSESSMENT";
150 INPUT ASSESSMENT
170 ON CLASS GOSUB 500,600,700,800
180 IF CLASS > 4 THEN GOSUB 850
200 PRINT "TAX CLASS IS ";CLASS
210 PRINT "ASSESSMENT IS ";ASSESSMENT
220 PRINT "ADJUSTED ASSESSMENT IS ";ADJUSTED
230 PRINT "TAX IS ";TAX
240 GOTO 999
250 REM
260 REM----------CLASS = 1----------
500 ADJUSTED = ASSESSMENT - 5000
510 IF ADJUSTED < 0 THEN ADJUSTED = 0
520 TAX = ADJUSTED * .025
540 RETURN
590 REM----------CLASS = 2---------
600 ADJUSTED = ASSESSMENT - 10000
610 IF ADJUSTED < 0 THEN ADJUSTED = 0
620 TAX = ADJUSTED * .037
640 RETURN
790 REM---------CLASS = 3---------
700 ADJUSTED = ASSESSMENT
```

```
710 TAX = ADJUSTED * .055
730 RETURN
790 REM---------CLASS = 4----------
800 ADJUSTED = ASSESSMENT
810 TAX = ADJUSTED * .077
830 RETURN
850 REM---------DEFAULT-----------
855 ADJUSTED = ASSESSMENT
860 TAX = ADJUSTED * .089
865 RETURN
999 END
```

You will note that the logical test in statement 120 has been inverted in both versions of the BASIC program. Here, statement 180 contains a test to assure that a second set of calculations is not performed for all cases. If it were absent, the default block would be performed even if one of the other CASE blocks had already been performed. Note also the use of comment statements to mark off the program blocks as well as the use of the **ON** . . . **GOSUB** in statement 170. It is often convenient to graphically depict the structure of such a program as in Figure 9.2.

Figure 9.2
Schematic of the Case Structure

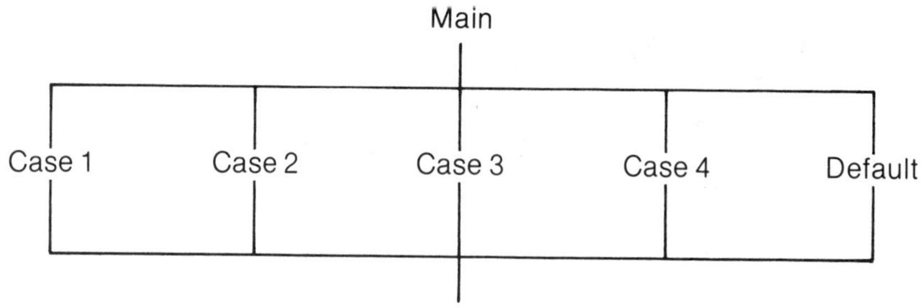

```
                        Main
          ┌────────┬────────┬────────┬────────┐
        Case 1   Case 2   Case 3   Case 4   Default
```

Let us summarize the case structure with a new pseudocode rule.

═══════════════ **PSEUDOCODE RULE 14** ═══════════════

The CASE or multiple alternative decision structure is expressed in pseudocode as follows:

    select(SWITCH)
        case 1: [ ]
        case 2: [ ]

case n: [ ]
default:[ ]

Here, SWITCH is a variable. Control is passed by the select statement to that case block with the same value as SWITCH. If no case block with that value is present, control passes to the default block. Any block can contain either a single statement or a block of statements enclosed in square brackets. If SWITCH has a value with a fractional part, that fractional part is truncated for use by the select statement. The value of the SWITCH, however, is not actually modified.

9.8 DEBUGGING TECHNIQUES

Much of our attention in this chapter is aimed at error prevention as well as error detection and correction. But we recommend a constructive attitude toward errors. While we wish to avoid them, we should use each error as a learning experience providing an opportunity for improving our problem-solving ability as well as our expertise with the syntax of a particular language.

Consider the following message:

?BAD SUBSCRIPT ERROR IN 210

The first step in error correction is to list line 210

LIST 210
210 X(I) = I

Next, it would seem wise to print the value of **I** and to list the entire program:

PRINT I
11

LIST

200 FOR I = 1 TO 15
210 X(I) = I
220 NEXT I

The cause of the error is easily determined. Since the array X is not dimensioned, it is given the default size of ten. Once the loop index exceeded ten, the bad subscript message was generated. The easiest solution to the error message is to add the following statement:

100 DIM X(15)

While this may be the first solution which occurs to us, we must be sure that we are not curing the wrong disease. What if we intended to have the loop index go from one to five but accidently keyed in a **1**, deleted the **1** (or so we thought) and then entered the 5? Adding statement 100 will eliminate the error message, but it will not solve the problem. This solution would replace an easy to detect error with a more elusive one. In this case, we must refer to the original program specifications including the algorithmic language version of the program in order to correct the real error.

Let us now consider the following situation. The following program fragment is entered and run producing an error message:

```
200 DIM LIST(25)
210 FOR I = 1 TO 25
220    LIST(I) = I * 2
230 NEXT I
```

?SYNTAX ERROR IN 200

But we are puzzled because upon careful reading the fragment seems syntactically correct. (You might want to think about this before reading on.) The error message in this case tells us no more than that something is wrong in line 200. In this case, we have used one of the fifty or so words that the Apple reserves for special use. The word **LIST** means list program statements. If one did not have access to a list of reserved words, one would have to experiment by imitating BASIC's syntax scanning. From left to right, first inspect the statement number, then the keyword **DIM**, then the variable name and then the size-fixing value. Everything is standard—as you have used in other dimension statements except the array name. The next thing to do is experiment with the variable name. Knowing that single alphabetic characters are always acceptable as variable names, use **L** as the array name in both statements 200 and 220 and then test the program.

Consider this situation. A small program has been written to compute and print the sale price of an item by subtracting a discount of ten percent of the original price and adding a three percent sales tax. Here is the program:

```
100 PRINT "ENTER ORIGINAL PRICE ";
110 INPUT P
120 TAX = P * .03
130 D = P * .1
140 P = P + TAX - D
150 PRINT "THE PRICE IS ";P
```

RUN
ENTER ORIGINAL PRICE? 59
THE PRICE IS 54.87

The sample run produces a result that seems to be reasonable. In fact, the result is almost correct—being off by only eighteen cents. But in this type of work, almost correct is the same as wrong. Yet, a program like this could be used for a long time before anyone detected the error. The program is overcharging customers by calculating the tax before discounting the original price. The tax should be computed on the discounted price.

Imagine that you sit down in front of an Apple to do some computing only to find that the person using it before you has left the machine on, with the following program displayed on the screen.

```
110  PØ = 2
120  P1 = 4
130  P2 = 6
140  P3 = 8
150  INPUT X
160  IF X <= 10 THEN Y = X * PO : GOTO 200
170  IF X <= 20 THEN Y = X * P1 : GOTO 200
180  IF X <= 30 THEN Y = X * P2 : GOTO 200
190  IF X <= 40 THEN Y = X * P3 : GOTO 200
200  PRINT Y
210  END
```

The program is simple but puzzling. Curiosity gets the better part of you and you decide to run it. You enter several values and receive the results indicated in Table 9.2.

Table 9.2
X-Input and Y-Output Values

Input	Output
12	48
2	0
1234	0
33	264
99	0

You are intrigued by a program that produces the same results when 2 and 1234 are used as input values. This is a classic debugging situation. You have tested a program and suspect that something is wrong because the output seems implausible.

In our attempt to evaluate this program we begin by listing it. Since we suspect the accuracy of the output value, our next step is to locate the line printing the output and the name of the output variable. In this case, we quickly determine that the output is being produced by line 200 and the output variable name is Y. Continuing our backward or upward scan of the program, we search for statements that assign a value to Y. Four such statements are quickly found. Statements 160 to 190 assign a value to Y depending upon the value of X. Further investigation reveals that X is the value we input at the keyboard. Studying the program further, we determine that no value will be calculated for Y if X is greater than forty. In such circumstances, we should expect the value zero to be printed since the Apple initializes all numeric variables and arrays to zero. Thus, we understand why an X value of 1234 produces a Y value of zero. But, we cannot see how an X value of two produces a zero as well. According to statement 160, a value of four should be produced. Further meditation reveals that the inconsistency is the result of a typing error. Line 110 assigns the value two to **PØ**—the second character is a zero, while in line 160 Y is multiplied by **PO**—both letters. By merely replacing the letter O with a zero, the program now works correctly. While it works correctly, only its original author knows what useful work it was intended to do.

Because you have become a proficient programmer, your instructor has asked you to help him check the programs of novice programmers. He has given them the assignment of writing a program that inputs a date in *Gregorian form* and outputs the same date in *Julian form*. The Gregorian form for January 9, 1980, for example, is 1-9-80. The Julian representation of the same date is 80009. The Gregorian form consists of the numeric representation of the month, followed by the day of the month, occupying two digits each, followed by the last two digits of the year. In contrast, the Julian form consists of the last two digits of the year followed by the number a particular day is from the beginning of the year. In the example above, January 9th is the 9th day of 1980, thus, the Julian date of 80009. Similarly, December 31, 1979 is the last day of the year, in Julian form, it would be 79365. With this background in mind, look at a program written by one student:

```
100 REM -- JULIAN DATE
110 DIM T(12)
120 DATA 31,28,31,30,31,30
121 DATA 31,31,30,31,30,31
125 FOR I = 1 TO 12
130    READ T(I)
135 NEXT I
140 REM
200 PRINT "MONTH ";: INPUT M
205 PRINT "DAY   ";: INPUT D
210 PRINT "YEAR  ";: INPUT Y
215 IF INT(Y / 4) * 4 = Y THEN T(2) = 29
220 S = 0
300 FOR I = 1 TO M - 1
305    S = S + T(I)
310 NEXT I
315 JD = S + D
```

```
325  Y = Y * 1000
330  JD = JD + Y
335  PRINT "JULIAN DATE IS ";JD
400  END
```

Reading the program, it looks pretty good. It even handles leap years correctly. The next step is to run the program.

```
MONTH ?3
DAY    ?10
YEAR   ?80
JULIAN DATE IS 80070

MONTH ?3
DAY    ?1
YEAR   ?79
JULIAN DATE IS 79060

MONTH ?12
DAY    ?31
YEAR   ?79
JULIAN DATE IS 79365

MONTH ?1
DAY    ?1
YEAR   ?80
JULIAN DATE IS 80032
```

Checking the results by hand we can see that all Julian dates are correct except the last one. In this case, the Julian date for January 1, 1980 (010180) is given as **80032**. We have discovered an important flaw in the program. It has treated January 1st as if it were February 1st. Scanning the program, we note that the day from the beginning of the year is calculated by summing the number of days in all months prior to the current month and then adding the day value. This occurs in the **FOR-NEXT** loop beginning in line 300. Since in this test case, **M** − **1** is equal to zero the loop should not be executed at all. What is needed now is the ability to trace program execution in order to see if the loop is executed as we suspect. The Apple and the TRS-80 have a trace facility that is useful for this purpose. With the Apple, the word **TRACE** is used to turn on the trace routine and the word **NOTRACE** is used to turn it off. With the TRS-80, the words **TRON** and **TROFF** are used for the same purpose. These commands can be used in direct mode or within programs as numbered statements.

While the trace facility is turned on, the statement number of each statement executed is displayed on the screen each time it is executed. Statement numbers are displayed each preceded by the "**#**" symbol and followed by a space. The Apple will print as many statement numbers as possible on the same line. Program input and output will be interspersed among statement numbers. If we run a trace on the entire program we see that forty-five statements were executed in the process of changing one date from Gregorian form into Julian form. (REMark statements are included in the trace.) To avoid a screenful of output, it is desirable to trace only the specific statements we are interested in studying. In this case, there is only one statement to trace, statement number 305. Adding the following statements to our program accomplishes the task:

301 TRACE
306 NOTRACE

If you are using a TRS-80, use TRON in place of TRACE and TROFF in place of NOTRACE. Next, we run the program:

RUN
MONTH ?1
DAY ?1
YEAR ?80
#305 #306 80032

The trace has proved that statement 305 was indeed executed. We will discuss this finding in a minute. First, let us address the subject of simulating a trace facility for machines that do not provide one. We can merely add a statement like this:

301 PRINT "#305 ";

Since statement 301 is immediately prior to statement 305, it will be executed if statement 305 is executed. More precisely, if statement 301 is executed, statement 305 will be executed also. There is the possibility that statement 301 might not be executed even though statement 305 is executed if there are **GOTO** statements that transfer control to statement 305.

One final technique that we might use to determine if the loop was executed is to cause the loop index to be printed. After the program has finished execution, we can type:

PRINT I

If a value other than zero is printed, we know that the loop was executed. In the case of this program, the value "**1**" will be printed.

All of our experiments confirm the fact that the loop was actually executed. The question remains as to why. ANSI standards for Minimal BASIC specify that **FOR-NEXT** loops should not be executed at all if the initial value of the loop index is already past the end value. In such cases, as in the **FOR-NEXT** loop in the Julian date program, the loop should not be entered at all. Yet, we know that the loop was entered as a result of the trace experiments. The fact is that the Apple does not conform to the ANSI specifications and neither do the PET nor the TRS-80. Most dialects of BASIC will perform this task as expected. But the conclusion to be drawn is that some programs will run correctly on some machines and incorrectly on others. The only way to be sure this program works correctly on all machines is to add a statement to prevent entry into the loop when the month value is one (January).

295 IF M = 1 THEN 315

Let us end our treatment of debugging with one final challenge in the form of another version of the Julian date program. Following is a program almost identical to the one displayed above, which produced incorrect results under some circumstances. However, the program following works correctly. Can you determine why it works and the one above does not? Do you approve of the modification? Has the author resorted to a *trick* to make the program work? Is such a program portable to other dialects of BASIC? If you were the instructor, would you accept the second version? Here is the program:

```
100  REM -- JULIAN V2
110  DIM T(12)
120  DATA 31,28,31,30,31,30
121  DATA 31,31,30,31,30,31
125  FOR I = 1 TO 12
130    READ T(I)
135  NEXT I
200  PRINT "MONTH  ";: INPUT M
205  PRINT "DAY    ";: INPUT D
210  PRINT "YEAR   ";: INPUT Y
215  IF INT(Y / 4) * 4 = Y THEN T(2) = 29
220  S = 0
300  FOR I = 0 TO M - 1
305    S = S + T(I)
310  NEXT I
315  JD = S + D
325  Y = Y * 1000
330  JD = JD + Y
335  PRINT JD
400  END
```

EXERCISE SET 9.1

The following programs illustrate some of the difficulties one encounters in debugging programs that run yet produce puzzling results. Programs that sometimes behave correctly and other times misbehave are particularly annoying.

1. Enter and run the following program. It is designed to allow us to examine the values of the function **Y = 2 * X^2 − 3 * X** in the interval from X = 4 to X = 5 by taking various step sizes.

   ```
   100  PRINT "X-Y PAIRS AS X RANGES FROM 4 TO 5"
   110  PRINT "IN STEPS OF VARIABLE SIZE."
   120  PRINT "ENTER STEP SIZE  ";
   130  INPUT S
   140  PRINT
   150  LET X = 4
   160  LET Y = 2 * X ^ 2 − 3 * X
   170  PRINT X,Y
   180  IF X = 5 THEN 200
   190  LET X = X + S
   200  END
   ```

   Run this with step sizes of .5, .25, .2, .1, and .05. Explain the behavior observed.

2. In this program we run a number through a rounding function (to two decimal places) and then compare its value with its original value.

   ```
   100  PRINT "ENTER A NUMBER  ";
   110  INPUT N
   120  LET N1 − INT (N * 100 + .5) / 100
   130  PRINT N,N1
   140  REM     TRANSFER TO END IF N = N1
   150  IF N =  N1 THEN 180
   160  PRINT "IF N = ";N;" AND N1 = ";N1;" WHY IS"
   170  PRINT "THIS STATEMENT EXECUTED?"
   180  END
   ```

   Run this program for some decimal numbers. Try for example 5.246, 3.46, 1.51, and 2.9. Can you explain the results you see?

3. This program simulates a problem of stocking an item of merchandise subject to variable demand. A program was to be designed to accumulate total sales and average days between restocking of the item. When the inventory on the shelf falls below five, twenty items are to be placed on the shelf. The following problem, turned in by a student, runs without error but produces meaningless results. Debug it.

   ```
   100  PRINT "ENTER NUMBER OF DAYS SIMULATION RUNS  ";
   110  INPUT DAYS
   120  REM     INITIALIZE
   130  SALES = 0
   140  STCK = 20
   ```

```
150 PRINT       "DAY    STOCK       SALES          FINAL STOCK"
160 FOR I = 1 TO DAYS
165 REM      SAVE STARTING STOCK VALUE
170 SAVSTCK = STCK
175 REM      DETERMINE DAILY CUSTOMERS
180 CUST = INT(RND(1) * 10 + 1)
185 REM      ACCUMULATE DAILY SALES
190 SALES = SALES + CUST
195 REM      REDUCE STOCK BY SALES
200 STCK = STCK - SALES
205 REM      DETERMINE IF RESTOCKING IS NECESSARY
210 IF STCK >= 5 THEN 240
220 STCK = STCK + 20
230 RESTCK = RESTCK + 1
235 REM      PRINT DAILY RESULTS
240 PRINT I;TAB(7)SAVSTCK,CUST,STCK
250 NEXT I
260 PRINT "TOTAL SALES IN ";DAYS;" DAYS IS ";SALES
270 PRINT "AVERAGE DAYS BETWEEN RESTOCKING IS ";DAYS / RESTCK
280 END
```

What lessons are learned from the errors in this program?

4. Below is another student program designed to reduce a fraction to lowest terms. The program runs without error messages. Sometimes it produces correct results, sometimes not. The program was built around an algorithm which finds all the factors of a whole number (other than the number and one). If no factors exist, then it prints a message that the number is prime. Here is the correct algorithm for that operation.

```
120 INPUT N
150 FOR I = 2 TO N / 2
160 IF N / I <> INT(N / I) THEN 180
170 PRINT I;" IS A FACTOR OF ";N
175 Q = 1
180 NEXT I
190 IF Q <> 1 THEN PRINT N;" IS PRIME"
200 END
```

Satisfy yourself that the program above works correctly. Then, enter and run the following program, which attempts to take advantage of this algorithm.

```
110 PRINT "ENTER NUMERATOR ";
120 INPUT N
130 PRINT "ENTER DENOMINATOR ";
```

```
140 INPUT D
150 FOR I = 2 TO N / 2
160 IF N / I <> INT(N / I) THEN 210
170 IF D / I <> INT(D / I) THEN 210
180 N = N / I
190 D = D / I
210 NEXT I
220 PRINT "THE REDUCED NUMERATOR IS  ";N
230 PRINT "THE REDUCED DENOMINATOR IS  ";D
240 END
```

Try the following data pairs:

N	D
9	30
9	45
4	14
12	20

You should find that sometimes the fraction is reduced to lowest terms. Other times it is not.

Review

New terms and syntax introduced in this chapter are reviewed here.

BUG   a term used to describe a program error. (Section 9.1)

DEBUG   the act of removing a program error or errors. (Section 9.1)

STRUCTURED PROGRAMMING   programming that recognizes the natural structure of the problem solution. Such programming uses fundamental control structures and modular construction to produce a linear arrangement of the major program blocks. (Section 9.2)

PROGRAM BLOCK   a major subsection of a program devoted to a specified task. Typical blocks provide for program identification, variable initialization, a main program loop, data identification, and subroutines. (Section 9.5)

SUBROUTINE   a discrete program segment that performs a specific function. (Section 9.4)

CASE STRUCTURE   a control structure that permits the selection of one option from among several. (Section 9.7)

BASIC SYNTAX

GOSUB a BASIC keyword that transfers control to the statement number following. For example, **200 GOSUB 1000** would transfer control to statement 1000 from statement 200. (Section 9.6)

RETURN a keyword that terminates a subroutine transferring control back to the statement following the most recent **GOSUB** executed. **GOSUB** and **RETURN** are a matched set—we cannot have one without the other. (Section 9.6)

ON VARIABLE GOTO a set of keywords used to implement a case structure. For example, **200 ON X GOTO 1000,2000,3000** will transfer control to statement 1000 if X = 1, to statement 2000 if X = 2, to statement 3000 if X = 3, or to the next statement following 200 if none of these conditions exist. (Section 9.7)

ON VARIABLE GOSUB a set of keywords used to implement a case structure. This syntax combines the multiple option of the **ON . . . GOTO** with the properties of the subroutine. (Section 9.7)

TRACE a BASIC keyword that causes the printing of a statement number as the statement is executed. This capability is useful in debugging a program. (Section 9.8)

NOTRACE a BASIC keyword used to terminate the **TRACE** feature. (Section 9.8)

10
FORMATTING AND GRAPHICS

10.1 INTRODUCTION TO FORMATTING AND GRAPHICS

We have emphasized certain basic techniques for improving the utility of our programs and the appearance of their output. In particular, we have discussed the following:

1. The value of user prompts,
2. Labeling of output with appropriate text,
3. Integration of text and data so that the output reads more naturally, and
4. Use of printing fields to organize the output.

All of these techniques might be considered cosmetic. If the program is doing what it is supposed to do, who cares how the output looks? We trust that you do not hold this view of programming. It is true that programs are written to solve problems rather than to display the ability of the programmer to format. However, they must not be so cursory or crude that they leave the user with more questions than answers. The user who has to study the internals of the program in order to interpret the output is likely to be discouraged with our *help*.

We feel that attention to appearance of the computer output is very important. To improve the appearance and readability of the output we must go beyond the basics discussed earlier. We are concerned with appearance for its own sake and because it makes possible a more rapid and meaningful evaluation of the output. Consider a simple example. Below are two outputs of the same program. In the first case, on the left, no attempt at formatting has been made. In the second case, on the right, the same data has been formatted before printing.

TIME	CHARGE	TIME	CHARGE
5	1.97847E−05	5.0	0.000020
10	2.41026E−04	10.0	0.000241
15	2.93630E−03	15.0	0.002936
20	.0357715	20.0	0.035772
25	.0435786	25.0	0.435786
30	5.30896	30.0	5.30896
35	64.6764	35.0	64.6764
40	787.919	40.0	787.919
45	9598.82	45.0	9598.82
50	116938	50.0	116938.

It is easier to interpret the trend of the righthand data in the second case.

We further believe that the ability to support our output with computer generated graphic material is seldom fully exploited. We will discuss methods of generating bar graphs, *X-Y* plots, and high resolution graphic material.

10.2 THE TAB FUNCTION

We mentioned in Chapter 6 that functions behave like processors. We enter a number called the argument of the function, the processor works on it, and a value is returned that bears some relation to the argument. In the case of the **TAB** function the output is not a number but an instruction to the computer to move the printing head (or cursor) right of the left-most printing position to the printing position given by the argument. Consider the following program fragment:

```
100 FOR I = 1 TO 3
110 PRINT "1234567890";
120 NEXT I
130 PRINT
140 PRINT "A";
150 PRINT TAB (9) "B";
160 PRINT TAB (21) "C"
```

Numbering of print positions differs from machine to machine. A run of the program for the three microcomputers looks like this:

Sec. 10.2   The Tab Function   **193**

================================ APPLE ================================

123456789012345678901234567890
A   B   C

The Apple uses a numbering system for the **TAB** function which starts with one **(1)** at the left margin—in the fashion of a typewriter. **PRINT TAB (9)** prints in position nine **(9)**.

============================ PET AND TRS-80 ===========================

123456789012345678901234567890
A   B   C

The PET and TRS-80 start tab positions at zero rather than at one. **PRINT TAB (9)** prints in position ten **(10)**.

Systems deal with positive and negative numbers in different ways. A run of the following demonstration program fragment demonstrates the differences between the Apple, the PET, and the TRS-80.

```
100   PRINT "1234567890"
110   PRINT 2
120   PRINT -3
130   PRINT "1234567890"
140   PRINT TAB(8)2
150   PRINT TAB(8)-3
```

================================ APPLE ================================

```
1234567890
2
-3
1234567890
       2
      -3
```

PET AND TRS-80

```
1234567890
        2
       -3
1234567890
         2
        -3
```

The **TAB** function is particularly valuable in formatting text headings. However, in formatting numbers we are frequently more interested in vertical decimal point alignment. The **TAB** function will not cause decimal point alignment if the data differs in the number of digits to the left of the decimal point. We touched upon decimal point alignment in Chapter 8 and will consider it again in this chapter.

The **TAB** function on microcomputers will generally not move the printing position left. Consider the following program fragment:

```
100  PRINT "123456789012345678901234567890"
110  PRINT TAB(25)"A";
120  PRINT TAB(10)"B"
```

The output is:

```
123456789012345678901234567890
                         AB
```

The print head, being beyond the designated print position in line 120, simply prints the character "**B**" in the next available print position (number twenty-six in this case).

The features of the **TAB** function on each machine are discussed as follows:

APPLE

The Apple **TAB** function will accept arguments up to position 255. **TAB** arguments over 255 give error messages. **TAB(0)** results in a tab move to position 256. This feature can be particularly troublesome when the program is computing the argument of the **TAB** function and fails to check for zero arguments.

Sec. 10.3 *Using a Print Image* **195**

PET

The PET accepts and executes **TAB** arguments up to and including 255. **TAB** argument values over 255 produce error messages.

TRS-80

The TRS-80 performs all **TAB** function arguments in excess of 63 by reducing the argument to modulus 64. That is, the computer tabs to the remainder of the value entered divided by 64. Then **TAB (65)** becomes **TAB (1)**, **TAB (132)** becomes **TAB (4)**, etc.

10.3 USING A PRINT IMAGE

A valuable formatting device is the **print image**, which is available on most minicomputers and on some microcomputers. The TRS-80 has such a feature although it is absent in the PET and in the Apple. With the print image an entire table can be formatted. We have developed a subroutine which will produce a print image. This subroutine is contained in the Library of Subroutines. (Appendix B, p.B21). We illustrate its use below.

Suppose we are to print an amortization schedule for a car loan in the sequence:

Month—Start Balance—Interest—Payment—Final Balance

Month numbers may run as high as forty-eight. Balances may need four digits to the left of the decimal point and payments may need three digits. Monthly interest may run as high as $150. With this information we can define an image for the actual entries. We give this image a character variable name:

    120 LET PU$ = "## $####.## $##.## $###.## $####.##"

(**PU** for "print using")

We develop a program to use this image:

    100 REM -- DEMONSTRATION PROGRAM FOR PRINT USING
    110 REM -- INITIALIZE
    120 LET PU$ = "## $####.## $##.## $###.## $####.##"
        130 LET NP(1) = 1
        140 LET NP(2) = 4000
        150 LET NP(4) = 130

```
160 REM     PRINT HEADER
170 PRINT "NO   BALANCE   INT   PAYMENT   BALANCE"
180 REM     PRINT TABLE
190 FOR I = 1 TO 10
200 LET NP(3) = INT(NP(2) * .14/12 * 100 + .5) / 100
210 LET NP(5) = NP(2) + NP(3) - NP(4)
215 REM     CALL PRINT USING SUBROUTINE
220 GOSUB 8600
230 REM     UPDATE MONTH AND BALANCE
240 LET NP(2) = NP(5)
250 LET NP(1) = NP(1) + 1
260 NEXT I
```

TRS-80 note: To run this program on the TRS-80 replace statement 220 with the following:

```
220 PRINT USING PU$;NP(1),NP(2),NP(3),NP(4),NP(5)
```

This program will print the first ten months of the amortization schedule as shown below:

NO	BALANCE	INT	PAYMENT	BALANCE
1	$4000.00	$46.67	$130.00	$3916.67
2	$3916.67	$45.69	$130.00	$3832.36
3	$3832.36	$44.71	$130.00	$3747.07
4	$3747.07	$43.72	$130.00	$3660.79
5	$3660.79	$42.71	$130.00	$3573.50
6	$3573.50	$41.69	$130.00	$3485.19
7	$3485.19	$40.66	$130.00	$3395.85
8	$3395.85	$39.62	$130.00	$3305.47
9	$3305.47	$38.56	$130.00	$3214.03
10	$3214.03	$37.50	$130.00	$3121.53

The print using subroutine causes the data to be rounded to the correct number of decimal points and entered in the correct format. If a number is out of range of its format statement (for example, too large) a warning indicator will be printed. We also note that the character data can be mixed within the print image. We are not limited to dollar signs but could print text such as the following:

```
150 LET PU$ = "MONTH ## BALANCE IS ###.##"
```

EXERCISE SET 10.1

1. Solve the following problems using the **TAB** function:
   (a) Generate three vertical lines in print positions 3, 15, and 27. The lines should extend vertically for ten print positions. Use a keyboard symbol of your choice to represent the elements in each line.

(b) A column of numbers stored in **X(1)** through **X(20)** is to be printed out. The numbers are between 100 and 999 in value and have decimal parts. The decimal point in all these numbers is to be in print position 27. Write a program that will produce the column.

(c) The following column headings are to be centered on columns 5, 20 and 35. Write a statement(s) that accomplishes this.

PAYMENT   INTEREST   BALANCE

(d) Write a program that will generate the quarterly balance on $5000 deposited in a bank at 6% annual interest compounded quarterly. Print the quarter number and the new balance in two columns starting at positions 7 and 12. Develop five years of data. The algorithm for computing the balance is:

Balance = Deposit * (1 + r / m) ^ (m * n)

where r is the decimal interest rate,
      m is the number of compoundings per year, and
      n is the number of quarters in the bank

Do not carry fractions of a cent.

2. Solve problem 1(d) using the print image technique.

3. Write a program that uses the print image to produce a table of daily net sales with sales tax and excise tax tabulated. Use the following image:

"##   NET = $####.##   ST = ###.##   ET = $####.##"

Sales tax is 5% of net sales and excise tax is 11% of net sales. Use the following data:

Day	Net Sales
1	$6537.20
2	$8421.25
3	$9320.75
4	$8778.10
5	$8329.50
6	$7922.35

10.4 TELETYPE GRAPHICS

The term **teletype graphics** refers to the use of standard symbols on a terminal to generate graphic material. Lines can be drawn, points can be plotted and symbolic representations of real objects can be generated with standard symbols on the keyboard. The development of graphic output in the form of charts and plots can enhance the readability and impact of the output.

We begin with a problem in which we wish to display the grade distribution on an examination. That distribution is:

A's = 2   D's = 5
B's = 6   F's = 2
C's = 8

Our program will set up an array to hold the count of each grade and then read the values into this array. In the following statements, an array **MARK** is dimensioned at size five (one location for each letter grade) and the data statement contains the actual count of the occurrences of each grade. The **FOR-NEXT** loop simply reads the values from the data statement into the array **MARK**.

```
150  DIM MARK(5)
160  FOR I = 1 TO 5
170  READ MARK(I)
180  NEXT I
350  DATA 2,6,8,5,2
```

Next we must instruct the computer to print a scale so we can read the bar graph. This can be done easily with the following **PRINT** statement. Note how the plus character represents the values of five and fifteen and the colon represents zero, ten, and so forth.

```
190  PRINT ":....+....:....+....:"
```

Now let us turn our attention to the printing of the bar graph itself. Since we have five different grades, we will want to produce five bars, one for each letter grade. We will accomplish this with a **FOR-NEXT** loop, which will execute five times. We will also use the **TAB** function to locate the print character at the proper column on the line. We will use the values stored in the array **MARK** to position the print head.

```
200  FOR I = 1 TO 5
210  PRINT ":";
220  PRINT TAB(MARK(I))"*"
230  NEXT I
```

Here is the output of the program:

```
:....+....:....+....:
: *
:     *
:       *
:    *
: *
```

This may not look much like a bar graph since our program only prints a single star, not a bar. We can improve this by nesting another loop within our **FOR-NEXT** loop. The new inner loop will cause a star to be printed at each column on a line beginning with column one and ending with the column represented by the value of the respective element of the array **MARK**. The inner loop is listed below:

```
220  FOR K = 1 TO MARK(I)
222  PRINT "*";
224  NEXT K
226  PRINT
```

Let us also add a **PRINT** statement to print scale values to make the output more readable.

```
185  PRINT "0          10         20"
```

Our revised program is reproduced below along with sample output. Some remarks have been added.

```
100  REM -- DEMONSTRATION BAR GRAPH
110  REM     INPUT VARIABLES: MARK(5)
120  REM     LOCAL VARIABLES: I, K
130  REM     OUTPUT VARIABLES: ALL GRAPHIC
140  REM     LOAD DATA ARRAY
150  DIM MARK(5)
160  FOR I = 1 TO 5
170  READ MARK(I)
180  NEXT I
183  REM     PRINT BAR GRAPH
185  PRINT "0          10         20"
190  PRINT ":....+....:....+....: "
200  FOR I = 1 TO 5
210  PRINT ":";
215  IF MARK(I) = 0 THEN 226
220  FOR K = 1 TO MARK(I)
222  PRINT "*";
224  NEXT K
226  PRINT
230  NEXT I
240  PRINT ":....+....:....+....:"
```

```
0          10         20
:....+....:....+....:
:**
:******
:********
:*****
:**
:....+....:....+....:
```

Line 215 is necessary only if you want to be able to graph a data set with a zero value. If **MARK (I) = 0**, the loop beginning at 220 will execute once.

Since the bars are not labeled with letter grades, we must rely on our understanding of the program itself to tell which bar represents grades of A, B, etc. One solution to this problem is to add the following statements to our program:

```
182  LET LTR$ = "ABCDF"
222  PRINT MID$(LTR$,I,1);
```

The output of this modification is shown below:

```
0          10         20
:....+....:....+....:
: A A
: B B B B B B
: C C C C C C C C
: D D D D D
: F F
:....+....:....+....:
```

10.5 TELETYPE GRAPHICS—X-Y PLOTS

We will next consider the simplest method of developing an *x-y* plot. We will plot the expression **y = .3 * x ^ 2 + 2** when the independent variable, **x**, runs from one to ten in steps of one. The generation of dependent variable values using a **FOR-NEXT** loop has been considered previously. A loop such as

```
130  FOR I = 1 TO 10
140  LET Y = .3 * I ^ 2 + 2
150  NEXT I
```

will generate the **y** value corresponding to each **x**. If we tab to the **y** value corresponding to each **x**, place a marker there and then superimpose the coordinate axes, we should have an *x-y* plot.

Consider the following program:

```
100  REM -- DEMONSTRATION OF X-Y PLOT
110  REM     LOCAL VARIABLE: Y
120  REM     DRAW Y AXIS
130  PRINT "0          10         20         30     Y-AXIS"
140  PRINT ":....+....:....+....:....+....:....+"
```

```
150 REM     DRAW X AXIS AND PLOT POINTS
160 FOR I = 1 TO 10
170 LET Y = .3 * I ^ 2 + 2
180 LET Y = INT(Y + .5)
190 PRINT ":";
200 IF I / 5 = INT(I / 5) THEN PRINT "-";I;
210 PRINT TAB(Y) "*"     [use TAB(Y + 1) on the Apple]
220 NEXT I
230 PRINT "X-AXIS"
240 END
```

Addition of one in line 210 for the Apple is necessary because the zero of the y-axis is in position one on the screen. The output of the program is displayed below:

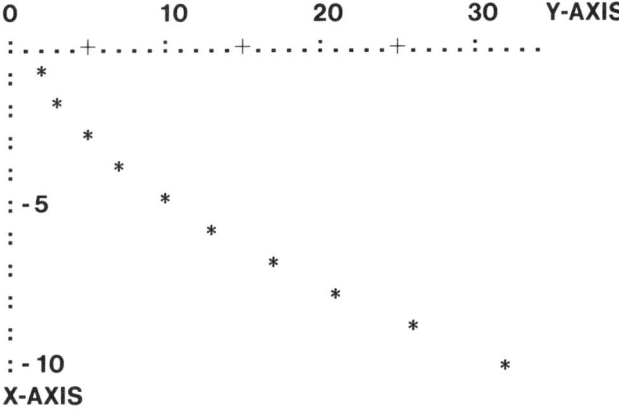

EXERCISE SET 10.2

1. Modify the bar graph program in Section 10.4 to present seven bars. The bars are to have the lengths 8, 9, 23, 9, 3, 8, and 5 and are to be labeled A, B, C, D, F, W, and I respectively.

2. Modify the *X-Y* program in Section 10.5 to plot the following:
    (a) **y = .2 * x ^ 2 + x + 3** (in the interval *x* = 1 to 10)
    (b) **y = 35 − .3 * x ^ 2** (in the interval *x* = 1 to 10)
    (c) **y = x + 10** (in the interval *x* = 1 to 10)
    (d) **y = 25 − 2 * x** (in the interval *x* = 1 to 10)

10.6 UP WITH THE BAR GRAPH

In Section 10.4 we treated simple bar graph programming. The horizontal orientation of line printers and terminals makes such applications easier to do if we use the vertical axis for the *x* variate. Displaying the *x* axis vertically may confuse some and outrage others. Confusion arises from the fact that visuals in textbooks and other sources commonly place the *x* variate on the horizontal axis. Here we will attempt to turn bar graphs upright so that they can stand on their own bottoms. The bar graph printed in section 10.4 is shown below.

```
       0          10         20
       :....+....:....+....:
       . **
       . ******
       . ********
       . *****
       . **
       :....+....:....+....:
```

Our goal here is to take the same data and produce a bar graph with a horizontal *x* axis. The easiest approach to this task may be to inspect the final product and then discuss the manner in which it was programmed. Here is the final product:

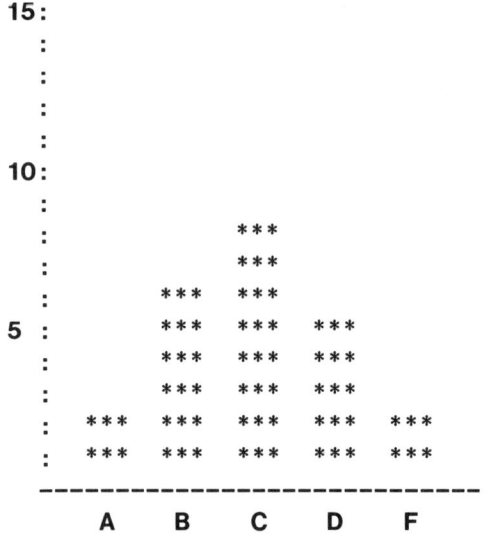

The program begins with an initialization block much like the one we used in Section 10.4.

```
150 DIM MARK(5)
160 FOR I = 1 TO 5
170 READ MARK(I)
180 NEXT I
350 DATA 2,6,8,5,2
```

Here is a loop which will generate the *k*-th line of the graph.

```
200 LET L$ = "  "
210 FOR I = 1 TO 5
220 IF MARK(I) >= K THEN LET L$ = L$ + "***":GOTO 240
230 LET L$ = L$ + "   "
240 LET L$ = L$ + "  "
250 NEXT I
```

L$ is an output string that will contain the appropriate parts of the bars corresponding to each printed line. Statement 200 inserts a two column blank spacer at the beginning of the output string. Inserting the spacer clears the previous content of the string. Statement 240 inserts a two column spacer between bars. Statements 220 and 230 determine the content of each bar—either blank or a field of stars. This loop must be performed one time for each output line; therefore, it must be nested inside another loop. Here is the program fragment with both loops present.

```
190 FOR K = 15 TO 1 STEP -1
200 LET L$ = "  "
210 FOR I = 1 TO 5
220 IF MARK(I) >= K THEN LET L$ = L$ + "**":GOTO 240
230 LET L$ = L$ + "   "
240 LET L$ = L$ + "  "
250 NEXT I
260 IF K / 5 = INT (K / 5) THEN PRINT K;
270 PRINT TAB(3)":";      (Use **TAB(4)** on the PET and the TRS-80.)
280 PRINT L$
290 NEXT K
```

The only task remaining is to print the *X* axis and label it. This can be accomplished as follows:

```
300 PRINT "    ";      (Use four blanks on the PET and the TRS-80.)
310 FOR I = 1 TO 30
320 PRINT "-"
330 NEXT I
335 PRINT
340 PRINT "    A    B    C    D    F"
```
(Insert one more blank in front of **A** on the PET and the TRS-80.)

We could develop a method for displaying *X-Y* plots upright as well. However, with the microcomputer graphics we can generate the graph in the correct orientation in a routine manner.

10.7 LOW RESOLUTION GRAPHICS

Low resolution graphics refers to the ability to produce graphic images by addressing an array of points on the video screen. These points may be the conventional printing positions or some subdivisions of these positions. We will first treat the low resolution graphics on the Apple.

Photo 10.1
The TRS-80 screen displays bricks that are used in low resolution graphics. (Photo courtesy of Radio Shack, a division of Tandy Corp.)

APPLE

The Apple microcomputer actually has four screen buffers. These screen buffers are memory areas containing information that may be displayed on the video monitor. Two buffers are used for text and low resolution graphics and the other two buffers are used for high resolution graphics. The first text buffer is the one normally displayed. It is used for text and low resolution graphics. The second text buffer is difficult to use and we will not discuss it further. Only one high resolution buffer is available on Apples with less than 24K of memory and no high resolution graphics is available if an Apple has less than 16K of memory.

A graphics system should be based on some sort of screen coordinate system. For the Apple that system has its zero point at the top left of the screen. Unfortunately, that is not very convenient as we normally plot right and up. The print element is a rectangular *brick* which is one half the size of a print position in the vertical direction. The brick is seven dots wide and four dots high. The screen grid consists of a forty by forty grid (1600 print positions). These positions are individually addressable through a **PLOT** command. The positions are numbered zero through thirty-nine starting from the top left of the screen. Note that this differs from the **TAB** positions that start at one, not zero.

To illustrate the low resolution graphics in an *x-y* plot, suppose we plot the equation $y = 32 - x$ on a set of axes at the lower left corner of the screen (*x* horizontal and *y* vertical). Let *x* range from one to thirty. Consider the following program fragment:

```
100  GR
110  COLOR = 15
120  FOR I = 1 TO 30
130  LET X = I
140  LET Y = 32 − X
150  LET Y = 39 − Y
160  PLOT X,Y
170  NEXT I
180  FOR I = 0 TO 39
190  PLOT 0,I
200  PLOT I, 39
210  NEXT I
```

We need to consider certain statements in this program in more detail. Statement 100 places the computer in graphics (low resolution) mode. This means that the top twenty lines on the screen are reserved for the *bricks,* and the bottom four printing lines are used for any text we want to print.

Should we wish to use the bottom four lines for *bricks* we must add the following statements immediately after the **GR** statement:

```
102 CALL – 1998
104 POKE – 16302,0
```

The first statement sets the entire screen buffer to black and the second statement causes the bottom four lines to be used for graphic display.

Statement 110 is necessary if we are to see the graphic image since the comand **GR** sets the color to zero (black). The number selected for color is a matter of preference. Values in the range of zero to fifteen are proper. If you have a black and white monitor, we recommend the value of fifteen for white.

Statement 150 is necessary if we are to restore the positive *y*-axis to its usual upward direction. This statement inverts the screen coordinate system.

Statement 160 is new syntax that instructs the computer to illuminate the *brick* at position *x,y*. Statements 190 and 200 produce a set of axes. A run of this program is shown below:

When the program above ends execution, the Apple will be displaying graphics. You can type **TEXT** followed by **RETURN** to resume normal text display.

The Apple low resolution graphics has some additional capability for line construction that is useful in bar graph and histogram construction. For example, a horizontal line may be drawn at any row of the screen by using the syntax:

Sec. 10.7   Low Resolution Graphics

150 HLIN X1, X2 AT Y

The line starts at position **X1** in row **Y** and ends at position **X2** in row **Y**. Similarly, a vertical line of variable length may be drawn at any column of the screen using the syntax:

150 VLIN Y1, Y2 AT X

To illustrate this capability consider the problem of constructing a histogram with the following characteristics:

Column	Quantity
3	5
4	15
5	22
6	37
7	15
8	18
9	4

The base of the histogram should be in row 39. A histogram differs from a bar graph in that the bars normally have no spaces between them. The following program fragment should produce the desired histogram.

```
100  GR
110  COLOR = 15
120  FOR I = 3 TO 9
130  READ Y
140  LET Y = 40 - Y
150  VLIN Y, 39 AT I
160  NEXT I
170  DATA 5,15,22,37,15,18,4
```

Statement 140, which effects a reversal of Y direction, uses forty rather than thirty-nine since no space is reserved for a *zero* bar.

Low resolution plots in the standard printing positions are also available on the Apple through the use of two special **TAB** commands. **HTAB X** moves the print position right of the left margin to X. **VTAB Y** moves the print position down from the top of the screen Y units. Consider the following program fragment:

```
100  HOME
110  PRINT "Y AXIS"
120  FOR I = 1 TO 19
130  PRINT ":"
```

208 *Formatting and Graphics*   *Ch. 10*

```
140 NEXT I
150 PRINT ":....:....:....:....: X AXIS"
160 FOR I = 0 TO 15
170 LET X = I
180 LET Y = X + 2
190 VTAB 21 - Y
200 HTAB X + 1
210 PRINT "*"
220 NEXT I
```

This program should plot the straight line Y = X + 2. The **HTAB** and **VTAB** then give us cursor control equivalent to that found on other machines. Cursor control on the PET is discussed below.

PET

Low resolution graphics on the PET is available only through the usual printing positions (twenty-five lines of length forty = 1000 printing positions). This compares with 1600 positions on the Apple and 6144 positions on the TRS-80 (Level II). PET graphics makes available special graphic characters that are convenient for certain applications. Although we are essentially using teletype graphics with the PET, the graphic symbols are contiguous to one another. As a result, straight lines need not be broken and bar graphs can be constructed with solid bars. We call your attention to the following characters, which are particularly useful:

    1   The upper case of the **@** key produces a horizontal bar centered on the printing position.

    2   The upper case of the **]** produces a vertical bar centered on the printing position.

    3   The upper case of the four lowest keys on the number pad join symbols 1 and 2 to form square corners.

4. Rounded corners are available in the upper case of U, I, J, and K.

    5   The upper case of keys 1, 2, 3, and 4 on the number pad are nice for doing brick work.

    6   The most intense symbol is obtained by the reverse blank space. Try the immediate command:

?"RVS SPACE SPACE"

A serious limitation of PET low resolution graphics is the absence of a screen coordinate system. As a result one must improvise a systematic method of reaching the various screen positions. One method of doing this is illustrated in the following program fragment:

```
100  PRINT CHR$(147)
110  FOR I = 1 TO 39
120  LET R$ = R$ + CHR$(29)
130  LET D$ = D$ + CHR$(17)
140  NEXT I
150  FOR I = 1 TO 10
160  LET X = I
170  LET Y = 2 * X + 3
180  LET Y = 24 - Y
190  PRINT CHR$(19);
200  PRINT LEFT$(D$,Y);
210  PRINT LEFT$(R$,X)"*"
220  NEXT I
```

This program fragment will plot the equation $y = 2x + 3$ over the interval $x = 1$ to 10.

Statement 100 clears the screen. Statements 110 and 120 load strings with character representations of ASCII codes for moving the cursor right and down respectively. Statement 190 sends the cursor *home* and is necessary because of the absence of a screen coordinate system. We must send the cursor *home* in order to have a standard reference point from which to move. Statements 200 and 210 cause the correct down and right movements prior to printing the point with "*". While this procedure is somewhat more cumbersome, the ability to select symbols to be printed and the ability to mix text and graphics are definite advantages.

TRS-80

The TRS-80 low resolution graphics has the most resolution of the three systems. Each of the 16 printing lines is subdivided into three giving a resolution of 48 in the vertical direction. Each of the 64 columns is divided into two giving a horizontal resolution of 128. Thus a total of 48 x 128 = 6144 positions are addressable. The TRS-80 has some of the desirable features of both the Apple and the PET. It has a screen coordinate system with the origin in the upper left corner (as with Apple). It has the ability to mix graphics and text (as with PET). The syntax for using the coordinate system is:

SET (X,Y)

Additional features are the ability to **RESET**, the ability to **PRINT @** a position (the original printing positions—not the graphics positions), and the ability to determine if a graphic point is **SET** or not.

In the Apple section we displayed the low resolution graphics plot of the equation $y = 32 - x$. That same plot for the TRS-80 follows.

The program which generated this plot is similar to that shown in the previous section on the Apple. Necessary changes to the previous program are replacement of statement 100 with **100 CLEAR**, each plot statement is replaced by a **SET( )** statement, and the value of thirty-nine in statements 150, 180, and 200 needs to be changed. This value should be forty-seven rather than thirty-nine. Note that the TRS-80 brick has four rows of dots in three columns.

EXERCISE SET   10.3

1. Modify the *upright* bar graph program in Section 10.6 to display seven bars. The bars are to have lengths 8, 9, 23, 9, 3, 8, and 5 and are to be labeled A, B, C, D, F, W, and I respectively.

2. Use low resolution graphics to solve the following problems:
   (a) Construct a bar chart (horizontal bars) representing the following percentage responses to a survey on job satisfaction (very satisfied) by category:

Challenge	45%
Financial Reward	37%
Comfort	32%

	Relations with Co-workers	44%
	Resource Adequacy	52%*

(b) Construct a bar chart (vertical bars) representing the following percentage responses to a survey:

Unsatisfactory	5%
Poor	12%
Fair	33%
Good	22%
Excellent	22%
Superior	6%

(c) Construct a histogram showing the following distribution of cars in a sample of 100 car owners:

25	Sub-compact
33	Compact
25	Mid-size
12	Large
5	Luxury

10.8 HIGH RESOLUTION GRAPHICS— FOR APPLES ONLY

High resolution graphics refers to the ability to produce graphic images by addressing a dense array of points on the video screen. We will discuss high resolution graphics on the Apple. The PET and the TRS-80 do not have high resolutions graphics except perhaps through special software.

The Apple II has a screen grid of 280 by 160 plotting points (extendable to 280 by 192). The numbers for the 280 horizontal positions run from 0 to 279 inclusive. For the vertical positions the numbers run from 0 (at the top of the screen) to 159 (or 191). High resolution graphics has the same point plotting capability that is found in low resolution graphics. Lines can be drawn with the added ability to draw a line between any two points. Thus, the vertical and horizontal line syntax is not necessary.

When we display the first high resolution graphics page with the **HGR** command, the bottom four lines of text space are usually reserved for the display of text.

We illustrate the new syntax with two program fragments. The first places a point in the 110-th column from the left and the bottom row of the high resolution screen.

```
100 HGR
110 HCOLOR = 3
120 HPLOT 109,159
```

*Source: Data from US Bureau of Census, 1978.

You should note the prefix **H** on each of these commands. We suggest three (white) for **HCOLOR** on black and white screens. Since the positions start at zero the 110-th column is position 109 just as the 160-th row is position 159.

Another version of this program is shown.

100 HGR
110 HCOLOR = 3
120 HPLOT 109,191

When you run this program, nothing appears to happen. If we add the following statement and rerun the program, a dot appears at the bottom of the screen:

105 POKE −16302,0

This statement sets a switch that causes the entire first page of the high resolutions graphics buffer to be displayed rather than a mixture of text and graphics.

The next program illustrates the line drawing capability. We are to connect the point plotted above with the point in screen position 59,75.

100 HGR
110 HCOLOR = 3
120 HPLOT 109,159 TO 59,75

This **HPLOT** command may be continued in the same statement to other points. For example, we might write line 120 as follows:

120 HPLOT 109,159 TO 59,75 TO 0,0

In using either high or low resolution graphics on the Apple it is important to know where to position the cursor so that text material to be displayed with graphics is not printed beneath the graphic image. If you go into graphics mode with the cursor above line 21, you may lose sight of any subsequent printed material. Therefore we suggest that you accompany each command for graphics with a **VTAB** command as shown below. The **HOME** command will clear the screen of any printed material that you do not want in the text window. We suggest the following sequence:

100 HOME: HGR: HCOLOR = 3: VTAB = 21

The command **TEXT** will clear the graphics from the screen leaving whatever may have been printed underneath. Try the following program:

100 HOME: HGR: HCOLOR = 3: VTAB = 21
110 HPLOT 0,0 TO 279,159
120 PRINT "TO CLEAR THE SCREEN PRESS ANY KEY."
130 GET A$: IF A$ = " " THEN 130
140 TEXT
150 PRINT "NOTE THAT THE GRAPHIC IMAGE DISAPPEARS."
160 PRINT "PRINTING CONTINUES DOWN THE PAGE."

The real advantage of the high resolution graphics mode is to produce point plots and line graphs. We consider two example programs and their output.

```
100  REM -- POINTPLOT 11-20-80
120  REM      LOCAL VARIABLES: I
130  REM      OUTPUT VARIABLES: X, Y
140  HGR: HCOLOR = 3: HOME: VTAB 21
150  REM      PLOT AXES
160  HPLOT 100,0 TO 100,150
170  FOR I = 0 TO 15
180  HPLOT 101,10 * I
190  NEXT I
200  HPLOT 0,100 TO 200,100
210  FOR I = 0 TO 20
220  HPLOT 10 * I,99
230  NEXT I
240  REM      PLOT CURVE
250  FOR I = -7 TO 10 STEP .1
260  LET X = I
270  LET Y = .2 * X ^ 3 - 2 * X ^ 2 - 7 * X + 50
280  HPLOT 100 + 10 * X, 100 - Y
290  NEXT I
300  REM      LABEL GRAPH
310  PRINT "GRAPH OF THE CURVE:"
320  PRINT "Y = .2X^3 - 2X^2 - 7X + 50 (-7 TO 10)"
330  PRINT "EACH DIVISION ON THE Y AXIS = 10 UNITS."
340  GET A$: IF A$ = " " THEN 340
350  END
```

Here is the output of this program:

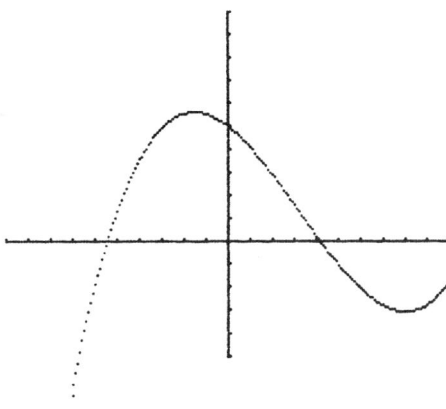

GRAPH OF THE CURVE:
Y = .2X^3 − 2X^2 − 7X + 50 (−7 TO 10)
EACH DIVISION ON THE Y AXIS = 10 UNITS.

And another example:

```
100  REM -- LINEGRAPH 11-22-80
110  REM     INPUT VARIABLES: SALES
120  REM     LOCAL VARIABLES: I, SVSALES
130  REM     OUTPUT VARIABLES: SALES
140  HGR: HCOLOR = 3: HOME: VTAB 21
150  REM     PLOT AXES
160  HPLOT 10,9 TO 10,159 TO 200,159
170  FOR I = 0 TO 15
180  HPLOT 11,9 + 10 * I
190  NEXT I
200  FOR I = 1 TO 6
210  HPLOT 28 * I,158
220  NEXT I
230  REM     PLOT LINE GRAPH
240  READ SVSALES
250  FOR I = 1 TO 5
260  READ SALES
270  HPLOT 28 * I,159 − SVSALES TO 28 * (I + 1),159 − SALES
280  NEXT I
290  DATA 48,69,79,34,56,120
300  PRINT " 75  76  77  78  79  80  SALES"
310  PRINT "EACH VERTICAL MARK = 10 THOUSAND UNITS."
320  END
```

The output is shown below.

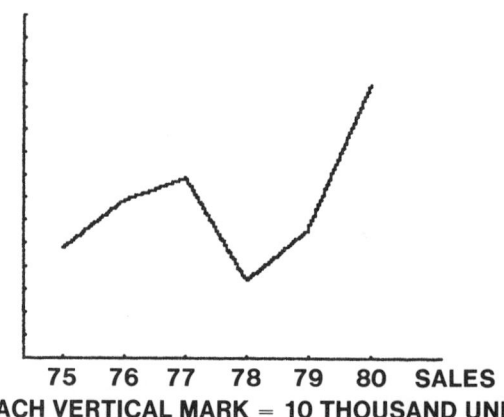

If the Apple you are using has 24K of memory or more, you can choose to use the second page of high resolution graphics for plotting. This is done by using **HGR2** instead of **HGR**. It is possible to have different images on each page and switch from one to the other as we will demonstrate in Chapter 13.

EXERCISE SET 10.4

1. Draw a set of coordinate axes that intersect at screen position (100,100). Each axis should extend 100 units in the positive direction (up or right) and 50 units in the negative direction (down or left).

2. Draw a box of side length 100 centered at (75,75).

3. Develop a program to plot the equation

    Y = (X ^ 2) / 7 − 32

    on the coordinate axes of problem 1. Let X range from -30 to +30.

4. One of the problems encountered in working with any plotting program is plotting off screen. Error messages result and our program stops. It is possible to check values to be plotted before they are executed. Establish coordinate axes that intersect at 100,150 and plot the equation

    Y = .5 * X ^ 2

    over the interval X = -20 to 20. Do not pass Y values larger than 150 to the **HPLOT** command.

5. Construct a line graph using the data below. Place each year's data fifteen spaces apart and let each vertical unit equal half a year. Draw curves joining the data points for both males and females.

Life Expectancy

Year	Male	Female
1920	53.5	54.5
1930	58.0	61.5
1940	61.0	65.0
1950	65.5	71.0
1960	66.5	73.0
1970	67.0	75.0

10.9 CONTROL OF DATA FORMAT

One of the advantages of BASIC over FORTRAN, and other more sophisticated computer languages, is the ability to obtain output without knowing much about formatting. FORTRAN, for example, requires specific formatting for each numerical output. As a result, one is forced to learn the formatting options early. BASIC, on the other hand, will make decisions for us on the format of the numerical output. This is fine so long as we are happy with the decisions inherent in the structure of the language. The example in Section 10.1 indicates one of the problems that arises. BASIC will print its output in scientific notation if the number is small ($<$ .01) or very large ($>=$ 1,000,000,000).

There is a related problem that affects not only the format but the meaning of our output. Suppose we were conducting an experiment in which we measure the speed of a moving object. Perhaps we have a timing gate that records the speed of a ball as it rolls past a point on an incline. We repeat the experiment several times and obtain the results listed in Table 10.1.

Table 10.1
Repeated
Measurements of the
Speed of a Ball

Trial	Speed
1	3.41 m/s
2	3.42 m/s
3	3.43 m/s
4	3.41 m/s

We compute the mean value for the four trials. If we do this on the computer we obtain an average speed of 3.4175 *m/s*. We have taken four numbers representing speeds measured to the hundredths of a meter per second. By averaging them we now have a velocity with four decimal places. This is wonderful. We have increased the precision of our answer by averaging—or have we? As you may suspect, data manipulation by itself cannot increase the precision of measured results. Thus, the number 3.4175 *m/s* could be misleading if reported as the average speed.

Scientists normally adhere to a set of rules that prescribe how many **significant digits** can appear in calculated results that are based on experimental measurements. Significant digits but not additional digits are reported. In Table 10.1, there are three significant digits in the experimental data. The average, if reported as calculated, shows five significant digits. We typically keep as many significant digits in a calculated result as were available in the least precise measured value involved. In averaging, perhaps one more significant digit may be kept in the result. In any case we would not keep more than four significant digits in the number 3.4175.

In summary, we often have problems not only of fixing the number of decimal places in any answer—which can be done easily enough using the **INT** function—but of deciding how many digits (regardless of their relation to the decimal point) should appear in the answer.

10.10 FORCING SCIENTIFIC NOTATION

We begin to deal with the problem of data format and significant digits by developing a program to place all numbers in scientific notation. This program will also serve to illustrate how we may control the format of numerical data by treating numbers as strings. We express the program in pseudocode form first. (TRS-80 users may skip this explanation and Section 10.11 since the **PRINT USING** in Level II BASIC will force scientific notation as well as the desired number of significant digits.)

```
SCINOTATION:
declare numeric NUM, P
declare string NUM$, SNUM$, EX$
put ("ENTER NUMBER")
get (NUM$)
set SNUM$ to the string value of NUM$
set NUM to the value of NUM$
set NUM$ to the string value of NUM (not redundant)
if (NUM is in decimal range)
    [move the decimal point until one non-zero digit is to its left
    fix the exponential part of the number
    concatenate the number and exponential strings]
put ("HERE IS THE NUMBER ";SNUM$)
put ("IN SCIENTIFIC NOTATION: ";NUM$)
end.
```

The statements associated with the single alternative decision structure require some refinement before they can be coded. In the first place, how can we determine if a number is in a certain range? Consider the following logical expression:

$$(L - X) * (X - S) >= 0$$

If X is between S (smallest value) and L (largest value) this condition evaluates as true. However, if X is outside this range the condition evaluates as false. You should convince yourself of this by trying values for L, S, and X. Since we know the range in which the computer maintains numbers in exponential form we need only replace L by

999999999 and S by .01. The logical expression then becomes:

if ((99999999 − ABS(NUM)) * (ABS(NUM) − .01)) >= 0

The next statement requires that we move the decimal point in NUM. Recall that in scientific notation only one nonzero digit appears left of the decimal point. We can do this by finding the range of the absolute value of NUM. Consider the following code:

```
220 LET M = 1
230 FOR P = −2 TO 8
240 IF ABS(NUM) < .1 * M THEN 270
250 LET M = M * 10
260 NEXT P
270 LET NUM = NUM * 100 / M
```

The value of **P** becomes the exponent on 10 when the number is written in scientific notation. Can you see why **P** ranges from −2 to 8? In the code we have chosen to work with powers of ten as whole numbers rather than in exponential form. This avoids minor errors, which creep in during exponentiation.

Establishing the value of the exponent on 10 is now easy. The following code should do the job:

```
280 LET EX$ = "0" + STR$(ABS(P))
290 IF P > −1 THEN EX$ = "E+" + EX$: GOTO 290
300 LET EX$ = "E−" + EX$
```

The "**0**" in statement 280 is to make the format of our exponent look like the computer's. Statements 290 and 300 make up a double alternative decision structure that determines the sign of the exponent based upon the value of **P**.

One other part of the program may need clarification. We are entering the number as a string rather than in its numerical form. This is necessary in order to retain the original form for comparison with the scientific notation form.

Here is the final program.

```
100 REM -- SCIENTIFIC NOTATION 8/20/80
110 REM     INPUT VARIABLES: NUM$
120 REM     LOCAL VARIABLES: P, EX$, NUM, M
130 REM     OUTPUT VARIABLES: SNUM$, NUM$
140 PRINT "ENTER NUMBER";
150 INPUT NUM$
160 REM     SAVE ORIGINAL ENTRY
170 LET SNUM$ = NUM$
180 LET NUM = VAL(NUM$)
185 LET NUM$ = STR$(NUM)
190 REM     IF NUMBER IS IN COMPUTER
200 REM       EXPONENTIAL RANGE, QUIT
```

```
210 IF (999999999 - ABS(NUM)) * (ABS(NUM) - .01) < 0 THEN 320
220 LET M = 1
230 FOR P = -2 TO 8
240 IF ABS(NUM) < .1 * M THEN 270
250 LET M = M * 10
260 NEXT P
270 LET NUM = NUM * 100 / M
280 LET EX$ = "0" + STR$(ABS(P))
290 IF P > -1 THEN EX$ = "E+" + EX$: GOTO 310
300 LET EX$ = "E-" + EX$
310 LET NUM$ = STR$(NUM) + EX$
320 PRINT: PRINT
330 PRINT "HERE IS THE NUMBER  ";SNUM$
340 PRINT "IN SCIENTIFIC NOTATION:  ";NUM$
350 END
```

10.11 SIGNIFICANT DIGITS

Now that we can force any number into scientific notation the problem of printing a number with the correct significant digits is not so difficult. We need only operate on the base part of the number and not the exponent. We will first run the number through the *processor*, which converts it to scientific notation. Then we will strip off the base part of the number and round it to the correct number of significant digits. Minor problems of the difference between positive and negative numbers and the padding of zeros remain. We illustrate one solution to this problem in the following program.

```
100 REM -- SIGNIFICANT DIGITS 8-20-80
110 REM     INPUT VARIABLES: NUM$, SIGD
120 REM     LOCAL VARIABLES: P, EX$
130 REM     OUTPUT VARIABLES: NUM$, SNUM$, SIGD
140 REM     PLACE NUMBER IN SCIENTIFIC NOTATION
150 GOSUB 9500
155 PRINT
160 PRINT "NOW ENTER THE NUMBER OF SIGNIFICANT"
165 PRINT "DIGITS  ";
170 INPUT SIGD
180 REM     SEPARATE BASE AND EXPONENT
190 LET NUM$ = MID$(NUM$,1,LEN(NUM$) -4)
195 LET EX$ = MID$(NUM$, LEN(NUM$) - 3,4)
200 REM     REDUCE TO SIGNIFICANT DIGITS
210 LET NUM = VAL(NUM$)
```

220 Formatting and Graphics

```
220 LET NUM = INT(NUM * 10^(SIGD - 1) + .5) / 10^(SIGD - 1)
230 LET NUM$ = STR$(ABS(NUM))
240 REM     ADD SIGNIFICANT ZEROES AS NEEDED
250 IF LEN(NUM$) > SIGD + 1 THEN 310
260 IF SIGD = 1 THEN 310
270 IF NUM = INT(NUM) THEN LET NUM$ = NUM$ + "."
280 LET NUM$ = NUM$ + "0"
290 IF LEN(NUM$) < SIGD + 1 THEN 280
300 REM     CONCATENATE AND PRINT RESULTS
310 IF NUM < 0 THEN LET NUM$ = "-" + NUM$
320 LET NUM$ = NUM$ + EX$
330 PRINT
340 PRINT "THE INPUT NUMBER (";SNUM$;") WRITTEN IN"
350 PRINT "SCIENTIFIC NOTATION WITH ";SIGD
360 PRINT "SIGNIFICANT DIGITS IS  ";NUM$;"."
370 END
```

10.12 REAL TIME DISPLAYS— FOR PETS ONLY

The PET has an internal clock that can be used to evaluate equations in which the time variable appears explicitly. The ability to evaluate quantities such as speed and position and to display and update their values in real (actual) time may be useful in many applications.

The internal clock can be set to zero by the statement:

LET TI$ = "000000"

From the instant this program statement is executed the clock runs using a basic unit of time equal to 1/60th of a second. **TI** is a variable in which the cumulative count of 60th's of seconds is kept. **TI$** is a variable in which the cumulative count of seconds is kept as a string variable. Both **TI** and **TI$** are set to zero by the instruction above. Thus, when **TI$** has the string value **"000001"**, **TI** has the numerical value of sixty.

The internal clock is initialized to zero when the PET is turned on. If we want to know how long the computer has been turned on, we can enter the immediate command **PRINT TI$**. Unless the clock has been reset under program control, the string printed will indicate the number of seconds the computer has been on.

Consider the following problem. An object falling in the gravitational field of the earth develops a downward velocity of $V = 32t$ ft/sec where t is elapsed time in seconds. Its downward displacement is given by $Y = 16t^2$ ft. These equations are valid in the absence of air resistance. Let us develop a program that will print out and update the velocity and position as the object falls. Consider the following program fragment:

```
100  PRINT CHR$(147): REM      CLEAR SCREEN
110  LET TI$ = "00000"
120  PRINT "TIME","VELOCITY","DISPLACEMENT"
130  FOR I = 1 TO 1000
140  IF TI/60 <> INT(TI/60) THEN 200
150  LET T1 = INT(TI/60)
160  LET V = 32 * T1
170  LET D = 16 * T1 * T1
180  PRINT "SQQQ": REM CURSOR CONTROL SYMBOLS
190  PRINT T1,V,D
200  NEXT I
210  END
```

Enter this program and observe the output. You should see time, velocity, and displacement updated each second for eighteen seconds.

EXERCISE SET 10.5

1. Use the program on significant digits to output the results of the following calculations:

    (a) Calculate **P** to three significant digits when **P = n*R*T/V**.

    n = 3.50
    R = 8.314
    T = 293
    V = 0.165

    (b) Calculate **K** to two significant digits when **K = .5*m*v^2**.

    m = 1.67E−27
    v = 2.5E7

    (c) Calculate **r** to two significant digits when **r = (E0*h^2)/(pi*m*e^2)**.

    E0 = 8.85E−12
    h = 6.62E−34
    pi = 3.14
    m = 9.1E−31
    e = 1.6E−19

2. Develop a program that will output any number in scientific notation with only one significant digit.

3. Develop a program that will output any number in scientific notation with two significant digits.

Review

In this Chapter we have been concerned with methods of producing formatted and graphic output. The following terms and syntax are highlighted:

PRINT IMAGE a string, including character information and formatted number images. The numbers are indicated symbolically while the character data appears explicitly in the image. (Section 10.3)

TELETYPE GRAPHICS graphic output produced by combinations of conventional symbols on a computer terminal. (Section 10.4)

LOW RESOLUTION GRAPHICS graphic output produced by addressing printing positions or their subdivisions on the screen. (Section 10.7)

HIGH RESOLUTION GRAPHICS graphic output in which each screen dot is addressable. (Section 10.8)

SIGNIFICANT DIGITS digits retained in a number because they indicate the actual precision of the number. Computer generation of numbers often introduces digits which are not significant. (Section 10.9)

REAL TIME DISPLAYS computer output that is updated in actual time to indicate the correct value of some time-dependent variable or variables. (Section 10.12)

BASIC SYNTAX

PRINT TAB( ) a combination of a command and a function that moves the printing position right on the current printing line. The argument of the function specifies the number of right moves. Arguments can range from 1 to 255. (Section 10.2)

APPLE ONLY

GR signifies entry into low resolution graphics mode. (Section 10.7)

COLOR = # (1 to 15) designates color of image in low resolution graphics mode. The **COLOR** statement is necessary even in black and white. (Section 10.7)

HLIN X1,X2 AT Y draws a horizontal *line* at vertical position **Y** extending from **X1** to **X2** in the horizontal direction. Syntax works in **GR** mode only. (Section 10.7)

VLIN Y1,Y1 AT X draws a horizontal line at horizontal position **X** extending from **Y1** to **Y2** in the vertical direction. Syntax works in **GR** mode only. (Section 10.7)

HTAB X moves the printing position **X** units from the left margin at the current printing line. (Section 10.7)

VTAB Y moves the printing position **Y** units down from the top of the screen. (Section 10.7)

PLOT X,Y places a standard marker in position **X,Y** on the screen. Syntax works in **GR** mode only. (Section 10.7)

HGR signifies entry into high resolution graphics mode. A four line text window is available in this mode. (Section 10.8)

HGR2 signifies entry into high resolution graphics mode with expanded vertical plotting positions (192) and no text window. (Section 10.8)

HCOLOR = # (1 to 7) establishes color of image in high resolution graphics mode. (Section 10.8)

HPLOT X,Y places a point in position **X,Y** on the screen. Syntax works in **HGR** and **HGR2** modes. (Section 10.8)

HPLOT X1,Y1 TO X2,Y2 draws a line from **X1,Y1** to **X2,Y2**. Syntax works in **HGR** and **HGR2** modes. (Section 10.8)

TRS-80 ONLY

SET (X,Y) places a standard marker in position **X,Y** on the screen. (Section 10.7)

PRINT @ X, (variable, expression, or string) prints the value or string beginning in print position **X**. (Section 10.7)

RESET (X,Y) changes status of standard marker at graphics position **(X,Y)**. (Turns a brick on if it is off, or off if it is on). (Section 10.7)

11

FILES

11.1 INTRODUCTION TO FILES

In programming examples presented so far, we have confined ourselves to entering data from the keyboard or storing it within the program itself using **DATA** statements. While the latter technique is surely superior to the former, whenever more than a few data values are involved, this method is still clumsy when it comes to updating and sharing files and it also consumes valuable computer memory that might otherwise be available for additional program statements. This factor is particularly important when one is using a microcomputer with a small memory increment.

BASIC syntax for file processing varies widely among computer systems. However, certain standard procedures must be taken on all such systems. In this chapter, we will first consider general concepts of file processing and, thereafter, take specific examples using the Apple, the PET, and the TRS-80 microcomputers. When we display BASIC syntax to accomplish file handling, we will use certain techniques that we have found to be effective with these machines without necessarily exhausting all possible methods of handling files.

11.2 FILES GENERALLY

A **file** is a collection of records with some type of logical organization. Each record in a file may contain one or more variables. Each record usually represents a specific case, often a person, about which or whom information is collected. For example, if a file contained information about the age, the sex and the residence of students, each record would contain attributes or variables which pertain to an individual student. We can call this a **logical record** because all the variables on the record are logically related to each other; they pertain to the same person. It is also possible to have information for the same case or person on two or more adjacent records. For example, the Bureau of the Census collects such a large amount of information about geographic areas that several large records are required to hold all the information. In such a case, several **physical records** (a physical record is a record that is physically separated from other physical records) are required to contain a single logical record, that is, all the information that pertains to a single geographic area. We will also see some examples in which it is desirable to deliberately choose separate physical records for logically related information.

The concept of a record may be more easily understood if we consider a record to be the equivalent of one line of output on the screen or printer. More technically, a physical record is a collection of characters (numbers, letters, and/or special symbols) terminated by a carriage return. This is the definition for a physical record, which, in most cases, is also a logical record. However, there are cases in which one logical record is composed of more than one physical record and it is also possible for several logical records to be contained in the same physical record. We will consider some examples of the former, but not the latter in this chapter. Generally speaking, physical records in the same file may be of varying lengths. The end of the record is detected by the presence of a carriage return—ASCII code 13. The Apple limits record size to 239 characters and the PET limits record size to 80 characters.

There are two basic file accessing methods: **sequential access** and **direct access** (sometimes called **random access**). Sequential access simply means that records in a file must be accessed—that is, processed—in the order in which they occur in the file. Thus, if we wish to read the record for the tenth student in the file, we must first read and ignore the records for the first nine students. Similarly, if there are 200 records in a file, we cannot read the 200th record without first reading the 199 records that precede it in the file. In contrast, random or direct access files allow us to read any record in a file directly without having to read those that precede it.

A useful analogy can be made between a sequential access file and a stack of file cards. Let us imagine that we have a stack of three by five file cards each containing the name of a student and certain other pieces of information. If we were looking for card number twenty, we would begin by counting each card as we proceed through the deck until we arrived at card twenty and then presumably use the information on it. A more realistic task would be to perform the same type of search beginning with the top card and continuing until we found the card with the name of the student about which we were seeking information. Social security numbers are also used for such identification purposes. In this case, we compare the name or social security number on each card with the name or social security number of the person whose card we are seeking. We process a sequential access file in the same way—by looking at each record beginning with the first until we find the record containing the desired information or come to the end of the file. In the latter case, the file does not contain information about the desired person.

11.3 SEQUENTIAL DISK FILES

Let us now consider an example of a sequential disk file using the Apple microcomputer. Developing the student information example mentioned in Section 11.2, let us suppose that we have a data set that looks like Table 11.1.

Table 11.1
Age, Sex, and Residence of Three Students

Student	Age	Sex	State
Jones	21	M	NY
Johnson	20	F	NJ
Brown	18	F	CT

This data set can be easily transformed into a series of **DATA** statements:

```
200  DATA JONES,21,M,NY
202  DATA JOHNSON,20,F,NJ
204  DATA BROWN,18,F,CT
```

(It should be noted parenthetically, that most versions of BASIC should process the string values in the **DATA** statements correctly. The PET, the TRS-80, and the Apple will do so. However, some versions of BASIC require that the string values be inclosed within double quotation marks.)

If we add the following statements, we will have a short program that will read our data and print it on the screen in tabular form.

```
100  REM---STORE      6-15-80
210  DATA *EOF*,0,*,*
220  READ N$,A,SX$,ST$
320  IF N$ = "*EOF*" THEN 900
330  PRINT TAB(1) N$; TAB(10)A;TAB(20)SX$; TAB(30)ST$
340  GOTO 220
900  END
```

Run the program to verify that it works as promised.

Now let us modify this program so that it writes a copy of the data on the disk rather than on the screen. In addition to the actual write transactions with the disk file, our program must instruct the computer to do four other things:

1 Open the file,
2 Name the file,
3 Specify the file to be a write only file, and
4 Close the file after use.

These four messages must be transmitted by the program to the Apple's disk operating system, which is often called **DOS** for short. The vehicle whereby we send these messages to the **DOS** is the ordinary **PRINT** statement with one special feature added. The **DOS** inspects every print line. When it finds a line beginning with a special marker (ASCII code 4 that can be entered either as **CHR$(4)** or as **CTRL/D**), it treats that line as a **DOS** instruction, intercepts the line, which is never printed, and performs the specified instruction. Thus, the **PRINT** statement with the **CTRL/D** on the front is the medium through which we send messages to **DOS**. The contents of these **PRINT** statements are not printed. Here is the final product:

```
100  REM---STORE      6-15-80
105  REM
110  D$ = CHR$(4)
115  PRINT D$"OPEN TESTDATA"
120  PRINT D$"WRITE TESTDATA"
195  REM
200  DATA JONES,21,M,NY
202  DATA JOHNSON,20,F,NJ
204  DATA BROWN,18,F,CT
210  DATA *EOF*,0,*,*
300  REM
310  READ N$,A,SX$,ST$
330  PRINT N$
332  PRINT A
334  PRINT SX$
336  PRINT ST$
338  IF N$ = "*EOF*" THEN 900
340  GOTO 310
900  PRINT D$"CLOSE"
```

Upon comparison, this program is very much like the first version with the following exceptions:

1 Statement 110 stores the character representation of ASCII code 4 in **D$**.

2 Statement 115 tells **DOS** to **OPEN** a file to be known as **"TESTDATA"**. (If a data file with the same name is already present on the disk, it will be used and its contents overwritten. If no such file exists, **DOS** will create one.)

3 Statement 120 tells **DOS** that the program will write to the file. From the time that statement 120 is executed until the file is closed, all **PRINT** statements will cause information to be printed to the disk file rather than on the screen.

4 Statement 900 tells **DOS** to close *all* files currently open. Since **TESTDATA** is the only file open, it will be closed when statement 900 is executed. If other files

Sec. 11.3 Sequential Disk Files 229

were open and we wished to close **TESTDATA** only, the following modification should be used:

900 PRINT D$"CLOSE TESTDATA"

One other important difference between this program and the first version concerns the print statements (lines 330 to 336). When we were printing data on the screen in the first program we used a single print statement with **TAB** instructions to obtain the desired columnar format. This approach is not appropriate to a disk file. Often it does not work as expected, but even if it does, a considerable amount of disk space would be wasted. Instead, in the second program, we have substituted four **PRINT** statements for the one previously used. Each **PRINT** statement writes one variable to the data file. Thus, each record in the file contains a single variable followed by a carriage return. Four physical records are required to make up one logical record. While it is possible to write more than one variable with the same print statement, computers vary in this regard and we recommend writing one variable per record which should be expected to work in all cases.

Our program has produced a data set on the diskette that consists of sixteen physical records—each ending with a carriage return. Each group of four physical records constitutes a logical record—with all values pertaining to the same student. Following you will find a symbolic representation of the data set. As you will note, the file is no more than a collection of numbers—fifty-six numbers to be exact. Each number is an ASCII code that represents a numeric, alphabetic, or special character. (See Appendix C for a listing of the ASCII coding system.)

74	79	78	69	83	13	50	49	13	77	13	78	89	13
J	O	N	E	S		2	1		M		N	Y	

74	79	72	78	83	79	78	13	50	48	13	70	13	78	74	13
J	O	H	N	S	O	N		2	0		F		N	J	

66	82	79	87	78	13	49	56	13	70	13	67	84	13
B	R	O	W	N		1	8		F		C	T	

42	69	79	70	42	13	48	13	42	13	42	13
*	E	O	F	*		0		*		*	

We have represented the file two ways: as ASCII numeric codes and as their character translations. You will note that some of the boxes are empty. They correspond to the carriage return code (ASCII 13) that has no graphic representation.

Recalling that physical records are defined as groups of symbols terminated by a carriage return, it is easy to recognize each physical record. Note that we have grouped physical records into logical records—each on a separate line. We have done so for the convenience of the reader but hasten to point out that this arrangement is unknown to our program and the computer. To the Apple, the file is a single list of ASCII codes, some of which are recognized as record separators—the carriage returns.

Now let us address ourselves to the task of reading the same file and producing on the screen the same table of information with which we began. Our program will be quite similar to the **STORE** program except that it will read from the disk and print on the screen in contrast to the **STORE** routine that did the opposite.

The program, called **GET7**, is displayed below. Note that statement 120 tells **DOS** that the program will read the file rather than write to it. No doubt you will also note that the program has only one **INPUT** statement in contrast to **STORE** (the program that created the file) that had four **PRINT** statements. The **INPUT** statement calls for values for each of four variables—and therefore will cause four separate records to be read from the disk file before it is satisfied. Statement 320 tests for the end of file condition.

```
100  REM -- GET7     6-15-80
105  REM
110  LET D$ = CHR$(4)
115  PRINT D$"OPEN TESTDATA"
120  PRINT D$"READ TESTDATA"
310  INPUT N$,A,SX$,ST$
320  IF N$ - "*EOF*" THEN 900
330  PRINT N$; TAB(10) A; TAB(20) SX$; TAB(30) ST$
340  GOTO 310
900  PRINT D$"CLOSE TESTDATA"
```

Sometimes, we must write programs to read data sets that do not have dummy end of file markers. When this is the case, we must resort to some other technique in order to avoid an error message and a premature halt to our program. The Apple has an error handling feature that allows our programs to control error processing if we wish to use it. If we place the following statement in our program, control will pass to statement 900 if an error occurs:

```
125  ONERR GOTO 900
```

More precisely, if an error is encountered during the execution of any statement after statement 125 is encountered, control will shift to statement 900. We can use such a statement to prevent program interruption as a result of the end of data on the disk file. Since it is our intention only to trap for one specific type of error, we must be able to separate disk end of file errors from other errors. We can do so by testing a memory location that contains an error code indicating which type of error has occurred. Apple error codes and their explanations are listed in Table 11.2.

Table 11.2
Apple Error Codes

Code	Explanation
0	**NEXT** without **FOR**
4	disk is write protected
5	out of data on disk data file
6	file not found
7	wrong volume
8	I/O error
9	disk full
10	file locked
11	bad file name or parameter
12	no buffers available (too many files open)
13	file type mismatch (you are probably trying to read a program as data)
16	syntax
22	**RETURN** without **GOSUB**
42	out of data
53	illegal quantity
69	overflow
77	out of memory
90	undefined statement
107	bad subscript
120	redimensioned array
133	division by zero
163	type mismatch
176	string too long
191	formula too complex
224	undefined function
255	control/C interrupt attempted

The Apple uses memory location 222 to store its error code. The contents of this location can be inspected by our program using the **PEEK** function which returns the contents of a memory location as a number. Since we are looking for a particular error, we test for its value. If **PEEK (222)** = **5** then our program has come to the end of data on a disk file. By incorporating such a test in a program, it can detect the end of file condition as illustrated in our next program.

Following is another version of the **GET** routine called **GET8** which is the same as **GET7** except for the use of the Apple error handling technique to trap for the end of file condition. Statement 900 closes the file as usual, but statement 910 checks to see if the error was an end of file condition. If it was, then control passes to statement 999;

otherwise the block of statements 915-930 is executed. They create a simulated error message indicating the error code and the line in which it occurred. Statement 930 rings the bell, or more precisely, causes the Apple to emit a bleep.

```
100  REM---GET8    6-15-80
105  REM
110  LET D$ = CHR$(4)
115  PRINT D$"OPEN TESTDATA"
120  PRINT D$"READ TESTDATA"
125  ONERR GOTO 900
310  INPUT N$,A,SX$,ST$
330  PRINT N$ TAB(10) A; TAB(20) SX$ TAB(30) ST$
340  GOTO 310
890  REM
900  PRINT D$"CLOSE TESTDATA"
910  IF PEEK (222) = 5 THEN 999
915  PRINT "***ERROR "; PEEK(222);" IN LINE ";
920  PRINT PEEK (218) + PEEK (219)*256
930  PRINT CHR$(7)
999  END
```

A common programming application using files is one in which information is entered from the keyboard for storage on disk. Here we will build a very simple payroll file on disk using information collected from the keyboard. This would be a relatively simple application were it not for the fact that it is virtually impossible to carry out I/O transactions with the keyboard while a disk file is open.

The Apple **DOS** maintains a file pointer that indicates the location to which the next character written to a sequential file will be stored. With one exception, we cannot modify the value of that pointer. When a program opens a sequential file with an **OPEN** command, the pointer is made to point to the beginning of the file. In contrast, when such a file is opened with the **APPEND** command, the file pointer is made to point to the position immediately following the location of the last character currently in the file. Thus, the **APPEND** command allows us to add records to the end of an existing file.

The **BUILDFILE** program, reproduced below, builds a simple payroll file. It does so by asking the user to input an employee's name **(N$)**, hourly pay rate **(R)**, and number of hours worked **(H)** in a given week. After these three values have been obtained from the keyboard, the disk file is opened, each value is written to the disk as a separate record, and the file closed. Because the **APPEND** command cannot be used to open a nonexistent file, the user is asked to indicate whether the file is new or old. If the user responds **"Y"**, the **OPEN** command is used to open the file the first time and the **APPEND** command is used thereafter. If the user responds that the file is not new, it is opened with the **APPEND** command and records are added to the existing file. Should a file already exist and the user nevertheless responds with **"Y"** indicating that the file is new, it will be opened with the **OPEN** command and its existing contents will be lost.

Note the use of the string variable **F$** to hold the file name and **A$** to contain either the string **"OPEN"** or **"APPEND"** as appropriate.

```
100 REM -- BUILDFILE    11-22-81
101 REM
102 REM     COLLECT INFORMATION
103 REM     AT KEYBOARD AND
104 REM     BUILD DISK FILE.
105 REM
110 D$ = CHR$(4)
115 ONERR GOTO 900
120 HOME
125 REM
126 REM==== GET FILE SPECIFICATIONS =====
127 REM
130 PRINT "ENTER FILE NAME: ";
135 INPUT F$
140 PRINT "IS FILE NEW: ";
145 INPUT R$
150 A$ = "APPEND"
155 IF LEFT$(R$,1) = "Y" THEN A$ = "OPEN"
190 REM
191 REM========= MAIN LOOP ==========
192 REM
200 PRINT "NAME: ";
205 INPUT N$
210 IF N$ = "EOF" THEN END
215 PRINT "HOURLY RATE: ";
220 INPUT R
225 PRINT "HOURS WORKED: ";
230 INPUT H
250 PRINT D$;A$;F$
260 PRINT D$;"WRITE";F$
270 PRINT N$
280 PRINT R
290 PRINT H
295 A$ = "APPEND"
300 PRINT D$;"CLOSE";F$
310 GOTO 200
400 REM
401 REM====== END OF MAIN LOOP ========
```

```
402 REM
900 ERR = PEEK(222)
910 IF ERR = 6 THEN PRINT "*** FILE NOT FOUND"; CHR$(7) : END
920 PRINT "*** ERROR ";ERR; CHR$(7)
```

The use of the **APPEND** command makes it difficult if not impossible to use a dummy trailer record as an end of file marker because such records would be written to the file each time it is closed. As a result, there might easily be dozens of such records in a file. Therefore, we advise you to use the **ONERR GOTO** statement to test for the end of file condition as illustrated by the **GETTEXT** routine below. **GETTEXT** can be used to read and display any text or data file.

```
100 REM -- GETTEXT
105 D$ = CHR$(4)
110 PRINT "ENTER FILE NAME: ";
115 INPUT F$
118 ONERR GOTO 200
120 PRINT D$;"OPEN";F$
125 PRINT D$;"READ";F$
130 INPUT S$
135 PRINT S$
140 GOTO 130
200 PRINT D$;"CLOSE"
210 ERR = PEEK(222)
220 IF ERR = 5 THEN PRINT "<EOF>" : END
230 PRINT "ERROR ";ERR; CHR$(7)
```

Note how both programs use the **ONERR GOTO** statement and test the error code generating a pseudo-error message if that code is not the expected one.

11.4 DIRECT ACCESS FILES

Direct access files, sometimes called random access files, allow one to select and retrieve records from a file in any order without having to process those records which precede them in the file. As already discussed, when we process sequential files, we must process all records in the order in which they occur in the file. Thus, if we desire to retrieve information from the twentieth record, we would have to retrieve and ignore the contents of the preceding nineteen records. Direct access files allow us to retrieve record twenty immediately, without processing the preceding records. In addition, we may read and write records to a direct access file in any order. In contrast, writing a record to a sequential access file in effect destroys all subsequent records in that file.

Direct access files must be stored on disks—either the hard disks or the flexible, floppy disks. Our discussion here will be limited to direct access files on the Apple although such files can also be processed by the PET and the TRS-80 when they have disk drives attached.

The method of processing direct access files on the Apple is similar to the method for processing sequential access files. Like other files, direct access files must be opened before they can be processed. Below is an open statement for a direct access file:

100 PRINT D$"OPEN DATAFILE,L40"

It is similar to the open statement used for sequential files with the exception of the **",L40"** at the end. This parameter indicates the length (that is, the maximum number of characters), of records in the file. Thus, **DATAFILE** will have records with forty characters each. If we wish to use a variable to indicate record length, the following statement will accomplish the same thing:

100 L=40
110 PRINT D$"OPEN DATAFILE,L"L

(As in previous examples, the variable **D$** contains the character representation of ASCII code 4.) We must be careful to make a note of the length of the records in a file because we must supply the length in every program that uses the file. The Apple **DOS** does not *know* what the record length is and if we specify an incorrect length, our program will produce erroneous and possibly disastrous results.

One additional caveat—our program should not attempt to read a record that has not yet been written. While this is a limitation, it is easily circumvented as we soon will see.

In order to illustrate the use of direct or random access files, we will create a small file made up of forty records consisting of twenty characters each. Our intention here is to store the names of United States Presidents in the order of their service in office. Thus, George Washington will be stored in the first record and Abraham Lincoln will be stored in the sixteenth record. We will write a program which will both store and retrieve records from the file.

Let us decide that our program will have three modules: one called **GET** to retrieve records; another called **PUT** to write records to the file; and a main routine that will call **PUT** and **GET** as required and handle interaction with the user. Schematically, our program looks something like this:

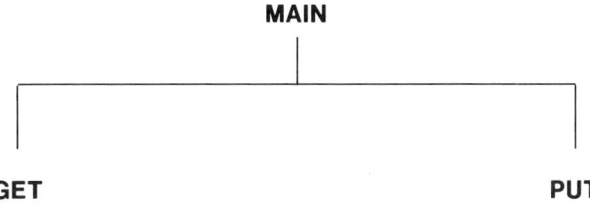

A program having this structure, first presented in algorithmic language and then in BASIC follows. We will use the algorithmic specifications for subroutines already presented in Chapter 9. GET and PUT are subroutines that read or write records respectively. First, we introduce here a pseudocode OPEN statement that specifies the type of information needed for direct access I/O. Such a statement, like the one in the GET routine, indicates both the file name and certain file attributes.

PSEUDOCODE RULE 15

The OPEN statement provides a facility for opening files as well as expressing attributes for the opened file.

    open "DATAFILE" (1,DA,IN,recordsize=20,filesize=40)

Most of this information is easily understood on the basis of the foregoing discussion.

    open   an algorithmic keyword.

    "DATAFILE"   the actual name of the file.

    1   a file identification number that is used in the GET and PUT statements. While 1 is not used in Apple syntax, the unit number is used on other microcomputers. It also provides for a method of distinguishing files when more than one file is in use.

    DA   indicates that the file is Direct Access. Use SA to indicate Sequential Access.

    IN   indicates that the file is to be opened for input. Use OUT for output.

    recordsize=20   indicates that each record in the file will have a capacity of twenty bytes.

    filesize=40   indicates the maximum number of records in the file. This parameter is not used in BASIC but is included here to provide documentation of an important file attribute.

The algorithmic expression of file characteristics is, admittedly, somewhat arbitrary. You may choose a different mode of expression if you wish. Our advice is that you use one method consistently. Doing so will give you an unambiguous guide for program coding and debugging. You will note that the *get* and *put* statements include file and record identifiers. The record identifier is required in direct access I/O. Thus, get 1:POINTER means "get from file one the record in the same relative position as the value of POINTER." Thus, if POINTER has the value 9, record number 9 is retrieved. So too with the put statement.

ALGORITHMIC LANGUAGE VERSION

MAIN:
declare string PRESIDENT$, CHOICE$
declare numeric POINTER
put ("*** PRESIDENTS ***")
loop
   put("SELECT: GET, PUT OR STOP (G/P/S)")
   get(CHOICE$)
   if(CHOICE$="S") break
   PUT ("WHICH RECORD")
   get(POINTER)
   if(CHOICE$ = "P")
   [put("ENTER NAME OF PRESIDENT ",POINTER)
     get(PRESIDENT$)
     call PUT   ]
   else
   [call GET
     put ("PRESIDENT # ",POINTER," IS ",PRESIDENT$)
     ]
end loop
end.
GET:
open "DATAFILE" (1,DA,IN,recordsize=20,filesize=40)
get 1:POINTER (PRESIDENT$)
close
return
end.
PUT:
open "DATAFILE" (1,DA,OUT,recordsize=20,filesize=40)
put 1:POINTER (PRESIDENT$)
close
return
end.

BASIC VERSION

```
100  REM --- PRESIDENTS V1    8-28-80
101  REM
110  D$= CHR$(4)
115  HOME : HTAB(5)
120  PRINT "***        PRESIDENTS          ***"
```

```
125 PRINT:PRINT
200 PRINT "SELECT: GET, PUT OR STOP  (G/P/S)";
205 INPUT CHOICE$
210 IF CHOICE$ = "S" THEN 300
215 PRINT "WHICH RECORD";
220 INPUT P
225 IF CHOICE$ <> "P" THEN 250
230 PRINT "ENTER NAME OF PRESIDENT  "P
235 INPUT PRESIDENT$
240 GOSUB 950
245 GOTO 260
250 GOSUB 900
255 PRINT "PRESIDENT " P " IS " PRESIDENT$
260 GOTO 200
300 END
900 REM----------GET RECORD
905 PRINT D$"OPEN DATAFILE,L20"
910 PRINT D$"READ DATAFILE,R";P
915 INPUT PRESIDENT$
920 PRINT D$"CLOSE"
925 RETURN
950 REM----------PUT RECORD
955 PRINT D$"OPEN DATAFILE,L20"
960 PRINT D$"WRITE DATAFILE,R";P
965 PRINT PRESIDENT$
970 PRINT D$"CLOSE"
975 RETURN
```

Because of the basic design of the program, it is possible that the user might attempt to have the program retrieve and display a record that has not yet been created and thus, produce an error message and premature program termination. The best solution to this problem is to write a small program to initialize the file to be used by the **PRESIDENTS** program. Such a program, which we will call **SKELETON** (because it writes skeleton records) will write forty blank records into the direct access file. **SKELETON** is displayed below. It is quite simple. You will note that it processes the file sequentially by using a loop index to select records. You will also note that **S$** has been initialized to a string containing eight blanks, rather than the twenty you might have expected given the record length. In fact, it does not matter how many blanks we write in each record as long as the number does not exceed the record length. The **DOS** pads out all records on the right with blanks to achieve the desired effect. After **SKELETON** is run, you can run **PRESIDENTS** without fear of errors caused by attempting to read nonexistent records.

```
100 REM -- SKELETON   9-2-80
101 REM
110 D$=CHR$(4)
120 L = 20
125 S$ = "                    "
150 PRINT D$"OPEN DATAFILE,L"L
200 FOR I=1 TO 40
210    PRINT D$"WRITE DATAFILE,R"I
220    PRINT S$
250 NEXT I
300 PRINT D$"CLOSE"
```

EXERCISE SET   11.1

1. Write a program that will open a sequential file called **RANDOM**, generate ten random integers in the range from one to six, and store them in this file.

2. Write a program that generates 100 random four letter words and stores them (four words to a record) in a sequential file called **WORD**. See Chapter 8 for a program that generates random words.

3. Write a program that will read and print to the screen every fourth record in a direct access file called **TEST**. Assume this file has forty records (each of length 30) in it. You are to read records 4, 8, 12, etc.

4. Identify any errors or omissions in the following program fragments. Assume the programs are to **RUN** properly with the statements shown. Add or correct statements to obtain a program that will execute properly.

   (a)
   ```
   100 PRINT "OPEN FIRSTNAME"
   110 PRINT "READ FIRSTNAME"
   120 INPUT A
   130 IF A = 999 THEN 160
   140 PRINT A
   150 GOTO 120
   160 END
   ```

   (b)
   ```
   100 PRINT D$ "OPEN TSTFILE1,L"
   110 PRINT D$ "WRITE TSTFILE1,R1"
   120 PRINT "RECORD 1"
   130 PRINT D$ "CLOSE"
   140 END
   ```

5. Describe in words what the following programs accomplish:

   (a)
   ```
   100 D$ = CHR$(4)
   110 PRINT D$ "OPEN DEMO"
   120 PRINT D$ "WRITE DEMO"
   ```

```
            130 FOR I = 1 TO 10
            140 X$ = "DEMO" + STR$(I)
            150 PRINT X$
            160 NEXT I
            170 PRINT D$ "CLOSE DEMO"
            180 END
    (b)     100 D$ = CHR$(4)
            110 PRINT D$ "OPEN TRIAL, L40"
            120 FOR I = 1 TO 20
            130 PRINT D$ "READ TRIAL, R";I
            140 INPUT T$
            150 PRINT T$
            160 NEXT I
            170 PRINT D$ "CLOSE"
            180 END
```

6. Describe the makeup of the two files **DEMO** and **TRIAL** used in problem 5 above. Consider file type, number of records and record length in each file.

11.5 PET FILES

In this section, we will treat sequential access files on the PET microcomputer using cassette tapes. From a functional standpoint, creating and using sequential access files with the PET is quite similar to processing such files using the Apple. The major difference is in the syntax used to express the instructions. As with the Apple, a file must be:

1. Opened,
2. Named (optional on the PET),
3. Declared either read or write, and
4. Closed after use.

In order to read from, or write to a file, a programmer must identify to the computer the file and the device upon which it resides. This is true for microcomputers like the PET and the Apple and for large scale machines like the IBM 370 series. With the PET, we use the **OPEN** statement to accomplish this goal. **OPEN** statements are found in many versions of BASIC and in other languages as well, on computers large and small, however the syntax we will demonstrate here is peculiar to the PET. The **OPEN** statement allows us to select a file identification number and link it with a particular data set on a particular device and also to specify other attributes for the file. A typical **OPEN** statement might be:

```
            100 OPEN 1,1,0,"DATA"
```

As noted earlier, before a file can be used, it must be opened. Therefore, an **OPEN** statement must be placed in the program, logically, prior to the first attempt to read or write to the file. Similarly, a file must be closed when a program is finished with it. This is accomplished with a **CLOSE** statement which has the following syntax:

400 CLOSE 1

The **CLOSE** statement includes the number of the file being closed. Essentially, the **CLOSE** statement revokes the previous **OPEN** statement, disassociating the device and file from the file number specified in the **OPEN** statement thus making the file undefined. For this reason, **OPEN** and **CLOSE** statements are used in pairs as indicated below:

100 OPEN 1,1,0,"DATA"
.
.
. Input transactions with file # 1
.
400 CLOSE 1

BASIC is fussy about the use of these two statements; we cannot open a file that is currently open nor close a file that is currently closed. Attempts to do so will cause fatal errors that will interrupt program execution.

Now let us consider the **OPEN** statement in greater detail.

100 OPEN 1,1,0,"DATASET1"

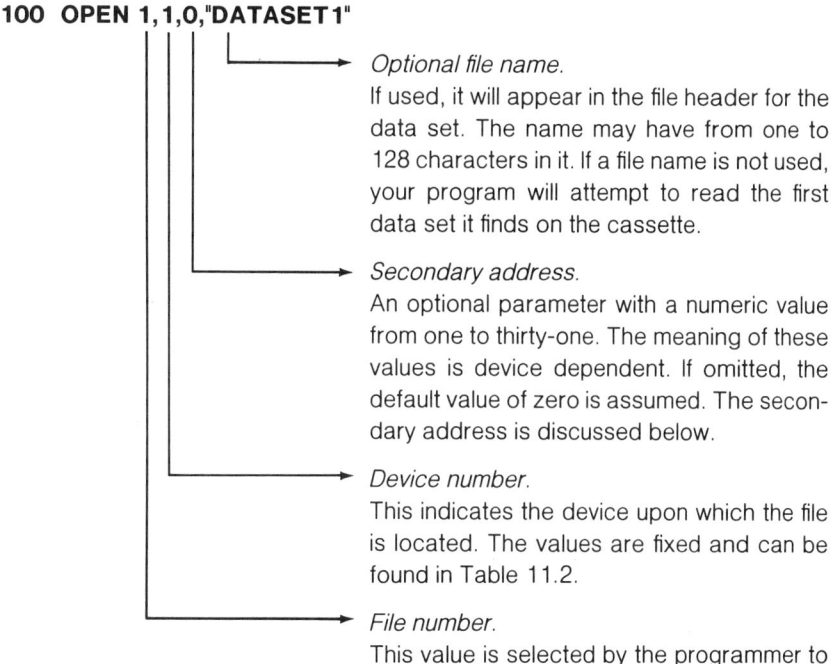

Optional file name.
If used, it will appear in the file header for the data set. The name may have from one to 128 characters in it. If a file name is not used, your program will attempt to read the first data set it finds on the cassette.

Secondary address.
An optional parameter with a numeric value from one to thirty-one. The meaning of these values is device dependent. If omitted, the default value of zero is assumed. The secondary address is discussed below.

Device number.
This indicates the device upon which the file is located. The values are fixed and can be found in Table 11.2.

File number.
This value is selected by the programmer to identify the file in **PRINT** and **INPUT** state-

ments. Any number in the range from 1 to 255 may be used.

Table 11.2
PET Devices

Number	Device
0	Keyboard (default for input)
1	Cassette #1
2	Cassette #2
3	Video screen (output default)

The third parameter in the **OPEN** statement, the zero in the following statement,

100 OPEN 1,1,0,"DATA"

is known to PET users as a secondary address. It is used to specify certain file attributes. A different set of values, and therefore, a different set of file attributes, apply to each type of device. The attribute options for the PET cassette files can be found in Table 11.3.

Table 11.3
File Attributes that Can Be Specified for the
Secondary Address for PET Cassette Tapes

Value	Meaning
0	Read only file.
1	Write only file.
2	Write only file with end of tape mark printed after end of file.

The default option—zero, or read only—is in effect if we decline to specify a value for the secondary address. As you can tell from looking over the list, a tape file cannot be simultaneously open for both read and write operations. While at first glance this may seem to be unnecessarily restrictive, it is, in fact, quite logical and can prevent accidental disasters. Were we able to open a file to be read and then write a record to that file, all the records beyond the point in the file at which the write occurred would be lost.

If it is necessary for a program to read a file and then rewrite the same file, we would accomplish the task by first opening the file as a read-only file, then reading all the desired records from the file. Then, we would close the file, rewind the tape and open the file again as a write-only file. PET BASIC does not support such statements as **RESTORE** or **RESET** with relation to tape files. Attempts to read from a write-only file and write to a read-only file will produce fatal errors.

Combining the techniques discussed so far, we can use the following program fragment to open a tape file and read and print its contents on the screen.

```
100  OPEN 1,1,0,"DATA"
120  INPUT #1,X$
130  PRINT X$
140  GOTO 120
150  CLOSE 1
```

Note the presence of the file label (#1) in the **INPUT** statement. By writing

```
120  INPUT #1, . . .
```

we tell BASIC specifically which file we wish to read; namely, file #1, that has been defined already in the **OPEN** statement. When the file label, the "#1", is omitted, BASIC assumes the keyboard for input and the screen for output. Note the comma that follows the file identification and precedes the variable list. Its absence will cause a syntax error message to be printed.

This program assumes that a file called **"DATA"** already exists on the cassette tape in tape drive one—the one that is mounted in the front panel of the older machines. The program fragment, however, ignores the very important matter of detecting and handling the end of file condition, which we will discuss next.

Usually our programs read data with an **INPUT** or **READ** statement that is placed within some type of loop that is repeated until no more records remain to be read. We must also provide for a means to exit such a loop when the last record has been read. Most computers will generate some type of error message if a program attempts to read beyond the end of a file. The PET may even crash if a program attempts to do so.* Because the PET is so sensitive to this problem, we must build into our program some protection that will prevent the error from occurring.

If we know how many records are in a file, we could use a **FOR-NEXT** loop containing an **INPUT** statement to read the appropriate number of records. However, it is generally better to let the computer do the counting. Two options remain: the first is to write a trailer record containing dummy values at the end of the data set when it is created, and the second option is to test for the end of file condition using the PET status word.

---

*A computer is said to crash when its operating system (master controlling program) fails. When the system crashes, the PET becomes inoperable. None of the keys have any effect on what the machine is doing and the video display may either freeze or become erratic. The only recourse is to reset the machine by turning it off and then on again. Of course, everything in the computer's memory is lost.

Let us explore the second alternative first. The PET monitors all input transactions with tape files and notes the status of these transactions in a variable known as the status word. The official variable name for the status word is **ST**. We can test **ST** with **IF . . . THEN** statements and print its contents as well. However, the PET protects itself from inadvertent modification of the status word by the user and issues a syntax error message whenever a program attempts to modify the contents of **ST**. For example, a statement like this: **ST=21** will cause a syntax error message to be printed. If input transactions occur without detectable problems, the status word will have a value of zero. Once the end of a file has been encountered, the status word will have the value of sixty-four. Thus, we can add the following statement to our program fragment and test for the end of file condition.

```
125  IF ST = 64 THEN 150
```

It is important to note that the PET uses the same memory location (**ST**) to record the status of transactions for all files. Therefore, **ST** must be tested immediately after a transaction occurs with the particular file in which we are interested. It is a good rule to make the status word test in the statement immediately following the **INPUT** statement.

The first option and more general approach to this problem is to write a dummy trailer record at the end of the data file when it is created, and then, make all programs reading the file test for the trailer record. Following you will find a simple program that accomplishes this task. It assumes that the trailer record **"EOF"** is found at the end of the data set.

```
100  REM-----GET     12-26-79
120  OPEN 1,1,0,"DATA"
130  INPUT #1, S$
140  IF S$ = "EOF" THEN 200
150  PRINT S$
160  GOTO 130
200  CLOSE 1
205  END
```

11.6 WHAT TO DO IF THE PET CRASHES

We include this section to deal with a peculiar file processing problem which is common to early models of the 8K PET. If you do not have such a machine you can skip this section. While the software problem has been corrected in more recent machines, we include this section because there are thousands of such machines in existence and we hope that this section will help owners and users of such machines process files more easily.

Because of a software error in the older PETs, the computer often crashes while reading data files from tapes. This is a source of great frustration that causes many PET users to give up attempting to store data sets on tape. The system crashes occur because the PET fails to find one or more blocks of data on the tape; therefore, the PET reads past the end of file mark and crashes. While this problem manifests itself when a program is reading a data file from tape, the problem originates when the data file is being created.

Those readers who are only interested in the solution of this problem may wish to skip this paragraph, which gives a mildly technical explanation of the problem. When writing tape files, the PET does not actually read or write individual records. Rather, it accumulates records in a buffer, or temporary storage area, until the buffer is full, and then transmits the entire contents of the buffer to the tape file. The contents of the buffer constitute a single block of data. The PET writes not records, but blocks of records to the tape. Blocks have 192 characters of data (that is, the length of the buffer is 192 characters). One of these characters is used to identify the type of block being written and the remaining 191 characters are actually data. Every data set on tape consists of a certain number of blocks of data. The first block is called a file header block, which identifies the type of file including the data set name if one has been specified in the **OPEN** statement in the program that created the file. This header block does not contain any of the data our program writes. The last block in each file is a trailer block that contains an end of file mark. All of the data written by our program will be found in blocks between the header and trailer blocks. All blocks are separated on tape by a blank space that is called an inter-record gap(IRG). All the special problems in reading data files with the PET are attributable to the fact that the PET sometimes does not make the inter-record gap long enough to assure the detection of the beginning of the following data block. As a result, programs reading data sets sometimes miss one or more data blocks, which leads to a system crash. Knowing the cause allows us to solve the problem by merely lengthening the inter-record gaps. We can do this by telling the PET to turn on its cassette motor for a while after it writes each block of data. A small subroutine to produce this result should be called after each **PRINT** statement which, writes to the tape file being created.

The subroutine below solves the PET file problem by putting more space between blocks of data on the tape as the data set is being created. To accomplish this goal, we need to know when the PET writes a block of data to the tape. This can be determined by counting the characters being printed to the output tape file. In order to facilitate the counting of characters being printed to the tape file, we must translate all information to be printed into strings using the **STR$** function. The string's length can then be determined using the **LEN** function.

```
700  REM---CASSETTE DRIVE ROUTINE
710  CH = CH + LEN(X$)+1
720  IF CH < 192 THEN RETURN
730  POKE 59411,53
```

```
740 FOR JJ = 1 TO 100 : NEXT JJ
750 POKE 59411,61
760 CH=CH-191
770 RETURN
```

Below is a small main program that causes the PET to generate fifty random numbers and then copy them to a tape file. The main program calls the cassette drive routine that starts and stops the cassette motor when necessary to produce the longer inter-record gaps needed to assure that the PET will read each data block in the file.

```
100 REM--PUT     12-26-79
105 POKE 243,122 : POKE 244,2
110 OPEN 1,1,2,"DATA"
120 CH=0
200 FOR I = 1 TO 50
210 X$ = STR$(RND(1))
220 PRINT #1, X$
230 GOSUB 700
240 NEXT I
250 X$ = "EOF"
255 PRINT #1, X$
260 GOSUB 700
270 CLOSE 1
280 END
```

Let us examine each statement in the main program first. Statement 100 is a **REM** statement that identifies the program for the benefit of the humans who use it. Statement 105 **POKEs** two values into memory to be sure that the PET knows where the cassette buffer begins in memory. (This is a precaution to eliminate another cause of system crashes.) Statement 110 tells the PET to open a file for output on tape drive #1, that the file will be referred to as file #1, and indicates that the file will be named **"DATA"**. Statement 120 initializes the variable **CH** at zero. This variable will be used to keep track of the number of characters in the PET's tape buffer. Statement 200 begins a **FOR-NEXT** loop that will be executed fifty times. Statement 210 causes the PET to generate a random number that is immediately translated into a string and stored in **X$**. Statement 220 causes the value of **X$** to be added to the buffer for cassette drive one. The loop ends with a call to the cassette drive routine followed by the **NEXT** statement. Once the loop has been executed fifty times, control passes to statement 250 that gives **X$** the value **"EOF"** to be used as an end of file marker. You can choose any such flag value you wish as long as it will not be confused with *real* data.* Statement 255 causes the trailer value to be printed to the tape buffer. The cassette drive routine is called a final time, the file is closed and the program ends.

---

*We treat the use of trailer values above beginning in Section 4.6.

The cassette drive routine, which is intended for general use in any program, begins with incrementing the variable **CH** by the number of characters in the record just printed to the tape buffer plus one. The one is for the carriage return character that is also printed to the buffer. If the buffer is not yet full, statement 720 returns control to the main program. If the buffer is full, meaning that a block of data has just been written on the tape, control continues with statement 730, which turns on the drive motor by poking a value into the proper memory cell. Statement 740 contains a loop that merely stalls the program for about a sixth of a second which causes the PET to continue to write a blank inter-record gap onto the tape. Statement 750 turns off the tape drive motor. Statement 760 deducts 191 from the count of characters currently in the buffer—the 191 characters just transferred to tape. Statement 770 returns control to the main program.*

A second version of the **GET** program is listed below. It is essentially the same as the earlier version with the addition of a status word test after each input statement. If the status word is found to have a value other than zero, some type of error has occurred and control shifts to statement 200, which begins a loop to print as characters the current contents of the tape buffer. It should be noted that nonprinting characters seem to be blanks. You may wish to remove the reference to the **CHR$** function in statement 220 so that the program will print the ASCII codes that are actually stored in the buffer. The type of approach represented by this program is recommended whenever you have problems reading a data file. It should prevent system crashes and help you determine the nature of the problem.

```
100  REM---GET V2     12-26-79
110  C=0
120  OPEN 1,1,0,"DATA"
140  INPUT #1, X$
145  IF ST <> 0 THEN 200
150  IF X$ = "EOF" THEN 250
160  C = C +1
170  PRINT C,X$
180  GOTO 140
200  PRINT "STATUS CODE IS ";ST
210  FOR I = 634 TO 825
220  PRINT CHR$(PEEK(I));
```

*The problem treated here has been corrected in newer machines. Our treatment here has been assisted by an article "Personal Electronic Transactions", in *Creative Computing* (April 1979, pages 28-32) by Gregory Yob and a brief mention in the *Commodore PET Users Club Newsletter* (Volume I, issue 3, page 17). Mr. Yob writes a regular column in *Creative Computing* concerning the PET. Similar articles appear monthly on the Apple and the TRS-80. Such articles, and similar ones in other computing magazines are a valuable source of information for owners and users of microcomputers.

```
230 NEXT I
250 PRINT C;"RECORDS READ FROM TAPE"
```

11.7 PET FILE APPLICATIONS

In Section 11.3 we presented a program called **STORE**, that created a sequential file containing student demographic information and a second program called **GET7**, that retrieved the file and displayed the information in tabular form on the screen. Here we present without further explanation the PET versions of these two programs. They use the error handling techniques we recommend for PET tape data files.

```
100 REM---PETSTORE    9-9-80
101 REM
105 POKE 243,122 : POKE 244,2
110 OPEN 1,1,1,   "TESTDATA"
115 CH = 0
200 DATA JONES,21,M,NY
202 DATA JOHNSON,20,F,NJ
204 DATA BROWN,18,F,CT
210 DATA EOF,0,*,*
300 REM
310 READ N$, A, SX$, ST$
312 X$ = N$
314 PRINT #1,X$
316 GOSUB 700
318 X$ = STR$ (A)
320 PRINT #1, X$
322 GOSUB 700
324 X$ = SX$
326 PRINT X$
328 GOSUB 700
330 X$ = ST$
332 PRINT #1, X$
334 GOSUB 700
338 IF N$ = "*EOF*" THEN 900
340 GOTO 310
699 REM
700 REM---CASSETTE DRIVE ROUTINE
701 REM
710 CH = CH + LEN(X$)+1
```

```
720 IF CH < 192 THEN RETURN
730 POKE 59411,53
740 FOR JJ=1 TO 100 : NEXT JJ
750 POKE 59411,61
760 CH = CH - 191
770 RETURN
800 REM
900 CLOSE 1
999 END

100 REM---PETGET7     9-9-80
101 REM
115 OPEN 1,1,0,"TESTDATA"
300 REM
310 INPUT #1, N$,A,SX$,ST$
320 IF N$ = "*EOF*" THEN 900
330 PRINT N$; TAB(10) A; TAB(20) SX$; TAB(39) ST$
340 GOTO 310
350 REM
900 CLOSE 1
999 END
```

11.8 TRS-80 TAPE FILE APPLICATIONS

Most of what we have said on files generally, and about sequential files in particular, also applies to the TRS-80. Following, we present two simple programs that process TRS-80 tape files. The first, called **TRSSTORE** (which should probably be called Radio Shack) writes a series of ten values to the tape file. The second program, **TRSRESTORE**, reads from tape and displays those values.

```
100 REM -- TRSSTORE
110 FOR I = 1 TO 10
120     PRINT #I
130 NEXT I

100 REM -- TRSRESTORE
110 FOR I = 1 TO 10
120     INPUT #X
130     PRINT X
140 NEXT I
```

Notice that neither a unit number nor a comma is required after the **#** symbol. Furthermore, no open or close statements are used. Care should be taken to make sure that the TRS-80 does not attempt to read beyond the end of file. Such an error would require you to use the reset key to regain control of the machine. Here, we use the loop to make sure that only ten records are read. A trailer value, as demonstrated in Section 11.6, is an even better solution.

While the TRS-80 is reading a file, two stars appear in the upper lefthand corner of the screen. The appearance of the left star indicates that a file has been encountered. The right star blinks to indicate that a record has been read successfully.

EXERCISE SET 11.2

1. Write a program that will generate 100 random integers in the range of from one to six and store them on tape. Use the value 999 as an end of file marker.

2. Interpret the following statements relating to PET files:
   (a) **OPEN 2,1,0,"TEST"**
   (b) **OPEN 1,"NAME"**
   (c) **OPEN 1,2,1,"TRIAL"**
   (d) **OPEN 2,1,2**

3. Repeat problem 2 in Exercise Set 11.1 on the PET.

Review

New terminology and BASIC syntax introduced in this Chapter are reviewed below.

FILE a collection of records with some type of logical organization. (Section 11.1)

LOGICAL RECORD a record in which all the variables are logically related in that they pertain to the same person or entity. (Section 11.2)

PHYSICAL RECORD a record that is physically separated from other records. The physical separation is a carriage return. (Section 11.2)

SEQUENTIAL ACCESS a method of file access in which each record must be accessed in the order in which it occurs in the file. (Section 11.2)

DIRECT (RANDOM) ACCESS a method of file access that allows direct reading of a specific record in a file. (Section 11.2)

DOS an abbreviation for disk operating system. (Section 11.3)

BASIC SYNTAX-APPLE ONLY

PRINT CHR$(4) "OPEN FILENAME" a BASIC statement that opens (or creates) a sequential file named **FILENAME**. (Section 11.3)

PRINT CHR$(4) "WRITE FILENAME" a BASIC statement that declares filename as a write-only file. From the time this statement is executed until the file is closed, all **PRINT** statements will be written to **FILENAME** rather than to the screen. (Section 11.3)

PRINT CHR$(4) "READ FILENAME" a BASIC statement that declares filename as a read-only file. From the time this statement is executed until the file is closed, all **INPUT** statements will obtain values from **FILENAME** rather than from the keyboard. (Section 11.3)

PRINT CHR$(4) "CLOSE FILENAME" a BASIC statement that closes file **FILENAME**. (Section 11.3)

PRINT CHR$(4) "OPEN FILENAME,L#" a BASIC statement that opens a direct access file in which each record has a length given by **#**. (Section 11.4)

PRINT CHR$(4) "READ FILENAME,R#" a BASIC statement that directs that record **#** will be read from direct access file **FILENAME**. (Section 11.4)

PRINT CHR$(4) "WRITE FILENAME,R#" a BASIC statement that directs that a new record **#** will be written to direct access file **FILENAME**. (Section 11.4)

ONERR GOTO # BASIC keywords that send control to statement **#** upon detection of an error condition. (Section 11.3)

BASIC SYNTAX-PET ONLY

OPEN #,#,#,"filename" a BASIC statement that opens a cassette tape file. The three numbers determine file number, device number, and secondary address in that order. (Section 11.5)

CLOSE # a BASIC keyword that closes the file whose number follows the symbol **#**. Example: **200 CLOSE #2**. (Section 11.5)

PRINT # a keyword that directs writing to the file whose number follows. Example: **100 PRINT #2,A$**. (Section 11.5)

INPUT # a keyword that causes the next record to be retrieved from the file identified by the number follows the "**#**" symbol and appropriate values to be stored in memory. Example: **100 INPUT #1,A$**. (Section 11.5)

12
MODELS AND SIMULATIONS

12.1 INTRODUCTION TO MODELS AND SIMULATIONS

We will use the term **model** to indicate a mathematical representation of a real-world system or problem. The use of the computer allows us to develop models that can represent the behavior of rather complex systems. Modeling can be thought of as a cyclic process in which one begins by formulating a real-world problem into precise mathematical language. We then allow the model to operate on input data and compare the output, which is interpreted back into real-world variables, with known results. If the agreement is poor, the model may be changed and the cycle repeated.

It is sometimes difficult to distinguish problems of modeling from those of **simulation**. The difference we will stress is that modeling focuses on the activities associated with the development of the model and verification of its validity. Modeling depends upon a comparison of model predictions with known results. Simulation uses the model to deal with problems that cannot be performed due to constraints of time, feasibility, or complexity. Obviously, some decisions about models have to be made before a simulation can begin.

Webster's dictionary gives one definition of simulation as "the imitative representation of the functioning of one system . . . by means of the functioning of another;" for example, a computer simulation of an industrial process.* The validity of a simulation depends upon how closely the device is able to replicate the essentials of the system represented. For example, a computer does an excellent job of tossing coins. In a few seconds it can perform statistical experiments involving coin tosses that would take

---

*Webster's New Collegiate Dictionary, (Springfield: G. & C. Merriam Co., 1979) p. 1074.

many hours if done by hand. However, the usual purpose of simulation is to conduct more complex operations that result in predictions about the future behavior of a system. Simulation is also used to conduct experiments that are not feasible in the laboratory because of hazards which they might impose.

We begin the chapter with a consideration of two models that are particularly suitable to computer solution. Both models involve matrix manipulations, which are quite tedious if done by hand.

12.2 LEONTIEF MODEL OF AN ECONOMY

We consider a model that utilizes arrays to develop the gross production rate of various commodities given the internal consumption of these commodities and the amount that is required for export. This model is called the *Leontief model*. Discussion of this model can be found in several texts on finite mathematics.*

The Leontief model involves a so-called *technological matrix* for an economy. Suppose we are dealing with five basic commodities—beef, grain, fertilizer, fuel, and transportation. The technological matrix might look like this:

	BEEF	GRAIN	FERTILIZER	FUEL	TRANSPOR-TATION	
$T =$	0.0	0.25	0.1	0.2	0.25	BEEF
	0.0	0.0	0.3	0.1	0.1	GRAIN
	0.2	0.0	0.0	0.1	0.1	FERTILIZER
	0.2	0.1	0.0	0.1	0.2	FUEL
	0.1	0.0	0.0	0.2	0.0	TRANSPORTATION

The interpretation of the element in the beef row and grain column is that it requires .25 units of grain to produce one unit of beef. Note that it also takes .1 unit of fertilizer, .2 units of fuel, and .25 units of transportation. Other rows have similar interpretations.

Next, define the array E to be the net amount of each commodity to be exported.

$$\text{Let } E = [2000 \quad 500 \quad 0 \quad 2000 \quad 0]$$

That is, we want to export beef, grain, and fuel but not fertilizer or transportation. To find the gross production required we must complete the following steps:

---

*See for example: Laurence C. Hoffman and Michael Orkin, *Mathematics with Applications*. (New York: McGraw-Hill, 1979) p.55.
William J. Adams, *Fundamentals of Mathematics for Business, Social, and Life Sciences*. (Englewood Cliffs: Prentice-Hall, Inc., 1979) pp.154-156.

Step 1 Subtract T from the identity matrix of the same size, as in the example below.

$$\begin{bmatrix} 1 & 0 & 0 & 0 & 0 \\ 0 & 1 & 0 & 0 & 0 \\ 0 & 0 & 1 & 0 & 0 \\ 0 & 0 & 0 & 1 & 0 \\ 0 & 0 & 0 & 0 & 1 \end{bmatrix} - \begin{bmatrix} 0.0 & 0.25 & 0.1 & 0.2 & 0.25 \\ 0.0 & 0.0 & 0.3 & 0.1 & 0.1 \\ 0.2 & 0.2 & 0.0 & 0.1 & 0.1 \\ 0.2 & 0.1 & 0.0 & 0.1 & 0.2 \\ 0.1 & 0.0 & 0.0 & 0.2 & 0.0 \end{bmatrix}$$

Step 2 Take the inverse of the result obtained in Step 1.

Step 3 Multiply E by the result in Step 2 to obtain a matrix G that represents the gross production of each quantity.

Consider the following main program:

```
100 REM---LEONTIEF MODEL - 12/15/80
110 REM     INPUT VARIABLES: B(I,J) — TECH. MATRIX
                             A(1,J) — EXPORT MATRIX
115 REM     LOCAL VARIABLES: A(I,I) — IDENTITY MATRIX
120 REM     OUTPUT VARIABLES: C(1,J)
130 REM---LOAD T AND THE IDENTITY MATRIX
140 DIM A(5,5),B(5,5),C(5,5)
150 FOR I = 1 TO 5
160 FOR J = 1 TO 5
170 IF I = J THEN A(I,J) = 1: GOTO 190
180 A(I,J) = 0
190 READ B(I,J)
200 NEXT J
210 NEXT I
220 REM---CALL SUBTRACTION SUBROUTINE
230 M = 5 : N = 5
240 GOSUB 8800
250 REM---RENAME C AS A
260 FOR I = 1 TO 5
270 FOR J = 1 TO 5
280 A(I,J) = C(I,J)
290 NEXT J
300 NEXT I
310 REM---CALL INVERSION SUBROUTINE
320 GOSUB 8400
330 REM---RENAME C AS B
340 FOR I = 1 TO 5
350 FOR J = 1 TO 5
360 B(I,J) = C(I,J)
```

```
370  NEXT J
380  NEXT I
390  REM---LOAD MATRIX A - NET PRODUCTION
400  FOR I = 1 TO 5: READ A(1,I): NEXT I
410  REM---CALL MULTIPLICATION SUBROUTINE
420  M = 1: N = 5: L = 5
430  GOSUB 8700
440  REM---PRINT GROSS PRODUCTION MATRIX
450  PRINT "GROSS PRODUCTION"
460  PRINT
470  PRINT "BEEF", C(1,1)
480  PRINT "GRAIN", C(1,2)
490  PRINT "FERTILIZER", C(1,3)
500  PRINT "FUEL", C(1,4)
510  PRINT "TRANSPORT.", C(1,5)
520  REM---DATA SET
530  DATA 0,.25,.1,.2,.25,0,0,.3,.1,.1,.2,0,0,.1,.1
540  DATA .2,.1,0,.1,.2,.1,0,0,.2,0
550  DATA 2000,500,0,2000,0
560  REM---END MAIN PROGRAM
570  GOTO 9999
```

Note that the subroutines are not shown here. They may be found in the Library of Subroutines (Appendix B). The two changes in array names above are made to accommodate the names used in the subroutines. If this program were to be used regularly, one would probably change the subroutines to avoid these extra steps.

A run of this program shows the following:

```
OPTION 1 = ADDITION (A + B)
OPTION 2 = SUBTRACTION (A - B)
ENTER THE OPTION NUMBER? 2

GROSS PRODUCTION

BEEF          3038.25
GRAIN         1613.96
FERTILIZER     788.012
FUEL          3543.95
TRANSPORT.    1708.55
```

The type of model used above is called **predictive**. It allows us to predict what we must do to satisfy a prescribed set of conditions (export so much of each commodity). It is also *deterministic* in that it specifies the exact quantity of each commodity needed in gross production. In Section 12.3 we will consider a model that is predictive but not deterministic.

12.3 MODEL OF A PASTURE ECOSYSTEM

This model traces the movement of phosphorus through a pasture ecosystem consisting of soil, grass, and cattle. In this model we again use matrices to describe information about the system under investigation. The model is based on certain statements about transition probabilities between parts of the ecosystem. Thus, although the model will provide predictions, those predictions will be probabilistic in nature. Consider the following matrix.

	SOIL	GRASS	CATTLE	OUTSIDE
SOIL	0.6	0.3	0.0	0.1
GRASS	0.1	0.4	0.5	0.0
CATTLE	0.75	0.0	0.2	0.05
OUTSIDE	0.0	0.0	0.0	1.0

To interpret this matrix, the first row represents the probabilities that phosphorus in the soil will move to each of the parts of the system, to include leaving the system, in one unit of time. Suppose the time unit is one day. Then after a day, a phosphorus molecule in the soil has a probability of .6 (60% chance) of staying there, a probability of .3 of going into the grass, and a probability of .1 of leaving the ecosystem. The probability of it moving to the cattle directly from the soil is zero. Note that each row total is one. Why must this condition be satisfied?

We might wish to know the following concerning this system:

1 The probability associated with a certain transition of the phosphorus after two or more time intervals (days in this case).

2 The number of time intervals the phosphorus stays in each part of the ecosystem before it leaves, given its starting location.

The answers to these questions are available by manipulating all or parts of the array above. Consider the first question.

Successive powers of the matrix give the transition probabilities for two, three, four and so on, time intervals. We can write a simple main program that will invoke the matrix multiplication routine to solve this problem.

```
100 REM---ECOSYSTEM TRANSITIONS-1/21/81
110 REM     INPUT VARIABLES: A(I,J)-TRANSITION MATRIX
115 REM     LOCAL VARIABLES: B(I,J)-POWER MATRIX
120 REM     OUTPUT VARIABLES: C(I,J)-POWER MATRIX
```

258 Models and Simulations Ch. 12

```
130  REM---REQUEST INPUT
140  PRINT "FOR HOW MANY UNITS OF TIME WILL YOU"
150  PRINT "RUN THE MODEL  ";
160  INPUT N
170  REM---LOAD A AND B
180  FOR I = 1 TO 4
190  FOR J = 1 TO 4
200  READ A(I,J)
210  B(I,J) = A(I,J)
220  NEXT J
230  NEXT I
240  REM---CALL MATRIX MULTIPLICATION SUBROUTINE
250  FOR I = 2 TO N
260  GOSUB 8700
270  PRINT "TRANSITION PROBABILITIES AFTER  ";I
280  PRINT "UNITS OF TIME."
290  PRINT
300  FOR J = 1 TO 4
310  FOR K = 1 TO 4
320  PRINT TAB(7*K)INT(C(I,J)*10^4+.5)/10^4
330  B(J,K) = C(J,K)
340  NEXT K
350  PRINT
360  NEXT J
370  PRINT
380  NEXT I
390  REM---DATA SET
400  DATA .6,.3,0,.1,.1,.4,.5,0,.75,.0,.2,.05,0,0,0,1
410  GOTO 9999
```

A run of this program for **N** = 3 is shown below.

**FOR HOW MANY UNITS OF TIME WILL YOU
RUN THE MODEL ?3**

**TRANSITION PROBABILITIES AFTER 2
UNITS OF TIME**

.39	.3	.15	.16
.475	.19	.3	.035
.6	.225	.04	.135
0	0	0	1

Model of a Pasture Ecosystem

TRANSITION PROBABILITIES AFTER 3 UNITS OF TIME

.3765   .237   .18   .2065
.529   .2185   .155   .0975
.4125   .27   .1205   .197
0   0   0   1

As an example of how these matrices are read we would say that a phosphorus molecule that originates in the cattle will have a 19.7% chance of being out of the ecosystem in three days. You should note the behavior of the probabilities in the last column in the matrices above.

To answer the second question, we need to rearrange the matrix a bit. First we separate all states of the system that are absorbing. An absorbing state is easily recognized as one from which the molecule cannot escape. Each absorbing state has a single entry in its row in which the number one appears. In this problem *outside* is an absorbing state. Rearrange the matrix to place absorbing state(s) in the upper left corner. In our problem we would have:

	OUTSIDE	SOIL	GRASS	CATTLE
OUTSIDE	1.0	0.0	0.0	0.0
SOIL	0.1	0.6	0.3	0.0
GRASS	0.0	0.1	0.4	0.5
CATTLE	0.05	0.75	0.0	0.2

We now separate the original matrix into four parts:

	ABSORBING	NONABSORBING		
ABSORBING	1.0	0.0	0.0	0.0
NONABSORBING	0.1	0.6	0.3	0.0
	0.0	0.1	0.4	0.5
	0.05	0.75	0.0	0.2

The lower right three by three matrix has special significance. If we give this matrix the same treatment given the technological matrix in the last section, (subtract it from the identity matrix and then find the inverse of the result) we will arrive at the following three by three array.

8.64865   4.32433   2.7027
8.1982   5.76577   3.60361
8.10811   4.05406   3.78379

The row sums for this array represent the answers to question 2. That is, the sums

8.64865 + 4.32433 + 2.7027 = 15.6 (SOIL ROW)
8.1982 + 5.76577 + 3.60361 = 17.6 (GRASS ROW)
8.10811 + 4.05406 + 3.78379 = 16.0 (CATTLE ROW)

represent days in the system before leaving. If the phosphorus started in the soil, it will take 15.6 days (on the average) to leave the ecosystem.

We have given no justification for the matrix manipulations above. We would suggest reference to a text on discrete mathematics for the reader who is interested in pursuing this further. Roberts' text deals with several matrix problems including the one above.*

EXERCISE SET 12.1

1. A food web can be modeled with a matrix. Consider the predator-prey relationships shown below.

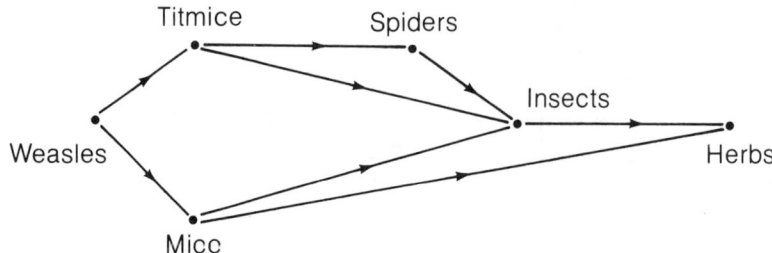

Model this diagram with a square matrix in which each species is represented on both rows and columns. A number one is placed in a predator row and prey column if it preys on the species in that column. Your matrix should look like this:

		1	2	3	4	5	6
Weasle	1	0	1	1	0	0	0
Titmice	2	0	0	0	1	1	0
Mice	3	0	0	0	0	1	1
Spider	4	0	0	0	0	1	0
Insect	5	0	0	0	0	0	1
Herb	6	0	0	0	0	0	0

(a) Form the second power of this matrix. You should find a matrix which identifies all the paths of length two between predator and prey.

*Fred S. Roberts, *Discrete Mathematical Models with Applications to Social, Biological and Environmental Problems*. (Englewood Cliffs: Prentice-Hall, Inc., 1976) pp.263-270.

(b) Form the third, fourth and fifth powers of this matrix. What interpretation can you give to each?

2. Develop a program to take a general matrix and separate out the nonabsorbing states as explained in the pasture ecosystem problem in Section 12.3. That is, produce a smaller matrix in which the rows and columns containing the number one (an absorbing state) are removed.

3. Consider the following transition matrix.

$$\begin{array}{c|cccc} \text{State} & 1 & 2 & 3 & 4 \\ \hline 1 & 0.4 & 0.2 & 0.2 & 0.2 \\ 2 & 0.5 & 0.0 & 0.5 & 0.0 \\ 3 & 0.25 & 0.25 & 0.4 & 0.1 \\ 4 & 0.0 & 0.0 & 0.0 & 1.0 \end{array}$$

Use the program above (ecosystem transitions) to predict the following:

(a) The probability of transition from state 3 to 2 in three units of time.

(b) The probability of transition from state 1 to state 4 in two units of time.

4. Matrix models are frequently used to describe communication networks. A matrix of ones and zeros is formed in which a one is placed in each row and column of communicating states. In the model below states 1, 2, and 3 communicate directly and states 4 and 2 communicate directly.

$$\begin{array}{c|cccc} \text{State} & 1 & 2 & 3 & 4 \\ \hline 1 & 0 & 1 & 1 & 0 \\ 2 & 1 & 0 & 1 & 1 \\ 3 & 1 & 1 & 0 & 0 \\ 4 & 0 & 1 & 0 & 0 \end{array}$$

Write a program that will form powers of this matrix. Examine the second and third powers of this matrix and interpret their meaning.

5. The row totals in any transition matrix such as that in problem 3 must total to one. Write a program that will read a general transition matrix from data lines and check that row totals meet this condition. The program should identify the location of any errors.

12.4 OKUN'S LAW SIMULATION

Simulation generally involves two processes with which the computer can help us. One process is the generation of sample input data. The second process is model testing using parameter variation and control. The capability of the computer to perform rapid calculations allows us to run numerous tests on a model making changes in one or more parameters, which will affect the outcome. In this section we develop a simulation of unemployment rates based on a model in which gross national product is a parameter.

Unemployment and approaches to its reduction were major concerns in the 1976 presidential campaign. As a candidate, Jimmy Carter set as a goal the reduction of unemployment from 7.9 percent in October of 1976 to 3.0 percent by the end of what he hoped would be his first term in office. This goal was also found in the Humphrey-Hawkins Bill, which was debated in Congress in 1976 but not passed. Soon after entering office, Mr. Carter modified his goal slightly and set as his target an unemployment rate of 4.75 percent by the start of 1981. By June of 1978, the unemployment rate had declined to 5.7 percent. While the goal of reducing the unemployment rate is not controversial, achieving results is a difficult, complex, and slow process.

Professor Arthur Okun, an economist and former presidential advisor, has demonstrated the existence of a regular relationship between the unemployment rate and the rate of growth of the gross national product (GNP) of the country. He has expressed this relationship in an equation from which we can predict changes in the unemployment rate on the basis of change in the rate of growth in the GNP. This equation will serve as the model on which our simulation will be built. We quote from an article from the *New York Times* concerning Professor Okun's theory: "... for every one percentage point that real gross national product grows by beyond the four percent trend rate, unemployment drops by one-third of a percentage point."*

We need to convert this relationship to computer code. If we let **U** = unemployment rate and **G** = the GNP, then we may write

LET U = U + (4 − G) * .33

This expression is the heart of our simulation. It says that the new unemployment is obtained by taking the old unemployment rate and incrementing it by one-third of the difference between 4% and the GNP growth rate. We can see that if **G > 4** the increment is negative and the unemployment rate decreases. If **G < 4** then the unemployment rate goes up.

At this point we begin to think about how we might develop a program around this expression. We consider these possibilities:

1   Let the user specify individual GNP growth rates for each year of the simulation. That is, treat **G** as a vector rather than a constant value.

2   Enter information into the program on numbers of people in the work force so that the simulation may generate numbers of people unemployed. This output may have more impact than a percentage figure.

New York Times, July 2, 1975, p. 48.

3 Organize the output so that it is labeled by year and formatted for easy reading.

Item 1 is taken care of with the following code:

```
200  PRINT "OKUN'S LAW SIMULATION"
205  PRINT
210  PRINT "INPUT LABEL";
212  LET Y = 1978
214  INPUT L$
216  PRINT "INPUT UNEMPLOYMENT RATE FOR ";Y
218  INPUT U
220  PRINT "YOU MAY USE A CONSTANT GNP GROWTH RATE"
222  PRINT "FOR THE ENTIRE TIME PERIOD OF THE"
224  PRINT "SIMULATION OR SPECIFY DIFFERENT GROWTH"
226  PRINT "RATES FOR EACH YEAR."
228  PRINT
230  PRINT "ENTER NOW EITHER THE CONSTANT GNP"
232  PRINT "GROWTH RATE FOR THE ENTIRE PERIOD,"
234  PRINT "OR ENTER A NEGATIVE NUMBER TO INDICATE"
236  PRINT "YOUR INTENTION TO SPECIFY GNP GROWTH"
238  PRINT "RATES FOR INDIVIDUAL YEARS.";
240  INPUT G(1)
242  IF G(1) > 0 THEN 300
244  PRINT "YOU HAVE CHOSEN TO SPECIFY INDIVIDUAL"
246  PRINT "GROWTH RATE FIGURES FOR EACH YEAR."
248  PRINT "NOW ENTER ELEVEN VALUES -- ONE FOR"
250  PRINT "EACH YEAR."
252  PRINT
254  FOR I = 1 TO 11
256  PRINT "FOR ";Y;
258  INPUT G(I)
260  LET Y = Y + 1
262  NEXT I
264  GOTO 330
300  FOR I = 1 TO 10
310  LET G(I + 1) = G(1)
320  NEXT I
330  PRINT
332  FOR I = 1 TO 11
334  READ C(I)
336  NEXT I
```

Note that we have loaded an array **G** with eleven values. In one case (loop from 300 to 320) these values were generated from the initial value. In the other case, (loop from 254 to 262) they were input individually by the user.

To provide output on the number of unemployed (Item 2 above), note that actual data on the size of the workforce can be obtained from census data and projections based on this data. This census data on the size of the workforce follows:

1978	98.8 million
1979	100.2 million
1980	101.7 million
1981	103.1 million
1982	104.4 million
1983	105.8 million
1984	107.2 million
1985	108.6 million
1986	109.6 million
1987	110.7 million
1988	111.7 million

This data will be included in the program on data lines and read into array **C**. (See loop from 332 to 336 above.)

Finally, we will format a heading and generate a table (Item 3 above). Consider the following code that will produce the essential data:

```
342  REM---PREPARE FOR PRINT USING SUBROUTINE
344  LET N = 4
346  LET PU$ = "####       #.#        #.#        #.#"
348  LET NP(1) = 1978
350  LET NP(3) = U
352  FOR I = 1 TO 11
354  LET NP(2) = G(I)
356  LET NP(4) = C(I) * NP(3) / 100
358  GOSUB 8600
360  LET NP(3) = NP(3) + (4 − G(I)) * .33
362  LET NP(1) = NP(1) + 1
364  NEXT I
```

The only problem that remains is the matter of making informed decisions about input values for the simulation. Since, according to Professor Okun, a reduction of the employment is contingent upon attaining a certain level of economic growth, we must first turn to the matter of projecting economic growth. Economic growth is commonly measured in terms of the growth of the GNP, the total value of all goods and services provided in the United States in a given year. The average growth rate for the GNP over the time period from 1946 to 1977 is 3.4 percent. Figures for individual years differ quite a bit from the average for the entire time period.

After studying past economic growth trends and projections of future growth, this simulation will allow us to make our own projections and observe their consequences. Here is a sample run of the program.

OKUN'S LAW SIMULATION

INPUT LABEL? TEST RUN #1
INPUT UNEMPLOYMENT RATE FOR 1978 ? 5
YOU MAY USE A CONSTANT GNP GROWTH RATE
FOR THE ENTIRE TIME PERIOD OF THE
SIMULATION OR SPECIFY DIFFERENT GROWTH
RATES FOR EACH YEAR.

ENTER NOW EITHER THE CONSTANT GNP
GROWTH RATE FOR THE ENTIRE PERIOD,
OR ENTER A NEGATIVE NUMBER TO INDICATE
YOUR INTENTION TO SPECIFY GNP GROWTH
RATES FOR INDIVIDUAL YEARS.? 3

TEST RUN #1

YEAR	GNP GROWTH RATE	UNEMPLOY- MENT RATE	UNEMPLOYED PERSONS*
1978	3.0	5.0	4.9
1979	3.0	5.3	5.3
1980	3.0	5.7	5.8
1981	3.0	6.0	6.2
1982	3.0	6.3	6.6
1983	3.0	6.7	7.0
1984	3.0	7.0	7.5
1985	3.0	7.3	7.9
1986	3.0	7.6	8.4
1987	3.0	8.0	8.8
1988	3.0	8.3	9.3

*MILLIONS OF PERSONS

Code to generate the table headings has not been shown.

12.5 A GENETICS SIMULATION

In this simulation, we illustrate the use of the random number generator to select outcomes of a process. We consider the particular trait of blossom color in a certain flower. We observe that the flowers have either blue or white blossoms and we know that the blue characteristic is dominant over the white characteristic. The genetic makeup of the flowers is displayed in Figure 12.1.

To simplify the problem we will assume that self-pollination occurs. If the parent has two dominant genes then the offspring must have two dominant genes. The same is true for two recessive genes. However, if the parent is hybrid, the offspring can be pure dominant, hybrid, or pure recessive. We will use random numbers to predict the result of this self-pollination.

In this problem we allow the program user to fix the percentage of gene makeup in the parent population. We make a random selection of plants to be self-pollinated from this parent pollination. Let **R** be the percentage of recessive (*white*) parents. **H** will be the percentage of hybrid (*blue but mixed gene*) parents. Then **100 - R - H** will be the percentage of pure dominant (*blue*) parents. Consider the following code:

```
340  LET S = RND(1)
350  IF S < R / 100 THEN Q = 1: GOTO 400
360  IF S > (R + H) / 100 THEN Q = 3: GOTO 400
370  LET S1 = INT(RND(1) * 2)
380  LET S2 = INT(RND(1) * 2)
390  LET Q - S1 + S2 + 1
400  LET C(Q) = C(Q) + 1
```

In line 340 we select the parent gene type. In line 350 we ask if we have selected a pure recessive (*white*) type. If so, we set **Q = 1**. In line 360 we ask if we have selected a pure dominant (*blue*) type. If so, we set **Q = 3**. In lines 370 and 380 we make selection of genes knowing that we are dealing with a hybrid cross. Line 390 determines a **Q** of **1**, **2**, or **3** depending on the genetic type of the offspring. Finally, line

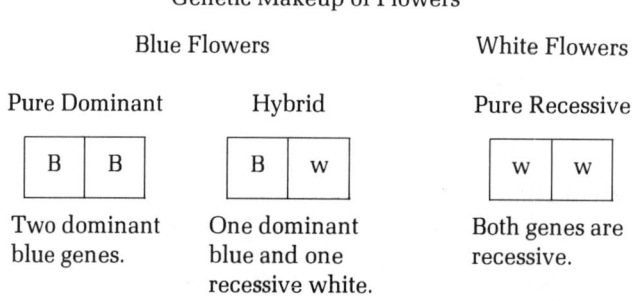

Figure 12.1
Genetic Makeup of Flowers

400 accumulates the total of each genetic type in array **C** using the method discussed in Section 7.5.

For this program to run correctly on the TRS-80 make the following changes:

```
340  LET S = RND(100)
350  IF S < R THEN Q = 1: GOTO 400
360  IF S > R + H THEN Q = 3: GOTO 400
370  LET S1 = RND(2)
380  LET S2 = RND(2)
390  LET Q = S1 + S2 - 1
```

With this code we can complete the entire simulation. The remainder of our program has to do with fixing parameters and printing the results.

```
100  REM -- POLLINATION 3/4/81
110  REM     INPUT VARIABLES: N, R, H
120  REM     LOCAL VARIABLES: I, S1, S2, Q
130  REM     OUTPUT VARIABLES: C(3)
140  DIM C(3)
150  PRINT "THIS PROGRAM SIMULATES THE SELF-POLLINA-"
160  PRINT "OF A POPULATION OF FLOWERS. GENOTYPES"
170  PRINT "ARE PURE RECESSIVE, HYBRID, AND PURE"
180  PRINT "DOMINANT."
190  PRINT
200  PRINT "HOW MANY SEEDS ARE TO BE POLLINATED ";
210  INPUT N
220  PRINT
230  PRINT "WHAT PERCENT OF THE POPULATION IS"
240  PRINT "PURE RECESSIVE ";
250  INPUT R
260  PRINT
270  PRINT "WHAT PERCENT OF THE POPULATION IS "
280  PRINT "HYBRID ";
290  INPUT H
300  PRINT 100 - R - H;" PERCENT OF THE POPULATION IS"
310  PRINT "PURE DOMINANT."
320  PRINT
330  FOR I = 1 TO N
340  LET S = RND(1)
350  IF S < R / 100 THEN Q = 1: GOTO 400
360  IF S > (R + H) / 100 THEN Q = 3: GOTO 400
370  LET S1 = INT(RND(1) * 2)
380  LET S2 = INT(RND(1) * 2)
390  LET Q = S1 + S2 + 1
400  LET C(Q) = C(Q) + 1
```

```
410 NEXT I
420 FOR I = 1 TO 3
430 LET C(I) = INT(C(I) / N * 1000 + .5) / 10
440 NEXT I
450 PRINT "RESULTS OF ";N;" CROSSINGS:"
460 PRINT
470 PRINT "% RECESSIVE      % HYBRID     % DOMINANT"
480 PRINT
490 FOR I = 1 TO 3
500 PRINT TAB(13 * I − 7)C(I);
510 NEXT I
520 END
```

In the exercises you will be asked to run this program for various genetic makeups of the parent population.

12.6 MONTE CARLO INVENTORY SIMULATION

In this section we display a more complex simulation that involves Monte Carlo methods. These methods were introduced briefly in Chapter 6. This simulation involves the manipulation of two parameters as well as the generation of random input data. The problem developed here has been suggested by Chou.*

Imagine that a merchant is trying to determine an optimal inventory plan for a given product. Factors affecting decisions concerning inventory might be:

1   Costs for holding each product unit in inventory each day,

2   Cost of placing an order, and

3   Cost in profits lost from failure to have an item in stock when demanded by a customer.

In addition to these costs, information concerning the need and availability of the product must be known if the simulation is to be meaningful. Suppose the merchant knows that he gets from zero to ten customers for the item each day with approximately equal probability. Furthermore, he knows that the delay in receiving an order varies from one to four days with equal probability. In the experiment the data on sales and delivery time will be generated using the random function. The other parameters may be varied to determine optimum values of minimum inventory and reorder quantity.

We begin the simulation each day (DAY) by adding merchandise received to the inventory. To determine if an order is received we need to have declared a day on

---

*Ya-Lun Chou, *Statistical Analysis*. (New York: Holt, Rinehart and Winston, 1975) pp.800-804.

Sec. 12.6   Monte Carlo Inventory Simulation

which the order was placed (ODAY). On that day the random number generator would have determined the waiting time (WT). We also need to have declared the inventory (INV) and the size of the reorder (SHIP). With these variables declared we can write:

    if (DAY = ODAY + WT)
        [increase INV by SHIP
        WT ← 0]

The next adjustment to inventory to be made is for daily sales. Daily sales (CUST) are determined by the random number generator.

    CUST ← RND(0−10)
    decrease INV by CUST

At this point we determine if we are at or below the reorder point. If we are, and if an order is not pending, an order is initiated. This can be done as follows:

    if (INV <= MININV)
        [if (DAY >= ODAY + WT)
            [increase TFEE by FEE
            WT ← RND(1−4)
            ODAY ← DAY]]

Here FEE is a single reorder cost and TFEE is the accumulation of these costs.

Next we determine losses incurred by our inability to provide for all customers. This situation will prevail if the adjusted inventory is negative.

    if (INV <= 0)
        [increase TLOSS by LOSS * ABS(INV)
        increase SALES by INV
        set INV to 0]

LOSS is the loss of profits due to lack of availability of the item. TLOSS is an accumulation of that loss and SALES is an accumulator for total items sold. The step "increase SALES by INV" may not be clear. Note that in this case the inventory is negative. We will later make an adjustment to increase sales by the number of customers. However, that adjustment will be excessive if all customers have not been supplied.

Finally, we compute total storage costs (TSC) by adding unit storage costs (UNITSC) for the inventory held over. Then total sales are accumulated.

    increase TSC by UNITSC * INV
    increase SALES by CUST

Having refined these steps we may write and code the entire algorithm. A complete program is given below.

```
100 REM -- INVENTORY 10/15/80
110 REM     INPUT VARIABLES: MININV, SHIP, UNITSC
120 REM                      FEE, LOSS, NDAYS
```

```
130 REM     LOCAL VARIABLES: ODAY
140 REM     OUTPUT VARIABLES: SVINV, CUST, TSC, TFEE
150 REM                       TLOSS, WT, SALES, INV
160 REM                       AVECST
170 HOME
180 TSC = 0:TFEE = 0:TLOSS = 0:SALES = 0
190 ODAY = 0:WT = 0
200 PRINT "THIS PROGRAM DEVELOPS AVERAGE INVENTORY"
210 PRINT "COSTS PER UNIT SALE BASED ON A MONTE"
220 PRINT "CARLO SIMULATION. REORDER TIMES OF"
230 PRINT "FROM 1 TO 4 DAYS AND CUSTOMER COUNTS"
240 PRINT "FROM 0 TO 10 ARE SIMULATED."
250 PRINT
260 PRINT "ENTER MINIMUM INVENTORY   ";
270 INPUT MININV
280 PRINT "ENTER SIZE OF REORDER   ";
290 INPUT SHIP
300 PRINT "ENTER UNIT STORAGE COST   ";
310 INPUT UNITSC
320 PRINT "ENTER REORDER COST   ";
330 INPUT FEE
340 PRINT "ENTER LOSS ON UNITS NOT SUPPLIED    ";
350 INPUT LOSS
360 PRINT "ENTER NUMBER OF DAYS SIMULATION WILL RUN   ";
370 INPUT NDAYS
380 PRINT
390 PRINT "INV    CUST TSC    TFEE TLOSS WT    SALES INV"
400 INV = INT(MININV + SHIP / 2)
410 FOR DAY = 1 TO NDAYS
420 SVINV = INV
430 IF DAY = ODAY + WT THEN INV = INV + SHIP:WT = 0
440 CUST = INT(RND(1) * 11)
450 INV = INV − CUST
460 IF INV > MININV THEN 550
470 IF DAY < ODAY + WT THEN 510
480 TFEE = TFEE + FEE
490 WT = INT(RND(1) * 4 + 1)
500 ODAY = DAY
510 IF INV > = 0 THEN 550
520 TLOSS = TLOSS + LOSS * ABS(INV)
530 SALES = SALES + INV
540 INV = 0
550 TSC = TSC + UNITSC * INV
```

```
560 SALES = SALES + CUST
570 PRINT SVINV;TAB(7)CUST;TAB(11)TSC;TAB(17)TFEE;
580 PRINT TAB(22)TLOSS;TAB(28)WT;TAB(33)SALES;TAB(38)INV
590 NEXT DAY
600 TCST = TSC + TLOSS + TFEE
610 AVECST = INT(TCSTS / SALES * 100 + .5) / 100
620 PRINT
630 PRINT "INVENTORY COST PER UNIT SALE EQUALS"
640 PRINT "          $";AVECST
650 END
```

A run of this program follows:

THIS PROGRAM DEVELOPS AVERAGE INVENTORY COSTS PER UNIT SALE BASED ON A MONTE CARLO SIMULATION. REORDER TIMES OF FROM 1 TO 4 DAYS AND CUSTOMER COUNTS FROM 0 TO 10 ARE SIMULATED.

ENTER MINIMUM INVENTORY ?15
ENTER SIZE OF REORDER ?15
ENTER UNIT STORAGE COST ?2
ENTER REORDER FEE ?30
ENTER LOSS ON UNITS NOT SUPPLIED ?20
ENTER NUMBER OF DAYS SIMULATION WILL RUN ?15

INV	CUST	TSC	TFEE	TLOSS	WT	SALES	INV
22	7	30	30	0	3	7	15
15	6	48	30	0	3	13	9
9	8	50	30	0	3	21	1
1	5	72	60	0	1	26	11
11	8	108	60	0	0	34	18
18	4	136	90	0	2	38	14
14	4	156	90	0	2	42	10
10	3	200	90	0	0	45	22
22	2	240	90	0	0	47	20
20	7	266	120	0	4	54	13
13	5	282	120	0	4	59	8
8	5	288	120	0	4	64	3
3	8	288	120	100	4	67	0
0	7	304	150	100	1	74	8
8	8	334	180	100	1	82	15

INVENTORY COST PER UNIT SALE EQUALS
   $7.49

EXERCISE SET 12.2

1. Run the genetics simulation problem in Section 12.5 with the following mix of genetic makeups in the parent population:
   (a) A 50-50 mix of pure dominant and pure recessive parents.
   (b) A 100 percent hybrid parent population.
   (c) A 50-50 mix of pure dominant and hybrid parents.

2. Modify the genetic simulation program to allow for a random cross pollination of the parent population. You will need to select each parent randomly after deciding on the genetic makeup of the parent population. Then select the gene contribution from that parent if it is a hybrid.

3. Develop a simulation for the total count obtained in the roll of a pair of dice. Accumulate the count of each of the eleven possible results for 10,000 rolls of the dice. From this experiment, what would you predict as the probability of getting a seven in a single roll of a pair of dice?

4. Develop a simulation for the shuffling of a deck of fifty-two cards. One way to do this is to place the cards (represented by the numbers one through fifty-two) into an array. Use the random number generator to select pairs of cards to be interchanged.

Review

There has been no new syntax introduced in this chapter. New terms are summarized here.

MODEL a mathematical representation of a system. (Section 12.1)

SIMULATION an imitation of the behavior of a system through the manipulation of a model. (Section 12.1)

PREDICTIVE MODEL a model that predicts the time behavior of a system. Such a model may specify exact outcomes (a deterministic model) or probable outcomes (a probabilistic model). (Section 12.2)

13

ADVANCED GRAPHICS TECHNIQUES

13.1 COMPUTER MAPPING

The high resolution graphics capacity of the Apple microcomputer, plus the increased availability of relatively low-cost printers that can put graphic images on paper, open the door to many interesting and useful graphics applications. The relatively simple plotting syntax available in Applesoft is an additional encouragement to this line of activity.

Figure 13.1 displays an outline map of the state of West Virginia and its fifty-five counties. With its highly irregular shape, it is a good example of the kind of precision graphing that one can do with the Apple. The program that created this map is not particularly complex—although we admit that 506 data statements were required to supply the X-Y coordinates. Although this task is more boring than difficult, it is still much easier than drawing such a map by hand.

In this chapter we will present a detailed treatment of the techniques required to create such graphic images, to store them on disk and the process of printing them on paper. We will also provide in an appendix (Section 13.9) information on the source of such data and its use. As we pursue this subject, bear in mind that computer mapping is merely a special case of a larger phenomena, and that anything that can be represented by pairs of Cartesian coordinates can be displayed using such techniques.

In Section 10.8 we introduced high resolution graphics techniques with the Apple. Here we will assume that you are familiar with that material and will build upon it. Let us

Figure 13.1
Outline Map of West Virginia and its 55
Counties Using 506 Coordinate Pairs

look at Table 13.1, a set of coordinates for a single county—in this case Brooke County, West Virginia.

Table 13.1
Coordinates for Brooke County

X	Y
362	106
361	54
343	52
334	99
362	106

All coordinates have values in the range from 0 to 1000. The Apple has the capacity to store two high resolution graphics images in memory simultaneously. It is common to describe these storage areas as pages of high resolution graphics storage. Recalling that each Apple high resolution graphics page has 280 horizontal positions (in a range from 0 to 279) and 192 vertical positions (in a range from 0 to 191) we recognize the fact that all the X values are out of range.

It is customary for the origin of an X-Y plot to be located in the lower left-hand corner. Thus, one might expect that plotting the position 0,0 would place a dot in the lower left-hand corner of the screen. In fact, these coordinates assume that the origin is in the upper left-hand corner. While this is unusual, it is consistent with Applesoft BASIC which makes a similar assumption. Thus, we are only required to scale the coordinates to bring them within plotting range.

Applesoft BASIC's **HPLOT** command has three variations:

1 **HPLOT X,Y**   which plots a single dot at **X,Y**.
2 **HPLOT TO X,Y**   which draws a line from the current plotting position to **X,Y**.
3 **HPLOT X1,Y1 TO X2,Y2**   which draws a line between the two pairs of coordinates.

Here we will use the first two instructions. For each county we wish to draw, we use **HPLOT X,Y** with the first pair of values and **HPLOT TO X,Y** for the remaining pairs. The main plotting loop will be:

```
140  READ X,Y
145  HPLOT FN S(X),FN S(Y)
150  FOR I = 1 TO 4
155     READ X,Y
160     HPLOT TO FN S(X),FN S(Y)
165  NEXT I
```

Since we have so few data pairs, we can count them and thus specify a loop count. With a larger data set it would probably be easier to use a pair of dummy values as trailer values. You will note that **X** and **Y** values are scaled before they are plotted. The scaling occurs in a user-defined function. This then is the heart of the mapping routine. Below we list the entire program:

```
100  REM -- ONECOUNTY      3-20-81
105  REM
110  HOME
115  INPUT "ENTER SCALE FACTOR AS A VALUE < .7 ";S
120  DEF FN S(Z) = Z * S
125  HGR : HCOLOR = 3
130  POKE - 16302,0
135  REM----------------------
140  READ X,Y
145  HPLOT FN S(X), FN S(Y)
150  FOR I = 1 TO 4
155     READ X,Y
160     HPLOT TO FN S(X), FN S(Y)
165  NEXT I
170  REM----------------------
175  GET R$: IF R$ <> CHR$(27) THEN 175
180  TEXT
185  DATA 362,106
190  DATA 361,54
195  DATA 343,52
```

```
200  DATA 334,99
205  DATA 362,106
```

Several statements may require explanation: Statement 115 asks the user to enter a scale factor as a percentage—with 1.0 equalling 100 percent. Thus, if you wish to reduce the scale to one-half, you would enter .50 for fifty percent. The scale factor is used by the user defined function in line 120 to scale the **X** and **Y** values as they are passed to it. Statement 125 selects high resolution graphics page one and the **POKE** in statement 130 closes the text window usually available at the bottom of the screen so that we can see the bottom thirty-two lines of the graphics page. Statement 175 delays program execution to keep the plot visible for as long as you wish. It does so by **GET**ting a character from the keyboard repeatedly until that character is the equivalent of ASCII code 27, the escape key. Once you push the escape key, execution continues, statement 180 restores the text page to the screen and the program ends.

We suggest that you try this program several times using different scale factors. You will discover that .7 is about the largest scale factor you can use without *going off* the right side of the screen. If you use a scaling factor that is too high, the Apple will *bleep* and print an **ILLEGAL QUANTITY** error message. But since the Apple was displaying the graphics page when the error occurred, you will not see the error message. You can restore the text page by typing **TEXT** followed by a carriage return.

You will note that increasing the scale factor not only makes the image larger, but also moves it away from the plot origin. This suggests that some additional processing of the data is required before plotting, something we will demonstrate in Section 13.2. Our treatment of the map creation process will take three steps which we will treat sequentially. They are:

Step 1   Creation of a map coordinates file,
Step 2   Determining the median *X* and *Y* value, and
Step 3   The actual process of drawing the map.

13.2 CREATING A MAP COORDINATES FILE

The most formidable aspect of such a mapping program is not the algorithm but the data entry task. The West Virginia map, Figure 13.1, displayed in Section 13.1 required 506 pairs of coordinates. Entering the coordinates is also an important task because we are creating the data set from which our map will be drawn. Here we will illustrate our mapping technique using a much smaller data set to draw a county outline map of the state of Connecticut. We have segmented the process into three steps, the first of which is the creation of a map coordinates file. To create such a file, we must first enter at the keyboard all the required coordinates. Each pair of coordinates becomes a separate data statement. Such a statement might look like this:

200 DATA 4,23132,45433

The first of the three values represents the county. Each county must have a separate code number. The other two values are the X and Y coordinates respectively. We have had to add the county code (which was not needed in the **ONECOUNTY** program) because we will need a way for the program to detect a change from one county to another.

Once all the coordinates have been entered, you will need to verify their accuracy by displaying them on the screen and checking them against the source document. When the verification process is complete, you will need a small program to read the values from the data statements and to write the values to a disk file. Here we will create a sequential data set on the Apple diskette. At this point you may wish to review our treatment of Apple sequential files in Chapter 11. We will assume that you are familiar with that material. This routine merely reads the values in the data set and writes them to the disk. You will note the three negative values at the end of the data set. They are used to indicate end of file. These values are written to the disk file. Here is the complete program.

```
100   REM -- BUILDCTMAP2    5-23-81
101   REM
102   REM
110   D$ =   CHR$   (4)
115   F$ = "CTMAPFILE#2"
120   PRINT D$"OPEN"F$
125   PRINT D$"WRITE"F$
130   READ ID,X,Y
135   PRINT ID
140   PRINT X
145   PRINT Y
150   IF ID > 0 THEN 130
155   PRINT D$"CLOSE"
160   END
170   REM----------------------
175   REM     CONNECTICUT MAP #2
180   REM     57 COORRDINATE PAIRS
185   REM----------------------
200   DATA 1,36,22
201   DATA 1,27,34
202   DATA 1,56,48
203   DATA 1,47,59
204   DATA 1,50,101
205   DATA 1,103,57
206   DATA 1,103,45
207   DATA 1,36,22
208   DATA 2,50,101
209   DATA 2,53,147
210   DATA 2,108,148
211   DATA 2,123,140
212   DATA 2,110,99
213   DATA 2,76,80
214   DATA 2,50,101
215   DATA 3,103,45
216   DATA 3,103,58
217   DATA 3,76,80
218   DATA 3,111,99
219   DATA 3,142,92
220   DATA 3,164,58
221   DATA 3,124,52
222   DATA 3,103,45
223   DATA 4,110,99
224   DATA 4,123,140
225   DATA 4,108,148
226   DATA 4,131,148
227   DATA 4,135,143
```

```
228  DATA 4,139,148
229  DATA 4,166,148
230  DATA 4,181,96
231  DATA 4,142,93
232  DATA 4,110,99
233  DATA 5,164,58
234  DATA 5,142,93
235  DATA 5,170,95
236  DATA 5,192,79
237  DATA 5,189,62
238  DATA 5,164,58
239  DATA 6,181,96
240  DATA 6,166,148
241  DATA 6,213,148
242  DATA 6,202,111
243  DATA 6,181,96
244  DATA 7,190,62
245  DATA 7,192,79
246  DATA 7,171,95
247  DATA 7,182,96
248  DATA 7,203,111
249  DATA 7,253,103
250  DATA 7,254,71
251  DATA 7,190,62
252  DATA 8,202,111
253  DATA 8,213,148
254  DATA 8,251,148
255  DATA 8,253,103
256  DATA 8,202,111
990  DATA -1,-1,-1
```

By creating a map coordinates file, it will be possible for a number of programs to read the same file. Creating this file also makes it possible to make the map drawing routine more general since the routine does not itself contain coordinates.

13.3 FINDING THE MIDRANGE OF THE COORDINATES

The second step of our map creation process is determining the midrange of the *X* and *Y* coordinates. Since county coordinates come in so many different forms, we need a generalized technique for standardizing the coordinates so that they fit on the Apple graphics screen. This task can be easily accomplished in a subroutine. More specifically, our task is to standardize the coordinates in terms of the center of the plotting screen. We can do so by finding the middle of the range of *X* coordinates and the middle of the range of *Y* coordinates. These midrange values will then be used to standardize the coordinates.

The first step in computing the midrange of the *X* and *Y* coordinates, is to find the minimum and maximum value of each set of coordinates. We presented a simple program fragment to find the largest value in an array in Section 9.4. Here we expand the same technique in order to find both the largest and the smallest value in each array. We begin by assuming that the first *X* value is both the largest and smallest value in the array. We make a similar assumption about the first *Y* coordinate. While this assumption is not likely to be true, it does make the process simple. We next begin to pass through each array replacing the current largest and smallest value in each array as new values are encountered. We use **X1** for the smallest *X* value and **X9** for the largest X value. This process is repeated with the Y values. Here is our subroutine:

```
365  REM------------------------
370  REM           MID-RANGE ROUTINE
375  REM------------------------
380  X1 = X(1)
385  X9 = X(1)
390  Y1 = Y(1)
395  Y9 = Y(1)
400  FOR I = 2 TO MAX
405     IF X(I) > X9 THEN X9 = X(I)
410     IF Y(I) > Y9 THEN Y9 = Y(I)
415     IF X(I) < X1 THEN X1 = X(I)
420     IF Y(I) < Y1 THEN Y1 = Y(I)
425  NEXT I
430  XM = (X9 + X1) / 2
435  YM = (Y9 + Y1) / 2
440  RETURN
```

Once the loop has been completed, we have the largest and the smallest of the X and Y values, which are then used to compute the midrange value for each array. We use **XM** and **YM** for the X and Y midrange values respectively. Control then returns to the main program.

13.4 DRAWING A MAP

Drawing a multi-county map, the third step in our process of creating a computer graphics map, is quite similar to drawing a single county map except for the additional statements needed to handle the change from one county to another. Our program must perform three basic tasks. It must: (1) read the coordinates and county identification codes from disk into arrays, (2) call the subroutine that finds the midrange of each set of coordinates, and (3) plot the coordinates. As in the **ONECOUNTY** routine, we must plot the first pair of coordinates for a given county using the **HPLOT** command and all subsequent pairs of coordinates for the same county using the **HPLOT TO** command. Thus, we must do something slightly different with the first pair of coordinates for each county. This is necessary because county coordinates usually come in alphabetical order, requiring our program to jump from the last coordinate of one county to the first coordinate of the next without drawing a line. In order to detect the change from one county to another, our data set must contain a county identification code, which is unique for each county.

Our plotting algorithm can be represented in pseudocode as follows:

```
DRAWMAP:
declare numeric ID(100),X(100),Y(100)
declare numeric LAG,YM,XM,HCOLOR,I,MAX,S
declare string C$
define function H(X) ← 140 + (X − XM) * S
define function V(Y) ← 96 − (Y − YM) * S
set LAG to 0
set S to 1.2
loop while I goes from 1 to 100
    get(ID(I),X(I),Y(I))
    if (ID(I) < 0) break
end loop
set MAX to I − 1
call MIDRANGE
HGR2
set HCOLOR to 3
loop while I goes from 1 to MAX
    if(ID(I) <> LAG)
       [ HPLOT FN H(X(I)), FN V(Y(I))
         LAG ← ID(I) ]
    else
       HPLOT TO FN H(X(I)),FN V(Y(I))
end loop
get(C$) until C$ = "   "
TEXT
end.


MIDRANGE:
set X1 to X(1)
set X9 to X(1)
set Y1 to Y(1)
set Y9 to Y(1)
loop while I goes from 2 to MAX
    if (X(I) > X9) X9 = X(I)
    if (Y(I) > Y9) Y9 = Y(I)
    if (X(I) < X1) X1 = X(I)
    if (Y(I) < Y1) Y1 = Y(I)
end loop
XM ← (X9 + X1) / 2
YM ← (Y9 + Y1) / 2
return
end.
```

The algorithm consists of three parts. The first loads the data into arrays, the second is the subroutine that computes the midrange of the coordinates, and the third part draws the map itself. As in previous examples, our input is expressed in generic terms and does not identify the source of the data. You will note that we have incorporated into our algorithmic language without change the special plotting commands supported by Applesoft BASIC. This illustrates the type of flexibility that we recommended in Chapter 3 in the development of your own pseudocoding techniques. The heart of this algorithm is a double alternative decision structure with either the true task or the false task being executed depending upon the result of the test "IF(ID(I) <> LAG)".

Because the selection of the true or false task is dependent upon whether the current value of ID is the same as the previous value and since each execution of the **INPUT** or **READ** statement destroys the present contents of the variable and replaces it with a new value, we must save the old value of ID in another variable which we call LAG.

Two functions are critical to the algorithm. The first— FN H —the horizontal function, standardizes X coordinates in terms of the center of the graphics screen. The vertical function—FN V— performs a similar task with the Y coordinates. Each function uses the appropriate midrange value computed by the subroutine as discussed in Section 13.3. Both functions also use the scaling factor S to scale the coordinates. You may have to experiment with S in order to get the best value. The Y coordinates in the data set assume the origin of the plot to be in the lower left-hand corner of the screen. Since the Apple assumes the origin to be in the upper left-hand corner, we use a minus sign in the vertical function. If your image comes out upside down, change this sign to "+" as follows:

define function V(Y) ← 96 + (Y − YM) * S

If your image comes out reversed, that is with the left-hand side of the image on the right-hand side of the screen, reverse the sign in the horizontal function. Better still, reverse the **X** and **Y** print statements in the **BUILDMAP** program. The BASIC version of the program is presented below:

```
100  REM -- DRAWMAP    5-23-81
105  REM
110  REM
115  HIMEM: 16383
120  DIM ID(100),X(100),Y(100)
125  D$ =CHR$(4)
130  LAG = 0
135  REM----------------------
140  REM         RUN PARAMETERS
145  REM----------------------
150  S = 1.2
155  F$ = "CTMAPFILE#2"
```

```
160  REM-----------------------
165  REM         LOAD ARRAYS
170  REM         FROM DISK
175  REM-----------------------
180  PRINT D$;"OPEN";F$
185  PRINT D$;"READ";F$
190  FOR I = 1 TO 100
195  INPUT ID(I),X(I),Y(I)
200     IF ID(I) < 0 THEN 210
205  NEXT I
210  MAX = I − 1
215  PRINT D$"CLOSE"
220  GOSUB 365
225  REM-----------------------
230  REM         DRAW MAP
235  REM-----------------------
240  HGR2 : HCOLOR = 3
245  DEF FN H(X) = 140 + (X − XM) * S
250  DEF FN V(Y) = 96 − (Y − YM) * S
255  REM-----------------------
260  REM         LOOP
265  REM-----------------------
270  FOR I = 1 TO MAX
275     IF ID(I) = LAG THEN 325
280  REM-----------------------
285  REM         NEW COUNTY
290  REM-----------------------
295     HPLOT FN H(X(I)),FN V(Y(I))
300     LAG = ID(I)
305     GOTO 330
310  REM-----------------------
315  REM         SAME COUNTY
320  REM-----------------------
325     HPLOT TO FN H(X(I)),FN V(Y(I))
330  NEXT I
335  REM-----------------------
340  REM         END LOOP
345  REM-----------------------
350  GET C$ : IF C$ <> CHR$(27) THEN 350
355  TEXT
360  END
```

```
365  REM----------------------
370  REM         MID-RANGE ROUTINE
375  REM----------------------
380  X1 = X(1)
385  X9 = X(1)
390  Y1 = Y(1)
395  Y9 = Y(1)
400  FOR I = 2 TO MAX
405     IF X(I) > X9 THEN X9 = X(I)
410     IF Y(I) > Y9 THEN Y9 = Y(I)
415     IF X(I) < X1 THEN X1 = X(I)
420     IF Y(I) < Y1 THEN Y1 = Y(I)
425  NEXT I
430  XM = (X9 + X1) / 2
435  YM = (Y9 + Y1) / 2
440  RETURN
```

This is a rather straightforward implementation of the algorithm. Figures 13.2 and 13.3 display two maps of the state of Connecticut. The map in Figure 13.2 was produced by this program using a data set containing fifty-seven pairs of coordinates and the map in Figure 13.3 was produced by the same program using a different data set that has 346 coordinate pairs. Our reason for displaying the program here with the smaller data set is frankly to save space.

There are some applications in which Figure 13.2, the map with less detail, would be more desirable. For example, you may recall watching election night coverage on

Figure 13.2
Map of Connecticut and its 8 Counties
Using 57 Coordinate Pairs

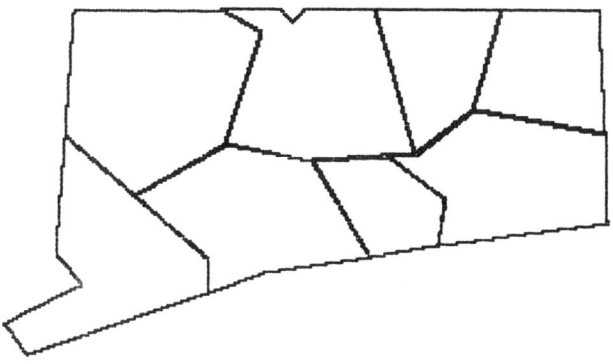

Figure 13.3
Map of Connecticut and its 8 Counties
Using 346 Coordinate Pairs

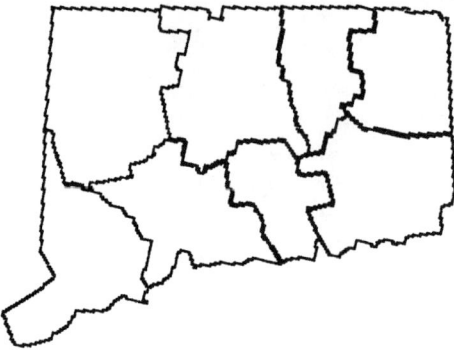

one of the major networks. Large maps indicating each state were used to indicate which presidential candidate the state supported. These maps did not display much state boundary detail. In this respect, the television map was quite similar to Figure 13.2.

13.5 SAVING GRAPHIC IMAGES ON DISK

The Apple may require several minutes to draw complex graphic images. This may be a disadvantage in those circumstances in which you may wish to change graphic images quickly. Fortunately, the Apple provides a means for saving a graphics image directly to the disk with a single command.

To save such an image, you must first run the program that creates the graphic display. Allow the program to create the image and end execution normally. Thereafter, enter one of the following commands.

If you used **HGR2**, enter the following command followed by a carriage return:

BSAVE image,A16384,L8192

In place of image enter a legitimate **DOS** file name. Make sure the file name is not already in use. Note that the command is **BSAVE**—which means binary save—in contrast with the standard **SAVE** command. The two parameters following the file name indicate the memory Address at which the save process is to begin and the Length of the memory segment to be saved. In this example, we have specified the beginning of the second page of high resolution graphics memory. If the graphic image was created using the **HGR** command in the program, then use the following:

BSAVE image,A8192,L8192.

If you enter a **CATALOG** command, the following would be displayed:

B 034 IMAGE

We assume the file is named **IMAGE**. You will note that thirty-four sectors of storage are required to store a single graphics image. Since each sector holds 256 characters, a total of 8704 characters of storage is required for each graphics image.

13.6 LOADING A GRAPHICS IMAGE FROM DISK

Once saved, a graphics image can be loaded and displayed with a three statement program as follows:

```
110  D$ = CHR$(4)
115  HGR2
120  PRINT D$"BLOAD IMAGE"
```

We assume that the file **IMAGE** contains a graphics image. You will note that we omitted the Address and Length parameters used in the **BSAVE** command illustrated above. Since these values are saved along with the map image by the **BSAVE** command, we need not supply them again.

The three line program given above is the quickest way of loading and displaying a binary map image, but it may not be the best way. You have no doubt noted how the image appears on the screen incrementally. This gradual process can be replaced with an instant picture using the following program:

```
100  REM -- DISPLAYMAP    5-15-81
105  D$ = CHR$(4)
110  HOME
115  PRINT "WHEN MAP APPEARS, PUSH ESCAPE TO END."
120  PRINT
125  INPUT "WHICH MAP FILE: ;"M$
130  PRINT D$;"BLOAD";M$;",A16384"
135  POKE - 16299,0
140  POKE - 16297,0
145  POKE - 16302,0
150  POKE - 16304,0
155  GET C$ : IF C$ <> CHR$(27) THEN 155
210  TEXT
215  END
```

Statements 120 through 126 use the Apple's so-called soft switches rather than the **HGR** commands. The effect of any one switch is partly dependent upon the setting of the others. You may wish to consult the Applesoft Reference Manual for a more detailed discussion. Here we present a brief description of what each does:

Statement 135: switches from page one high resolution graphics (beginning at 8192) to page two (beginning at 16384).

Statement 140: selects high resolution graphics.

Statement 145: selects full screen graphics rather than mixed graphics and text.

Statement 150: switches from text to graphics.

This approach makes it relatively easy for us to load two map images and switch from one to the other. Consider this modification of the program just presented:

```
100 REM -- DOUBLEMAP    4-6-81
101 REM
105 D$ = CHR$(4)
110 PRINT D$"BLOAD CT MAP"
115 PRINT D$"BLOAD WV MAP,A8192"
120 POKE -16299,0
122 POKE -16297,0
124 POKE -16302,0
126 POKE -16304,0
150 GET C$ : IF C$ <> CHR$(27) THEN 150
160 POKE -16300,0
170 GET C$ : IF C$ <> CHR$(27) THEN 170
180 TEXT
190 END
```

Note that two map images were loaded one after the other. For the Figure 13.3, we specified the location or address in memory into which the image was to be stored. This was necessary since the image was originally stored from page two of the high resolution graphics storage but, we wished to load it into page one. Statement 160 was added to switch the display to page one of high resolution graphics from page two.

13.7 PRINTING GRAPHIC DISPLAYS

A number of printers are available for use with the Apple, some of which can print high resolution graphics images as well as text. One such device is the Apple Silentype printer. It is a small and compact thermal printer that often is available with the Apple

Photo 13.1
Apple Silentype Printer prints high resolution graphics with images as well as text. (Photo courtesy of Apple Computer Inc.)

microcomputer. Our treatment of printing graphics images here will be confined to the use of the Silentype. We further assume that the controller board for the printer is in slot number one of the Apple's backplane.

A graphics image can be transferred to the printer by statements within a program or by commands entered at the keyboard. Only two commands are required:

PR#1
CTRL/Q

Each command is typed at the keyboard and followed by a carriage return. Should the printer controller board be in a slot other than one, substitute that number for the "**1**" in **PR#1**. The **CTRL/Q** is entered by holding the control key down and then striking the **Q**. These commands will cause the Apple to print the image on high resolution graphics page one on the printer. It will be printed white on black as the image appears on the screen. You may **POKE** various locations to change these defaults as we will indicate in the following program.

Here we present a small program that loads a binary image from disk into the second high resolution graphics page. The statements down to number 155 should be familiar if you have read Section 13.6. Statement 160 initializes the printer. The **PRINT** statement is essential for the correct initialization of the printer. The next three statements modify default printer characteristics. Statement 165 causes the printer to print the darkest possible image. The values **POKE**d into this location can range from zero to seven with zero the lightest image and seven the darkest image. Statement 170 selects the second high resolution graphics page for display, the one beginning at memory location 16384. A value of thirty-two, which is the default, causes page one to be printed and a value of sixty-four causes page two to be selected. Statement 175 causes the inverse image to be printed—that is, it causes the image to be printed black on white, the opposite of the screen image. A value of 255 causes white on black printing and a value of zero causes black on white printing. Statement 180 causes a **CTRL/Q** to be printed thus beginning the printing process. Statements 190 to 200 merely restore the default values once the image has been printed. Statement 205 turns off the printer. It is important to note that these **POKE** instructions will have an effect only if the printer is turned on at the time. Remember that statement 160 turned on the printer.

```
100 REM -- PRINTMAP    5-15-81
105 D$ = CHR$(4)
110 HOME
115 PRINT "WHEN MAP APPEARS, PUSH ESCAPE TO PRINT."
120 PRINT
125 INPUT "WHICH MAP FILE:  ";M$
130 PRINT D$;"BLOAD";M$;",A16384"
135 POKE - 16299,0
140 POKE - 16297,0
145 POKE - 16302,0
150 POKE - 16304,0
155 GET C$ : IF C$ <> CHR$(27) THEN 155
160 PR#1 : PRINT
165 POKE - 12528,7   : REM    DARKEST IMAGE
170 POKE - 12525,64  : REM    HRES PAGE 2
175 POKE - 12525,0   : REM    PRINT INVERSE
180 PRINT CHR$(17)
185 REM ----- RESTORE DEFAULTS
190 POKE - 12528,5
195 POKE - 12525,32
200 POKE - 12524,255
205 PR#0
210 TEXT
215 END
```

13.8 ADDING TEXT TO YOUR GRAPHICS

We have already noted that the TRS-80 has the very convenient feature of allowing one to print character data along with a low resolution graphic image. Printing character data with Apple high resoluton graphics is not quite so easy. On the Apple, one can produce a shape table to represent the character or figure to be drawn. Special commands can then be used to position the character or figure on the screen. Constructing the shape table is not an easy task. The best solution is to borrow someone else's shape table.*

A technique we have used involves converting each figure to be printed into a character string. All characters are formed from a seven row by five column dot matrix. For example, if we look closely at the letter *S* on the screen, we will see that it is formed of fifteen dots located in a seven by five array. If we could code the information in that array in such a way that we could retrieve the illuminated dots, we could use the **HPLOT** commands to print the array and, thus, the character of interest. Consider the empty matrix in Figure 13.4.

In Figure 13.5 we will darken those squares that are illuminated in the letter *S*.

Let us use a binary system to indicate whether the dot is illuminated or not:

0 = off

1 = on

Arranging the array for *S* in row order we find the following:

01110   (first row)
10001   (second row)
10000   (third row)
01110   (fourth row)
00001   (fifth row)
10001   (sixth row)
01110   (seventh row)

You should be able to see the letter *S* spelled out in 1s. We form these digits into a one-dimensional array by concatenating the seven rows in order.

S$ = "01110100011000001110000011000101110"

*See, for example, an article in *Creative Computing,* entitled "Hi-Res Text for the Apple," January 1981, by Paul Hitchcock, pages 126-129, Volume 7.

290 *Advanced Graphic Techniques* Ch. 13

Figure 13.4
An Empty Matrix

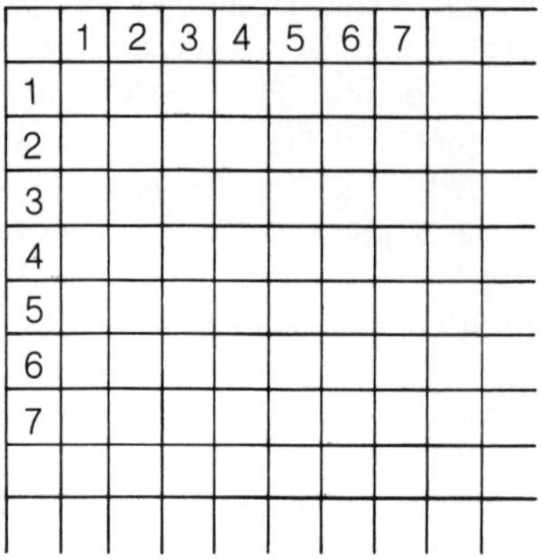

Figure 13.5
The Letter *S* in a 7-Row by 5-Column Matrix

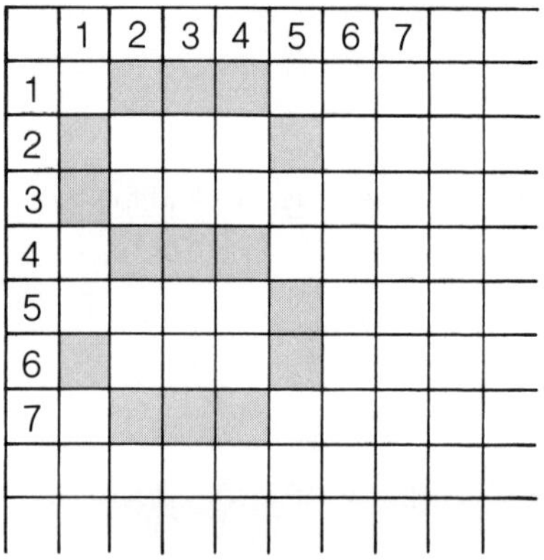

We can print the letter in high resolution graphics using the following fragment:

```
100  HGR:HCOLOR = 3
110  S$ = "0111010001100000111000001100010 1110"
120  X = 10 : Y = 10
130  GOSUB 1000
140  GOTO 9999
1000 REM -- SUBROUTINE TO PLOT ARRAY
1010 FOR I = 1 TO 7
1020 FOR J = 1 TO 5
```

```
1030  IF MID$(S$,(I − 1) * 5 + J,1) = "1" THEN
      HPLOT X + J, Y + I
1040  NEXT J
1050  NEXT I
1060  RETURN
9999  END
```

This fragment will produce the letter *S* in a matrix which has its top-left corner at 11,11 on the screen. Try it.

It would be better yet if we could place this string in a random access file with a record number that corresponds to its place in the ASCII coding system so that it can be retrieved in a systematic way. This can be easily done once we decide on the extent of our character set. It is also important that we extract a continuous set of characters from the character set (no gaps allowed). For example, if we decide to have all the digits and the letters, our set must run from ASC(48) which corresponds to 0, to ASC(90) which corresponds to Z.

Assuming such a file is built, we can expand the program above to print any string of characters on the high resolution screen as follows:

```
100   HGR: HCOLOR = 3
110   D$ = CHR$(4)
120   HOME: VTAB 22
130   PRINT "ENTER CHARACTER STRING";
140   INPUT C$
150   PRINT "ENTER COORDINATES OF PRINT LOCATION"
160   INPUT X,Y
170   FOR K = 1 TO LEN(C$)
180   PRINT D$;"OPEN HIRES,L36"
190   C = ASC(MID$(C$,K,1)) − 47
200   PRINT D$;"READ HIRES,R";C
210   INPUT S$
220   GOSUB 1000
230   PRINT D$;"CLOSE HIRES"
240   X = X + 7
250   NEXT K
260   GOTO 9999
1000      (add subroutine above)
          .
          .
          .
9999  END
```

This program fragment provides for the entry of a character string and the selection of its printing location. The string is then segmented and each character

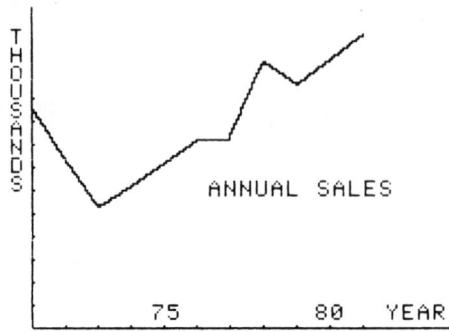

Figure 13.6
Graph Produced as Output by Combining
Graphics and Characters

identified with a record number in line 190. The character data is retrieved from the file in lines 200 and 210. Line 240 advances the printing position for printing the next character.

It should be noted that this technique can be used to develop your own character set or special symbols and logos. The Subroutine Library (Appendix B, page B24), contains a program, which permits combining graphics and characters in a trial and error fashion. All the Apple characters are available in a supporting data file. A sample of the output of this program (an annotated graph) is shown in Figure 13.6.

13.9 APPENDIX

We are happy to acknowledge the assistance of Mr. William Detweiler of the Office of Health Services Research of West Virginia University who provided the map coordinates for West Virginia and Connecticut as well as some good advice.

In preparation for the 1980 Census, the Bureau of the Census entered into agreements with most of the fifty states for the creation of State Data Centers within individual states to meet the need for the distribution of Census data. If you are interested in obtaining map coordinates for your state, you should contact the State Data Center in your state. A reference librarian in a college or public library should be able to get the address of your state data center.

In this chapter, we have written as if there were but one set of coordinates for a given state. The fact is, there are likely to be several sets of coordinates for any state. Map coordinates provided by the Bureau of the Census are very precise and take into consideration detailed boundary gyrations. As a result, many pairs of coordinates are often required to draw each map. State Data Centers are likely to have alternative sets of coordinates that sacrifice some boundary detail in order to obtain a smaller number of coordinates. These data sets are easier to work with and generally produce very good results. When you get a set of map coordinates you should determine the following before getting started:

1 Do the coordinates assume the plot origin to be in the upper lefthand corner of the screen or the lower lefthand corner? Since the Apple assumes the plot origin to be in the upper lefthand corner, you will have to change the sign in the vertical function if the coordinates assume the opposite.

2 Some map coordinates may come with the vertical (Y) coordinate first, followed by the horizontal (X) coordinate. In such a case, you will have to transpose them as you enter them into the program or adjust the **READ** statement to read the Y coordinate first.

3 Use the **HIMEM:** command to protect your program from accidental catastrophe. This command specifies the highest memory location available to your BASIC program including variable storage space. When your Apple is powered up, Applesoft normally sets **HIMEM:** to the highest memory address available. But this exposes some of your program to the risk of destruction by execution of either **HGR** or **HGR2** commands if the program is large enough to extend into the area used for storage of high resolution graphics. Execution of these commands causes the graphics storage area to be cleared to blank perhaps destroying many statements. Nothing can be more frustrating than to spend hours entering coordinates only to have such an accident destroy much of your work. If you have a 32k or 48k machine, we recommend that you use the following:

HGR2
HIMEM: 16384

If you have a 16k machine, you will have to use:

HGR
HIMEM: 8192

The value assigned to **HIMEM:** is not modified by the following commands: **CLEAR, RUN, NEW** and **DEL**. Also please note that the colon is part of the name **HIMEM:**. You can cause the Apple to display the value of **HIMEM:** by entering the following:

PRINT PEEK(116) * 256 + PEEK(115)

The printed value is a decimal.

APPENDICES

A	ALGORITHMIC LANGUAGE SUMMARY	**A 1**
B	LIBRARY OF SUBROUTINES	**B 1**
	DATAFL	**B 1**
	BUBBLE	**B 2**
	MEDIAN	**B 4**
	SIGMA	**B 5**
	XYSORT	**B 7**
	YXSORT	**B 8**
	PMCORR	**B10**
	MATADD	**B12**
	MATMUL	**B15**
	MATINV	**B17**
	SCIENTNOT	**B19**
	SIGNIFDIGIT	**B20**
	PRINT USING	**B21**
	CHARGEN	**B24**
C	ASCII CODES	**C 1**
D	THE EDITOR AND CROSS-REFERENCE TABLE GENERATOR	**D 1**

A ALGORITHMIC LANGUAGE SUMMARY

1 VARIABLE DECLARATION

PURPOSE: to provide a means for the declaration of size and type of variables and arrays. There are two variable types: numeric and string. Only arrays have size declarations.

EXAMPLES

    declare numeric X,Y,ALPHA,TABLE(20)
    declare string NAME$
    declare string LABELS$(20)

2 GENERIC INPUT STATEMENT

PURPOSE: to retrieve values for variables at run time. No input device is implied.

EXAMPLES

    get(X,Y,ALPHA)
    get(NAME$)

3 GENERIC OUTPUT STATEMENT

PURPOSE: to display values of variables and constants on an output device.

EXAMPLES

    put (X,Y,ALPHA)
    put("THE ANSWER IS",ANSWER)

4 ARITHMETIC ASSIGNMENT STATEMENT

PURPOSE: to assign the value of the variable, constant or expression on the right side of the replacement operator ('←') to the variable named on the left side.

EXAMPLES

    AREA ← PI * RADIUS ^ 2
    X ← Y
    AMOUNT ← 25

5 INITIALIZATION OF ACCUMULATORS AND COUNTERS

PURPOSE: to provide a means for initializing the values of accumulators and counters.

EXAMPLES

    set SUM to 0
    set COUNT to 0
    set LAST to 100

6 INCREMENT ACCUMULATORS AND COUNTERS

PURPOSE: to provide a means to increase or decrease the value of accumulators, counters and constants.

EXAMPLES

    increase SUM by AMOUNT
    increase COUNT by 1
    decrease BALANCE by AMOUNT

7 END OF PROGRAM MARKER

PURPOSE: to provide a means of marking the end of a program unit.

EXAMPLE

    end.

8 START OF PROGRAM MARKER

PURPOSE: to mark the start of a program unit (main routine or subroutine) and to name that unit.

EXAMPLES

    MAIN:
    SORT:

9 HALT PROGRAM EXECUTION

PURPOSE: To end execution of a program.

EXAMPLE

    stop

10 SIMPLE LOOPS

PURPOSE: to provide a means for a simple loop, the content of which is executed repeatedly until the structure is exited.

EXAMPLE

    loop
        ... block of statements ...
    end loop

11 LOOP EXIT

PURPOSE: to provide a means of exiting a loop.

EXAMPLE

    break
    if(condition) break

12 INDEXED LOOP

PURPOSE: to provide a facility for a repeating loop to be performed a specified number of times with a structure index.

EXAMPLE

    loop while COUNTER goes from START to STOP by STEP
        ... block of statements ...
    end loop

13 NEXT LOOP ITERATION

PURPOSE: to cause the next iteration of a loop to be initiated immediately. If the loop is indexed, the loop control variable is incremented and tested against its terminal value immediately. If there is no loop index, control passes immediately to the logical test.

EXAMPLE

    loop while INDEX goes from 1 to 10
        ... statements ...
            if(condition) next
        ... statements ...
    end loop

14 SINGLE ALTERNATIVE DECISION STRUCTURE

PURPOSE: to provide for the execution of a block of statements if a condition is true.

EXAMPLE

    if(condition)

    [. . . block of statements . . .

        ]

15 DOUBLE ALTERNATIVE DECISION STRUCTURE

PURPOSE: to provide for the execution of one block of statements if a logical condition is true and another block of statements if the condition is false.

EXAMPLE

    if(condition)

    [. . . true task . . . :

        ]

    else

    [. . . false task . . .

        ]

16 MULTIPLE ALTERNATIVE DECISION STRUCTURE

PURPOSE: to provide a process for selecting a single alternative from a series of three or more. The multiple alternative decision structure, or the case structure as it is sometimes known, is illustrated below:

EXAMPLE

        select (SWITCH)

           case 1: [. . . block of statements . . .]

           case 2: [. . . block of statements . . .]

           case n: [. . . block of statements . . .]

           default: [. . . block of statements . . .]

Here SWITCH is a variable. Control is passed by the select statement to that case block with the same value as SWITCH. If no case block with that value is present, control passes to the default block. If SWITCH has a value with a fractional part, that fractional part is truncated for use by the select statement. The value of SWITCH, however, is not actually modified. Any number of case blocks may be present so long as each has a distinct value.

17 FUNCTION DEFINITION

PURPOSE: to provide a pseudocode facility for defining a mathematical function.

EXAMPLE

>   define function H(X) = . . . mathematical expression . . .

Here *H* is the function name and *X* is a dummy argument or parameter variable. Its value is local to the function. See Section 6.4 for a more detailed treatment.

18 SUBROUTINES

PURPOSE: to provide a means of modularizing programs through the use of subroutines.

EXAMPLE

>   invoking a subroutine
>   >   call SORT:
>
>   subroutine
>   >   SORT:
>   >   .
>   >   .
>   >   .
>   >   return
>   >   end.

19 FILE PROCESSING

PURPOSE: to provide a means for opening and closing files and reading from and writing to them.

EXAMPLES

>   to open a file:
>
>   open "DATAFILE" (1,DA,IN,recordsize=20,filesize=40)

where DATAFILE is the name of the file and 1 is a file identification number to be used in subsequent read, write and close statements. Files may be direct access (DA) or sequential access (SA) and input (IN) or output (OUT). The record size indicates the maximum number of characters in each record and the file size indicates the maximum number of records in the file.

    to read from a file:

    get 1 (X)

specifies that a value should be retrieved from file number 1 for the variable X. The lack of a pointer variable implies sequential access.

    get 1:P (X)

specifies that a value is to be retrieved for X from file number 1 record P. This specifies random or direct access.

    to close a file:

    close 1

B LIBRARY OF SUBROUTINES

This library includes several subroutines that perform recurring tasks. Included with each subroutine is a discussion of its purpose and usage. A complete listing and sample *main* program which calls the subroutine are listed. The output of the main program is displayed.

DATAFL

PURPOSE: **DATAFL** is a subroutine that generates a distribution of integers in a specified interval. The distribution varies from flat to peaked at the center of the interval depending upon the value of a parameter K. As K increases the distribution approximates a normal distribution.

USAGE: In order that the **DATAFL** subroutine function properly, your main program must dimension an array $X()$ to hold the data generated. It must also pass the number of data elements to be generated, their maximum and minimum values, and a parameter K which determines the degree of peaking about the center of the interval. The distribution is flat for $K = 1$.

SUBROUTINE LISTING

```
8300 REM -- SUBROUTINE DATAFL 1-20-81
8310 REM -- INPUT VARIABLES: R0, R1, N, K
8320 REM -- LOCAL VARIABLES: I, J
8330 REM -- OUTPUT VARIABLES: X(I)
8340 FOR I = 1 TO N
8345    X(I) = 0
8350    FOR J = 1 TO K
8360       X(I) = X(I) + RND (1)
8370    NEXT J
8375    X(I) = INT (X(I) * (R1 - R0 + 1) / K) + R0
8380 NEXT I
8390 RETURN
9999 END
```

MAIN PROGRAM LISTING

```
100 REM -- MAIN PROGRAM (DATAFL)
110 REM -- INITIALIZE FOR 15 DATA ELEMENTS
```

```
120 DIM X(15)
130 PRINT "ENTER SMALLEST DATA VALUE  ";
140 INPUT R0
150 PRINT "ENTER LARGEST DATA VALUE  ";
160 INPUT R1
170 PRINT "ENTER THE 'PEAKING' PARAMETER  ";
180 INPUT K
190 N = 15
200 REM -- CALL SUBROUTINE
210 GOSUB 8300
220 REM -- PRINT OUTPUT
230 FOR I = 1 TO N
240 PRINT X(I)
250 NEXT I
260 GOTO 9999
```

TYPICAL OUTPUT

ENTER SMALLEST DATA VALUE ?3
ENTER LARGEST DATA VALUE ?17
ENTER THE 'PEAKING' PARAMETER ?3
8
12
14
11
14
10
6
11
12
8
12
13
10
11
12

BUBBLE

PURPOSE: The subroutine **BUBBLE** sorts a one-dimensional array (vector) named $X()$ into ascending order via the interchange method.

USAGE: Before the subroutine is called the array $X()$ should be dimensioned and loaded with values. A variable named N should contain the value of the dimension of X(). Upon return, the vector will be sorted in ascending order. Note that the original vector will be lost so if it is needed in its original order, the programmer should copy it into another array before the subroutine is called.

SUBROUTINE LISTING

```
8900 REM -- SUBROUTINE BUBBLE 12-1-80
8902 REM -- INPUT VARIABLES: X(), N
8904 REM -- LOCAL VARIABLES: I, J, S
8906 REM -- OUTPUT VARIABLES: X() - SORTED
8910 FOR I = N TO 2 STEP -1
8920     FOR J = 1 TO I - 1
8930         REM -- IF X(J) > X(J + 1) THEN
8940         IF X(J) < = X(J + 1) THEN 8970
8950             S = X(J)
8955             X(J) = X(J + 1)
8960             X(J + 1) = S
8965         REM -- ENDIF
8970     NEXT J
8980 NEXT I
8990 RETURN
9999 END
```

MAIN PROGRAM LISTING

```
100 REM -- MAIN PROGRAM (BUBBLE)
110 REM -- INITIALIZE
120 DIM X(15)
130 N = 15
140 REM -- LOAD ARRAY X()
150 FOR I = 1 TO N
160     READ X(I)
170 NEXT I
180 REM -- CALL SUBROUTINE
190 GOSUB 8900
200 REM -- PRINT OUTPUT
210 FOR I = 1 TO N
220     PRINT X(I)
230 NEXT I
240 REM -- DATA
250 DATA 9,5,10,15,9,11,12,9,8,12,13,14,6,7,11
260 GOTO 9999
```

TYPICAL OUTPUT

```
5
6
7
8
9
9
9
10
11
11
12
12
13
14
15
```

MEDIAN

PURPOSE: **MEDIAN** is a subroutine that computes the median value of an array of numeric values. The array must already be sorted in ascending order. The subroutine **BUBBLE** is available in the library for sorting arrays.

USAGE: In order that the **MEDIAN** subroutine function properly, your main program should load an array called $X()$ with the values from which the median is to be selected. A variable N should be assigned a value equal to the number of items in $X()$. After subroutine execution is completed, the variable $M9$ will contain the value of the median of the array.

SUBROUTINE LISTING

```
9200 REM -- SUBROUTINE MEDIAN 12-5-80
9202 REM -- INPUT VARIABLES: N, X()
9204 REM -- LOCAL VARIABLES: I9
9206 REM -- OUTPUT VARIABLES: M9, X()
9210 I9 = INT (N / 2 + 1)
9220 M9 = X(I9)
9230 REM -- IF N IS EVEN THEN
9240 IF INT (N / 2) * 2 < > N THEN 9270
9250     M9 = (X(I9) + X(I9 - 1)) / 2
9260 REM -- ENDIF
9270 RETURN
9999 END
```

MAIN PROGRAM LISTING

```
100 REM -- MAIN PROGRAM (MEDIAN)
110 REM -- INITIALIZE
120 DIM X(15)
130 N = 15
140 REM -- LOAD ARRAY X()
150 FOR I = 1 TO N
160    READ X(I)
170 NEXT I
180 REM -- CALL SUBROUTINE
190 GOSUB 9200
200 REM -- PRINT OUTPUT
210 FOR I = 1 TO N
220    PRINT X(I); SPC(2);
230 NEXT I
240 PRINT: PRINT
250 PRINT "THE MEDIAN OF THIS ARRAY IS  ";M9
260 REM -- DATA
270 DATA 4,5,8,8,9,9,9,9,9,10,10,11,12,12,14
280 GOTO 9999
```

TYPICAL OUTPUT

4   5   8   8   9   9   9   9   9   10   10   11   12   12   14

THE MEDIAN OF THIS ARRAY IS 9

SIGMA

PURPOSE: **SIGMA** is a subroutine that computes the mean of a series of numeric values and the standard deviation using two separate algorithms, one for a population and the other for a sample.

USAGE: To use **SIGMA,** the array of values should already be in a vector named $X()$ and the variable N should be initialized to the size of $X()$. Upon return, the variable $M8$ will contain the value of the mean of $X()$. $S9$ will contain the standard deviation for $X()$ assuming $X()$ to be a population while $S8$ will contain the standard deviation of $X()$ assuming it to be a sample.

SUBROUTINE LISTING

```
9100 REM -- SUBROUTINE SIGMA 12-12-80
9102 REM -- INPUT VARIABLES: N, X()
9104 REM -- LOCAL VARIABLES: I, S1, S2
```

```
9106 REM -- OUTPUT VARIABLES: M8, S8, S9
9108 S1 = 0
9110 S2 = 0
9120 FOR I = 1 TO N
9130     S1 = S1 + X(I)
9140     S2 = S2 + X(I) * X(I)
9150 NEXT I
9160 M8 = S1 / N
9170 S9 = SQR (N * S2 - S1 * S1) / N
9180 S8 = SQR ((N * S2 - S1 * S1) / (N * (N - 1)))
9190 RETURN
9999 END
```

MAIN PROGRAM LISTING

```
100 REM -- MAIN PROGRAM (SIGMA)
110 REM -- INITIALIZE
120 DIM X(15)
130 N = 15
140 REM -- LOAD ARRAY X
150 FOR I = 1 TO N
160     READ X(I)
170 NEXT I
180 REM -- CALL SUBROUTINE
190 GOSUB 9100
200 REM -- PRINT OUTPUT
210 FOR I = 1 TO N
220     PRINT X(I); SPC(2);
230 NEXT I
240 PRINT : PRINT
250 PRINT "THE MEAN OF THE ARRAY IS  ";M8
260 PRINT
270 PRINT "THE STANDARD DEVIATION IS  ";S8;" (SAMPLE)"
280 PRINT
290 PRINT "THE STANDARD DEVIATION IS  ";S9;" (POPULATION)"
300 REM -- DATA
310 DATA 9,5,10,9,11,12,9,14,8,10,9,8,9,12,4
320 GOTO 9999
```

TYPICAL OUTPUT

```
9  5  10  9  11  12  9  14  8  10  9  8  9  12  4
THE MEAN OF THE ARRAY IS 9.26666667
THE STANDARD DEVIATION IS 2.54857569 (SAMPLE)
THE STANDARD DEVIATION IS 2.46215804 (POPULATION)
```

XYSORT

PURPOSE: The subroutine **XYSORT** is a tandem sort that uses the same algorithm used in **BUBBLE** to sort the values of two vectors $X()$ and $Y()$ on the value of $X()$.

USAGE: Before the subroutine is called the arrays $X()$ and $Y()$ should be dimensioned and loaded with values. A variable named N should contain the limit of the arrays. Upon return, the vectors will be sorted on $X()$ in ascending order. Note that the original vectors will be lost. If they are needed, the programmer should copy them into another array before the subroutines are called.

SUBROUTINE LISTING

```
8900 REM -- SUBROUTINE XYSORT 2-20-81
8902 REM -- INPUT VARIABLES: N, X(), Y()
8904 REM -- LOCAL VARIABLES: S, I, J
8906 REM -- OUTPUT VARIABLES: X(), Y() SORTED
8910 FOR I = N TO 2 STEP -1
8915    FOR J = 1 TO I - 1
8920       REM -- IF X(J) > X(J + 1) THEN
8925       IF X(J) < = X(J + 1) THEN 8980
8930          S = X(J)
8935          X(J) = X(J + 1)
8940          X(J + 1) = S
8945          S = Y(J)
8950          Y(J) = Y(J + 1)
8960          Y(J + 1) = S
8970       REM -- ENDIF
8980    NEXT J
8985 NEXT I
8990 RETURN
9999 END
```

MAIN PROGRAM LISTING

```
100 REM -- MAIN PROGRAM (XYSORT)
110 REM -- INITIALIZE
120 DIM X(15), Y(15)
130 N = 15
140 REM -- LOAD ARRAY X
150 FOR I = 1 TO N
160    READ X(I)
170 NEXT I
180 REM -- LOAD ARRAY Y
190 FOR I = 1 TO N
```

```
200     READ Y(I)
210 NEXT I
220 REM -- CALL SUBROUTINE
230 GOSUB 8900
240 REM -- PRINT OUTPUT
250 PRINT "X VALUES","Y VALUES"
260 PRINT
270 FOR I = 1 TO N
280     PRINT X(I),Y(I)
290 NEXT I
300 REM -- DATA
310 DATA 9,5,10,9,11,12,9,14,8,10,9,8,9,12,4
320 DATA 24,12,25,20,30,29,23,33,18,23,23,14,20,28,10
330 GOTO 9999
```

TYPICAL OUTPUT

X VALUES	Y VALUES
4	10
5	12
8	18
8	14
9	24
9	20
9	23
9	23
9	20
10	25
10	23
11	30
12	29
12	28
14	33

YXSORT

PURPOSE: The subroutine **YXSORT** is a tandem sort that uses the same algorithm used in **BUBBLE** to sort the values of two vectors X() and Y() on the value of Y().

USAGE: Before the subroutine is called the arrays X() and Y() should be dimensioned and loaded with values. A variable named N should contain the limit of the arrays. Upon return, the vectors will be sorted on Y() in ascending order. Note that the original vectors will be lost. If they are needed, the programmer should copy them into another array before the subroutine is called.

SUBROUTINE LISTING

```
8900 REM -- SUBROUTINE YXSORT 2-20-81
8902 REM -- INPUT VARIABLES: N, X(), Y()
8904 REM -- LOCAL VARIABLES: S, I, J
8906 REM -- OUTPUT VARIABLES: X(), Y() SORTED
8910 FOR I = N TO 2 STEP -1
8915    FOR J = 1 TO I - 1
8920       REM -- IF Y(J) > Y(J + 1) THEN
8925       IF Y(J) < = Y(J + 1) THEN 8980
8930          S = Y(J)
8935          Y(J) = Y(J + 1)
8940          Y(J + 1) = S
8945          S = X(J)
8950          X(J) = X(J + 1)
8960          X(J + 1) = S
8970       REM -- ENDIF
8980    NEXT J
8985 NEXT I
8990 RETURN
9999 END
```

MAIN PROGRAM LISTING

```
100 REM -- MAIN PROGRAM (YXSORT)
110 REM -- INITIALIZE
120 DIM X(15), Y(15)
130 N = 15
140 REM -- LOAD ARRAY X
150 FOR I = 1 TO N
160    READ X(I)
170 NEXT I
180 REM -- LOAD ARRAY Y
190 FOR I = 1 TO N
200    READ Y(I)
210 NEXT I
220 REM -- CALL SUBROUTINE
230 GOSUB 8900
240 REM -- PRINT OUTPUT
250 PRINT "X VALUES","Y VALUES"
260 PRINT
```

```
270 FOR I = 1 TO N
280     PRINT X(I),Y(I)
290 NEXT I
300 REM -- DATA
310 DATA 9,5,10,9,11,12,9,14,8,10,9,8,9,12,4
320 DATA 24,12,25,20,30,29,23,33,18,23,23,14,20,28,10
330 GOTO 9999
```

TYPICAL OUTPUT

X VALUES	Y VALUES
4	10
5	12
8	14
8	18
9	20
9	20
9	23
10	23
9	23
9	24
10	25
12	28
12	29
11	30
14	33

PMCORR

PURPOSE: The subroutine **PMCORR** computes Pearson's product moment correlation coefficient for pairs of data values. Additionally, it computes the slope and intercept of the best fit straight line using the method of least squares.

USAGE: Before the subroutine is called, two arrays $X()$ and $Y()$ should be dimensioned and loaded with pairs of data values. For example, $X(1)$ and $Y(1)$ will be treated as a pair. The variable N should be assigned the value of the size of $X()$ and $Y()$. When control returns to the main program, $R9$ will have the value of the correlation coefficient, A will have the value of the y-intercept, and B will have the value of the slope.

SUBROUTINE LISTING

```
9700 REM -- SUBROUTINE PMCORR 12-15-80
9702 REM -- INPUT VARIABLES: N, X(), Y()
9704 REM -- LOCAL VARIABLES: J, S1 THRU S7
```

```
9706 REM -- OUTPUT VARIABLES: R9, A, B
9710 REM -- INITIALIZE
9715 S1 = 0 : S2 = 0 : S3 = 0 : S4 = 0 : S5 = 0
9720 FOR J = 1 TO N
9725     S1 = S1 + X(J)
9730     S2 = S2 + Y(J)
9735     S3 = S3 + X(J) * Y(J)
9740     S4 = S4 + X(J) * X(J)
9745     S5 = S5 + Y(J) * Y(J)
9750 NEXT J
9755 S6 = N * S3 - S1 * S2
9760 S7 = SQR ((N * S4 - S1 * S1) * (N * S5 - S2 * S2))
9765 R9 = S6 / S7
9770 B = S6 / (N * S4 - S1 * S1)
9780 A = (S2 - B * S1) / N
9790 RETURN
9999 END
```

MAIN PROGRAM LISTING

```
100 REM -- MAIN PROGRAM (PMCORR)
110 REM -- INITIALIZE
120 DIM X(15), Y(15)
130 N = 15
140 REM -- LOAD ARRAY X
150 FOR I = 1 TO N
160     READ X(I)
170 NEXT I
180 REM -- LOAD ARRAY Y
190 FOR I = 1 TO N
200     READ Y(I)
210 NEXT I
220 REM -- CALL SUBROUTINE
230 GOSUB 9700
240 REM -- PRINT OUTPUT
250 PRINT "X VALUES","Y VALUES"
260 PRINT
270 FOR I = 1 TO N
280     PRINT X(I),Y(I)
290 NEXT I
300 PRINT
310 PRINT "THE CORRELATION COEFFICIENT IS  ";R9
320 PRINT
```

```
330 PRINT "THE SLOPE OF THE LINE OF BEST FIT IS  ";B
340 PRINT
350 PRINT "THE Y INTERCEPT OF THE LINE OF BEST FIT IS  ";A
360 REM -- DATA
370 DATA 9,5,10,9,11,12,9,14,8,10,9,8,9,12,4
380 DATA 24,12,25,20,30,29,23,33,18,23,23,14,20,28,10
390 GOTO 9999
```

TYPICAL OUTPUT

X VALUES	Y VALUES
9	24
5	12
10	25
9	20
11	30
12	29
9	23
14	33
8	18
10	23
9	23
8	14
9	20
12	28
4	10

THE CORRELATION COEFFICIENT IS .951306075
THE SLOPE OF THE LINE OF BEST FIT IS 2.47947217
THE Y INTERCEPT OF THE LINE OF BEST FIT IS −.843108763

MATADD

PURPOSE: **MATADD** is a subroutine that forms the sum or difference of two matrices of numerical values.

USAGE: In order that the **MATADD** subroutine function properly, your main program must load and dimension two arrays A() and B(). An array C() must also be dimensioned the same size but not loaded. These arrays must each have equal numbers of rows and equal numbers of columns (though row numbers need not equal column numbers). If subtraction is to be performed, the subtrahend must be selected as matrix B(). The subroutine will return the sum (or difference) matrix C() of the same dimension as A() and B().

Library of Subroutines **B13**

SUBROUTINE LISTING

```
8800 REM -- SUBROUTINE MATADD 11-26-80
8802 REM -- INPUT VARIABLES: M, N, A(), B()
8804 REM -- LOCAL VARIABLES: O, I, J
8806 REM -- OUTPUT VARIABLES: C()
8810 PRINT "OPTION 1 = ADDITION (A + B)"
8815 PRINT "OPTION 2 = SUBTRACTION (A - B)"
8820 PRINT "ENTER THE OPTION NUMBER  ";
8825 INPUT O
8830 IF O < > 1 THEN 8865
8835 FOR I = 1 TO M
8840    FOR J = 1 TO N
8845       C(I,J) = A(I,J) + B(I,J)
8850    NEXT J
8855 NEXT I
8860 GOTO 8895
8865 IF O < > 2 THEN 8810
8870 FOR I = 1 TO M
8875    FOR J = 1 TO N
8880       C(I,J) = A(I,J) - B(I,J)
8885    NEXT J
8890 NEXT I
8895 RETURN
9999 END
```

MAIN PROGRAM LISTING

```
100 REM -- MAIN PROGRAM (MATADD)
110 REM -- INITIALIZE
120 DIM A(3,4), B(3,4)
130 M = 3 : N = 4
140 REM -- LOAD AND PRINT MATRIX A
150 PRINT "MATRIX A" : PRINT
160 FOR I = 1 TO M
170    FOR J = 1 TO N
180       READ A(I,J)
190       PRINT A(I,J); SPC( 3);
200    NEXT J
210    PRINT
220 NEXT I
230 REM -- LOAD AND PRINT MATRIX B
240 PRINT : PRINT "MATRIX B" : PRINT
250 FOR I = 1 TO M
```

```
260     FOR J = 1 TO N
270         READ B(I,J)
280         PRINT B(I,J); SPC( 3);
290     NEXT J
300     PRINT
310 NEXT I
320 PRINT
330 REM -- CALL SUBROUTINE
340 GOSUB 8800
350 REM -- PRINT OUTPUT
360 PRINT : PRINT "MATRIX C" : PRINT
370 FOR I = 1 TO M
380     FOR J = 1 TO N
390         PRINT C(I,J); SPC( 3);
400     NEXT J
410     PRINT
420 NEXT I
430 REM -- DATA
440 DATA 1,2,3,1,2,3,4,2,1,2,1,0
450 DATA 1,3,3,0,1,4,3,1,1,3,4,2
460 GOTO 9999
```

TYPICAL OUTPUT

MATRIX A

1 2 3 1
2 3 4 2
1 2 1 0

MATRIX B

1 3 3 0
1 4 3 1
1 3 4 2

OPTION 1 = ADDITION (A + B)
OPTION 2 = SUBTRACTION (A − B)
ENTER THE OPTION NUMBER ?1

MATRIX C

2 5 6 1
3 7 7 3
2 5 5 2

MATMUL

PURPOSE: **MATMUL** is a subroutine that forms the product of two matrices of numerical values.

USAGE: In order that the **MATMUL** subroutine function properly, your main program must dimension and load two arrays A() and B(). Matrix C() must also be dimensioned but not loaded. These arrays are to be multiplied in the order A() * B(). To perform a matrix multiplication the number of columns of A() must equal the number of rows of B(). The program passes M (rows of matrix A()), N (columns of matrix A()) and L (columns of matrix B()). The subroutine returns an M by L matrix called C().

SUBROUTINE LISTING

```
8700 REM -- SUBROUTINE MATMUL 1-25-81
8702 REM -- INPUT VARIABLES: M, N, L, A(), B()
8704 REM -- LOCAL VARIABLES: I, J, K
8708 REM -- OUTPUT VARIABLES: C()
8710 FOR I = 1 TO M
8720     FOR J = 1 TO L
8730         C(I,J) = 0
8740         FOR K = 1 TO N
8750             C(I,J) = C(I,J) + A(I,K) * B(K,J)
8760         NEXT K
8770     NEXT J
8780 NEXT I
8790 RETURN
9999 END
```

MAIN PROGRAM LISTING

```
100 REM -- MAIN PROGRAM (MATMUL)
110 REM -- INITIALIZE
120 DIM A(3,4), B(4,3)
130 M = 3 : N = 4 : L = 3
140 HOME
150 REM -- LOAD AND PRINT MATRIX A
160 PRINT "HERE IS MATRIX A" : PRINT
170 FOR I = 1 TO M
180     FOR J = 1 TO N
190         READ A(I,J)
200         PRINT A(I,J); SPC( 2);
210     NEXT J
220     PRINT
```

```
230  NEXT I
240  REM -- LOAD AND PRINT MATRIX B
220  PRINT : PRINT "HERE IS MATRIX B" : PRINT
230  FOR I = 1 TO N
240     FOR J = 1 TO L
250        READ B(I,J)
260        PRINT B(I,J); SPC( 2);
270     NEXT J
280     PRINT
290  NEXT I
300  REM -- CALL SUBROUTINE
310  GOSUB 8700
320  REM -- PRINT OUTPUT
330  PRINT : PRINT "HERE IS THE PRODUCT MATRIX" : PRINT
340  FOR I = 1 TO M
350     FOR J = 1 TO L
360        PRINT C(I,J); SPC( 2);
370     NEXT J
380     PRINT
390  NEXT I
400  REM -- DATA
410  DATA 1,2,3,1,2,3,4,2,1,2,1,0
420  DATA 1,3,3,0,1,4,3,1,1,3,4,2
430  GOTO 9999
```

TYPICAL OUTPUT

HERE IS MATRIX A

1 2 3 1
2 3 4 2
1 2 1 0

HERE IS MATRIX B

1 3 3
0 1 4
3 1 1
3 4 2

HERE IS THE PRODUCT MATRIX

13 12 16
20 21 26
4   6   12

MATINV

PURPOSE: **MATINV** is a subroutine that computes the inverse of a square matrix of numerical values.

USAGE: In order that the **MATINV** subroutine function properly, your main program should dimension and load a square array called A(). An array C() of the same size as A() must also be dimensioned. The subroutine returns the matrix C() as the inverse. Not every matrix has an inverse. If the subroutine returns a divide by zero error message during execution, your matrix inverse probably does not exist.

SUBROUTINE LISTING

```
8400 REM -- SUBROUTINE MATINV 11-28-80
8402 REM -- INPUT VARIABLES: M, A()
8404 REM -- LOCAL VARIABLES: R, S, I, J
8406 REM -- OUTPUT VARIABLES: C()
8410 FOR I = 1 TO M
8415    FOR J = 1 TO M
8420       C(I,J) = A(I,J)
8425    NEXT J
8430 NEXT I
8435 FOR I = 1 TO M
8440    R = C(I,I)
8445    FOR J = 1 TO M
8450       IF J = I THEN 8465
8455       C(I,J) = C(I,J) / R
8460       GOTO 8470
8465       C(I,J) = 1 / R
8470    NEXT J
8472    FOR J = 1 TO M
8474       IF J = I THEN 8490
8476       S = - C(J,I)
8478       FOR K = 1 TO M
8480          IF K = I THEN 8486
8482          C(J,K) = C(I,K) * S + C(J,K)
8484          GOTO 8488
8486          C(J,K) = C(I,K) * S
8488       NEXT K
8490    NEXT J
8492 NEXT I
8494 RETURN
9999 END
```

MAIN PROGRAM LISTING

```
100  REM -- MAIN PROGRAM (MATINV)
110  REM -- INITIALIZE
120  DIM A(3,3)
130  M = 3
140  HOME
150  REM -- LOAD AND PRINT MATRIX A
155  PRINT "HERE IS MATRIX A": PRINT
160  FOR I = 1 TO M
170      FOR J = 1 TO M
180          READ A(I,J)
190          PRINT A(I,J); SPC( 2);
200      NEXT J
210      PRINT
220  NEXT I
230  PRINT
240  REM -- CALL SUBROUTINE
250  GOSUB 8400
260  REM -- PRINT OUTPUT
270  PRINT "HERE IS THE INVERSE OF MATRIX A"
280  PRINT
290  FOR I = 1 TO M
300      FOR J = 1 TO M
310          PRINT C(I,J); SPC( 2);
320      NEXT J
330      PRINT
340  NEXT I
350  REM -- DATA
360  DATA 1,3,3,1,4,3,1,3,4
370  GOTO 9999
```

TYPICAL OUTPUT

HERE IS MATRIX A

1	3	3
1	4	3
1	3	4

HERE IS THE INVERSE OF MATRIX A

7	-3	-3
-1	1	0
-1	0	1

SCIENTNOT

PURPOSE: **SCIENTNOT** is a subroutine that places any input number into standard scientific notation (one digit to the left of the decimal point multiplied by a power of ten).

USAGE: In order that **SCIENTNOT** function properly, you must pass the number to be placed in scientific notation as a string. The subroutine will return the original string under a new name and a new number string (in scientific notation) with the original name.

SUBROUTINE LISTING

```
9500 REM -- SCIENTNOT 8-2-80
9502 REM -- INPUT VARIABLES: NUM$
9504 REM -- LOCAL VARIABLES: P, EX$, NUM, M
9506 REM -- OUTPUT VARIABLES: SNUM$, NUM$
9510 SNUM$ = NUM$
9515 NUM = VAL (NUM$)
9520 NUM$ = STR$ (NUM)
9525 REM -- IF NUMBER IS ALREADY EXPONENTIAL, QUIT
9530 IF (999999999 - ABS (NUM)) * (ABS (NUM) - .01) < 0 THEN 9585
9535 M = 1
9540 FOR P = -2 TO 8
9545     IF ABS (NUM) < .1 * M THEN 9560
9550     M = M * 10
9555 NEXT P
9560 NUM = NUM * 100 / M
9565 EX$ = "0" + STR$ (ABS (P))
9570 IF P > -1 THEN EX$ = "E+" + EX$: GOTO 9580
9575 EX$ = "E-" + EX$
9580 NUM$ = STR$ (NUM) + EX$
9585 RETURN
9999 END
```

MAIN PROGRAM LISTING

```
100 REM -- MAIN PROGRAM (SCIENTNOT)
110 PRINT "ENTER THE NUMBER TO BE PLACED"
120 PRINT "IN SCIENTIFIC NOTATION  ";
130 INPUT NUM$
140 REM -- CALL SUBROUTINE
150 GOSUB 9500
160 REM -- PRINT RESULT
```

```
170  PRINT
180  PRINT "HERE IS THE NUMBER  ";SNUM$
190  PRINT "IN SCIENTIFIC NOTATION:  ";NUM$
200  GOTO 9999
```

TYPICAL OUTPUT

ENTER THE NUMBER TO BE PLACED
IN SCIENTIFIC NOTATION ?561.3

HERE IS THE NUMBER 561.3
IN SCIENTIFIC NOTATION: 5.613E+02

SIGNIFDIGIT

PURPOSE: **SIGNIFDIGIT** is a subroutine that places any input number into standard scientific notation with a specified number of significant digits.

USAGE: In order for this subroutine to function properly, you must pass the number as a string. The number of significant digits is passed as a numerical variable. You must also merge the subroutine **SCIENTNOT** with your program since it is called by this subroutine. This subroutine returns the original string as **SNUM$** and the new string under the original name.

SUBROUTINE LISTING

```
9400  REM -- SUBROUTINE SIGNIFDIGIT 8-1-80
9402  REM -- INPUT VARIABLES: NUM$, SIGD
9404  REM -- OUTPUT VARIABLES: NUM$, SNUM$
9410  REM -- PLACE NUMBER IN SCIENTIFIC NOTATION
9415  GOSUB 9500
9420  EX$ = MID$ (NUM$, LEN (NUM$) - 3,4)
9425  NUM$ = MID$ (NUM$,1, LEN (NUM$) - 4)
9430  NUM = VAL (NUM$)
9435  NUM = INT (NUM * 10 ^ (SIGD - 1) + .5) / 10 ^ (SIGD - 1)
9440  NUM$ = STR$ ( ABS (NUM))
9445  REM -- ADD ZEROES AS NEEDED
9450  IF LEN (NUM$) > = SIGD + 1 THEN 9480
9455  IF SIGD = 1 THEN 9480
9460  IF LEN (NUM$) = 1 THEN NUM$ = NUM$ + "."
9465  NUM$ = NUM$ + "0"
9470  IF LEN (NUM$) < SIGD + 1 THEN 9465
9475  REM -- CONCATENATE AND PRINT
9480  IF NUM < 0 THEN NUM$ = "-" + NUM$
```

```
9485 NUM$ = NUM$ + EX$
9490 RETURN
9999 END
```

MAIN PROGRAM LISTING

```
100 REM -- MAIN PROGRAM (SIGNIFDIGIT)
110 REM -- PROMPT FOR NUMBER
120 PRINT "ENTER THE NUMBER TO BE PLACED"
130 PRINT "IN SCIENTIFIC NOTATION ";
140 INPUT NUM$
150 PRINT
160 PRINT "NOW ENTER THE NUMBER OF SIGNIFICANT"
170 PRINT "DIGITS ";
180 INPUT SIGD
190 REM -- CALL SUBROUTINE
200 GOSUB 9400
210 REM -- PRINT OUTPUT
220 PRINT
230 PRINT "THE NUMBER (";SNUM$;") WRITTEN IN"
240 PRINT "SCIENTIFIC NOTATION WITH ";SIGD
250 PRINT "SIGNIFICANT DIGITS IS ";NUM$;"."
260 GOTO 9999
```

TYPICAL OUTPUT

**ENTER THE NUMBER TO BE PLACED
IN SCIENTIFIC NOTATION ?546.2**

**NOW ENTER THE NUMBER OF SIGNIFICANT
DIGITS ?5**

**THE NUMBER (546.2) WRITTEN IN
SCIENTIFIC NOTATION WITH 5
SIGNIFICANT DIGITS IS 5.4620E+02.**

PRINT USING

PURPOSE: **PRINT USING** is a subroutine that produces numerical output in a prescribed format. The output can include character data.

USAGE: In order that **PRINT USING** function properly, you must have established the print image in a character string called **PU$**. Within **PU$**, locations for number images must be indicated by the symbol "#". The number of numerical images in the string **(N)** and an array **(NP(N))** containing the data to be printed in the image must also be passed to the subroutine.

SUBROUTINE LISTING

```
8600  REM -- SUBROUTINE PRINTUSING 2-19-81
8602  REM -- INPUT VARIABLES: PU$, NP(N), N
8604  REM -- LOCAL VARIABLES: L, R, S, X, Y, S$
8606  REM -- OUTPUT VARIABLES: N$
8610  N$ = "":S = 0
8612  FOR J = 1 TO N
8614     L = 0:R = 0
8616     X = NP(J):Y = INT (X)
8618     FOR I = S + 1 TO LEN (PU$)
8620        S$ = MID$ (PU$,I,1)
8622        IF S$ = "#" THEN GOSUB 8672: GOTO 8630
8624        N$ = N$ + S$
8626     NEXT I
8628     REM -- ADJUST PARAMETERS
8630     I = I + L + R:S = I - 1:R = R - 1
8632     REM -- CHECK FOR OUT OF BOUNDS
8634     IF LEN ( STR$ ( ABS (Y))) < = L THEN 8640
8636     X$ = "E?": GOTO 8664
8638     REM -- SKIP ROUNDING OF INTEGERS
8640     IF X = Y THEN 8646
8642     REM -- ROUND AND TRUNCATE
8643     IF R < 0 THEN X = INT ((X * 10 + 5)/10:  GO TO 8646
8644     X = INT (X * 10 ^ R + .5) / 10 ^ R
8646     X$ = STR$ (X)
8648     REM -- ADJUST FOR SPECIAL VALUES
8650     IF X = 0 AND R > 0 THEN X$ = X$ + ".": GOTO 8660
8652     IF X * (X - 1) < 0 AND R > 0 THEN X$ = "0" + X$
8654     IF X * (X + 1) < 0 AND R > 0 THEN X$ = "-0" + STR$ ( ABS (X))
8656     IF VAL (X$) = Y AND R > 0 THEN X$ = X$ + "."
8658     REM -- PAD ZEROES
8660     IF LEN (X$) - LEN (STR$ (Y)) - 1 > = R THEN 8664
8662     X$ = X$ + "0": GOTO 8660
8664     Z$ = MID$ (B$,1,I - 1 - LEN (X$) - LEN (N$))
8666     N$ = N$ + Z$ + X$
8668  NEXT J
8670  PRINT N$: GOTO 8694
8672  FOR L = 1 TO 20: REM -- LOOP TO FIX L
8674     S$ = MID$ (PU$,I + L,1)
8676     IF S$ = "#" THEN 8682
```

```
8678    IF S$ = "." THEN GOSUB 8686
8680    GOTO 8684
8682 NEXT L
8684 RETURN
8686 FOR R = 1 TO 20: REM -- LOOP TO FIX R
8688    S$ = MID$ (PU$,I + L + R,1)
8690    IF S$ < > "#" THEN RETURN
8692 NEXT R
8694 RETURN
9999 END
```

MAIN PROGRAM LISTING

```
100 REM -- MAIN PROGRAM (PRINT USING)
110 REM -- INITIALIZE
120 HOME
130 B$ = "            "
140 READ PU$
150 REM -- PRINT HEADING
160 PRINT "HERE IS THE INPUT STRING:"
170 PRINT : PRINT PU$
180 PRINT : PRINT "AND THE OUTPUT:"
190 PRINT
200 PRINT " NO.   BALANCE   PAYMENT    INT   BALANCE"
210 PRINT
220 READ N,NP(1),NP(2),NP(3)
230 FOR M = 1 TO 20
240    NP(4) = INT (NP(2) * .08 / 12 * 100 + .5) / 100
250    IF NP(2) + NP(4) > = NP(3) THEN 290
260    NP(3) = NP(2) + NP(4)
270    NP(5) = 0
280    GOTO 300
290    NP(5) = NP(2) + NP(4) - NP(3)
300    REM -- CALL SUBROUTINE
310    GOSUB 8600
320    IF NP(5) = 0 THEN 390
330    NP(1) = NP(1) + 1
340    NP(2) = NP(5)
350 NEXT M
360 REM -- DATA
370 DATA " ##   $####.##   ###.##   ##.##   $####.##"
380 DATA 5,1,4600,480
390 GOTO 9999
```

TYPICAL OUTPUT

HERE IS THE INPUT STRING:

$####.##   ###.##   ##.## $####.##

AND THE OUTPUT:

NO.	BALANCE	PAYMENT	INT	BALANCE
1	$4600.00	480.00	30.67	$4150.67
2	$4150.67	480.00	27.67	$3698.34
3	$3698.34	480.00	24.66	$3243.00
4	$3243.00	480.00	21.62	$2784.62
5	$2784.62	480.00	18.56	$2323.18
6	$2323.18	480.00	15.49	$1858.67
7	$1858.67	480.00	12.39	$1391.06
8	$1391.06	480.00	9.27	$ 920.33
9	$ 920.33	480.00	6.14	$ 446.47
10	$ 446.47	449.45	2.98	$ 0.00

CHARGEN

PURPOSE: The subroutine **CHARGEN** permits the addition of text to graphic images using a trial and error method of formatting.

USAGE: Before the subroutine is called the graphics to be annotated should be prepared in a subroutine beginning at line 7000.

SUBROUTINE LISTING

```
6000 REM -- CHARGEN 2-25-81
6010 REM -- INPUT VARIABLES, C$, M, S
6020 REM -- LOCAL VARIABLES, C(40), D$, M1(40,4), S$(20)
6025 REM                    R$, A$, I, J, K, Q, X1, Y1, X2
6030 REM -- OUTPUT VARIABLES, GRAPHICS ONLY
6040 REM -- INITIALIZE
6050 DIM C(40), M1(20,4), S$(20)
6060 D$ = CHR$(4)
6070 PRINT "DO YOU NEED DIRECTIONS (Y/N) ";
6080 INPUT R$
6090 IF R$ = "Y" THEN GOSUB 6500
6100 REM -- DRAW GRAPHICS TO BE ANNOTATED
6110 GOSUB 7000
```

```
6120 REM -- SELECT LOCATION FOR CHARACTER DATA
6130 GOSUB 6600
6140 REM -- ENTER CHARACTER DATA AND DRAW
6150 GOSUB 6700
6160 REM -- GIVE OPTION TO ERASE
6170 PRINT "DO YOU WANT TO CHANGE THIS (Y/N) ";
6180 INPUT R$
6190 IF R$ = "N" THEN 6240
6200 PRINT "WE ERASE AND START OVER"
6210 HCOLOR = 0:X0 = M1(Q,1):Y0=M1(Q,2): Q = Q - 1
6220 GOSUB 6720
6230 X0 = 0: Y0 = 0: HCOLOR = 3:GOTO 6120
6240 PRINT "WILL YOU ENTER ADDITIONAL TEXT (Y/N) ";
6250 INPUT R$
6260 IF R$ = "Y" THEN X0 = 0:Y0 = 0:GOTO 6120
6270 REM -- REDRAW GRAPHICS
6280 TEXT : HOME
6290 PRINT "NOW WE REDRAW THE FIGURE -"
6300 FOR J = 1 TO 1000: NEXT J
6310 HGR: HCOLOR = 3
6320 GOSUB 7000
6330 REM -- REDRAW TEXT
6340 FOR N = 1 TO Q
6350    C$ = S$(N):X0 = M1(N,1):Y0 = M1(N,2)
6360    M = M1(N,3):S = M1(N,4)
6370    GOSUB 6720
6380 NEXT N
6390 VTAB 22: PRINT "TO SAVE THIS ENTER --"
6400 PRINT "BSAVE NAME,A$2000,L$2000"
6410 RETURN
6500 REM -- PROGRAM INSTRUCTIONS
6502 HOME
6504 PRINT "FEATURES OF THIS PROGRAM ARE:"
6506 PRINT : PRINT "      1. ALL CHARACTERS ON THE APPLE"
6508 PRINT "         KEYBOARD ARE AVAILABLE (EXCEPT"
6510 PRINT "         THE COMMA).": PRINT
6512 PRINT "      2. THREE MODES OF PRINTING ARE"
6514 PRINT "         AVAILABLE WITH SINGLE OR"
6516 PRINT "         MULTIPLE CHARACTERS."
6518 PRINT : PRINT "      3. SIZE OF FIGURES CAN BE SCALED."
6520 PRINT : PRINT "PRESS ANY KEY TO CONTINUE"
6522 GET A$: IF A$ = " " THEN 6530
```

```
6524 HOME
6526 PRINT "PRINTING MODES:": PRINT
6528 PRINT "MODE 1 - HORIZONTAL E.G '123'"
6530 PRINT : PRINT "VERTICAL DOWN E.G. 1"
6532 PRINT "                          2"
6534 PRINT "                          3"
6536 PRINT : PRINT "MODE 3 — READING UPWARD"
6538 PRINT
6540 PRINT "USE THE NORMAL CURSOR KEYS TO MOVE THE"
6542 PRINT "DOT WHICH APPEARS IN THE UPPER LEFT"
6544 PRINT "CORNER OF THE SCREEN. POSITION THE"
6546 PRINT "DOT WHERE THE FIRST CHARACTER IS TO BE"
6548 PRINT "PRINTED. THEN PRESS 'S' AND ENTER THE"
6550 PRINT "CHARACTER(S) TO BE PRINTED."
6552 PRINT : PRINT "WRITE SOME TEXT IN EACH MODE"
6554 PRINT "IN THE BOX WHICH IS DRAWN."
6556 PRINT "PRESS ANY KEY TO CONTINUE."
6558 GET A$: IF A$ = " " THEN 6558
6560 HOME : RETURN
6600 REM -- MOVE TO PRINT POSITION
6602 HPLOT 0,0
6604 VTAB 22
6606 PRINT "NOTE THE DOT IN THE UPPER LEFT CORNER."
6608 PRINT "MOVE TO THE PRINT POSITION NOW."
6610 PRINT "PRESS 'S' TO STOP."
6612 FOR I = 1 TO 1000
6614    GET A$: IF A$ = " "THEN 6614
6616    HCOLOR = 0: HPLOT X0,Y0
6618    IF A$ = "S" THEN HPLOT X0,Y0: HCOLOR = 3: GOTO 6632
6620    IF A$ = "M" THEN Y0 = Y0 + 1
6622    IF A$ = "I" THEN Y0 = Y0 - 1
6624    IF A$ = "K" THEN X0 = X0 + 1
6626    IF A$ = "J" THEN X0 = X0 - 1
6628    HCOLOR = 3: HPLOT X0,Y0
6630 NEXT I
6632 RETURN
6700 REM -- CHARACTER SELECTION AND DRAWING
6702 PRINT "ENTER THE CHARACTER(S) TO BE PRINTED"
6704 INPUT C$
6706 Q = Q + 1: S$(Q) = C$
6708 PRINT "IN WHAT MODE (1, 2, OR 3)";
6710 INPUT M
```

```
6712 PRINT "ENTER SCALE (1 = NORMAL, 2 = DOUBLE,"
6714 PRINT "AND SO ON.";
6716 INPUT S
6718 M1(Q,1) = X0:M1(Q,2) = Y0:M1(Q,3) = M: M1(Q,4) = S
6720 FOR K = 1 TO LEN (C$)
6722    PRINT D$;"OPEN HIRES,L36"
6724    C(K) = ASC ( MID$ (C$,K,1)) −31
6726    PRINT D$;"READ HIRES,R";C(K)
6728    INPUT N$
6730    GOSUB 6800
6732    IF M = 1 THEN X0 = X0 + 7 * S
6734    IF M = 2 THEN Y0 = Y0 + 8 * S
6736    IF M = 3 THEN Y0 = Y0 − 6 * S
6738    PRINT D$; "CLOSE HIRES"
6740 NEXT K
6742 RETURN
6800 REM -- DRAWING SUBROUTINE
6802 FOR I = 1 TO 7
6804    FOR J = 1 TO 5
6806       IF M < > 3 THEN 6822
6808       IF MID$ (N$,5 * (I−1) + J,1) = "0" THEN 6834
6810       FOR II = 1 TO S
6812          X1 = X0 + S * I:Y1 = Y0 − S * J − II + 1
6814          X2 = X0 + S * I + S − 1
6816          HPLOT X1,Y1 TO X2,Y1
6818       NEXT II
6820       GOTO 6834
6822       IF MID$ (N$,5 * (I−1) + J,1) = "0" THEN 6834
6824       FOR II = 1 TO S
6826          X1 = X0 + J * S:Y1 = Y0 + I * S + II − 1
6828          X2 = X0 + J * S + S − 1
6830          HPLOT X1,Y1 TO X2,Y1
6832       NEXT II
6834    NEXT J
6836 NEXT I
6838 RETURN
7000 REM -- GRAPHICS SAMPLE
7005 HGR: HCOLOR = 3
7010 HPLOT 50,20 TO 150,20 TO 150,140
7020 HPLOT 50,20 TO 50,140 TO 150,140
7030 RETURN
9999 END
```

MAIN PROGRAM LISTING

```
100 REM -- MAIN PROGRAM (CHARGEN)
110 REM -- CALL SUBROUTINE
120 GOSUB 6000
130 GOTO 9999
```

TYPICAL OUTPUT

(NONE SHOWN)

C ASCII CODES

Below we present ASCII codes for the characters and functions most likely to be useful.

ASCII CODE	Apple	PET	TRS-80
00			
01			
02			
03			
04			
05			
06			
07	Bell		
08	Backspace		Backspace
09			
10	Line feed		Line feed
11			
12	Form feed		Form feed
13	Return	Return	Return
14			Turn on cursor
15			Turn off cursor
16			
17		Cursor down	
18		Reverse screen	
19		Cursor home	
20		Delete	
21			
22			
23			
24			Cursor left
25			Cursor right
26			Cursor down
27	Escape		Cursor up
28			Cursor home
29		Cursor right	Cursor to left end of line

ASCII Code	Apple	PET	TRS-80
30			Erase to end of line
31			Clear to end of frame
32	Space	Space	Space
33	!	!	!
34	"	"	"
35	#	#	#
36	$	$	$
37	%	%	%
38	&	&	&
39	'	'	'
40	(	(	(
41	)	)	)
42	*	*	*
43	+	+	+
44	,	,	,
45	-	-	-
46	.	.	.
47	/	/	/
48	0	0	0
49	1	1	1
50	2	2	2
51	3	3	3
52	4	4	4
53	5	5	5
54	6	6	6
55	7	7	7
56	8	8	8
57	9	9	9
58	:	:	:
59	;	;	;
60	<	<	<
61	=	=	=
62	>	>	>
63	?	?	?
64	@	@	@
65	A	A	A
66	B	B	B
67	C	C	C
68	D	D	D

ASCII Code	Apple	PET	TRS-80
69	E	E	E
70	F	F	F
71	G	G	G
72	H	H	H
73	I	I	I
74	J	J	J
75	K	K	K
76	L	L	L
77	M	M	M
78	N	N	N
79	O	O	O
80	P	P	P
81	Q	Q	Q
82	R	R	R
83	S	S	S
84	T	T	T
85	U	U	U
86	V	V	V
87	W	W	W
88	X	X	X
89	Y	Y	Y
90	Z	Z	Z
91	[	[	Cursor up
92	Back slash		Cursor down
93	]	]	Cursor left
94	^		Cursor right
95	Underscore	Left arrow	Underscore
145		Cursor up	
146		Reverse off	
147		Clear screen	
157		Cursor left	

D THE EDITOR AND CROSS-REFERENCE TABLE GENERATOR

In this appendix we describe two programs, mentioned several times in text, that we recommend for use in documenting your programs. They are available on diskette from the authors. One produces a formatted listing of a program and the other creates a cross-reference table of the variables used in a program.

EDITOR

The **EDITOR** makes a formatted list of your program. It indents the contents of **FOR-NEXT** loops and does a page turn after every sixty lines. To run the **EDITOR** do the following:

1   Load your program.

2   Save your program under the name **XSOURCE** on a disk which also contains the **EDITOR** software.

3   Enter **EXEC EDITOR**.

Note that you do not use the **RUN** command but rather the **EXEC** command. While the **EDITOR** is running, a number of Applesoft prompts will appear on the screen and the disk drive will be intermittently active. Be sure that a printer controller board is installed in slot number one and that the printer is turned on and ready to go before entering **EXEC EDITOR**.

CROSS-REFERENCE TABLE GENERATOR

The cross-reference table generator works like the editor. Follow these three steps:

1   Load your program.

2   Save your program under the name **XSOURCE** on a disk which also contains the cross reference generator software.

3   Enter **EXEC CROSSREF**.

This program will take several minutes to run. While it is running Applesoft prompts will appear on the screen and the disk drive will be intermittently active. The program will prompt for a choice of hardcopy or not. If you select the hardcopy option, be sure the printer is ready to run. When you choose hardcopy the output will be about eighty columns wide. When you do not select hardcopy, the output will fit on the forty column screen. You may have to use **CTRL/S** to slow down screen output.

Both the editor and the cross-reference table generator work on the same principle. They first capture your program as a text file and then process it. Thus, you can produce a second edited listing by merely entering: **RUN EDIT**. This is adequate because the text file has already been created. So too, if you want a cross-reference table for a file just processed by the editor, merely enter: **RUN XREF**. Both programs assume that the printer controller board is in slot one. If it is not, change the program.

INDEX

ABS, 92
Accumulator, 60-62
Algorithm, 39
Algorithmic language, 40
Algorithmic language summary, A1
ALU, 6
APPEND, 232
Append files, 232
Apple error codes, 231
Arithmetic assignment statement, 21
Arithmetic logic unit, 6
Arithmetic operations, 24
array
   as an accumulator, 117-118
   declaration, 114
   defined, 109
   one-dimensional, 115
   sorting, 118-121
   two-dimensional, 124-26
ASC, 138
ASCII codes, C1
   coding system, 135

Bad data checking, 156
Bar graphs, 198-200, 202-204
BASIC, 1, 6, 19
BLOAD, 285

Break, 56
BSAVE, 284
Bubble sort, 154
Bug, 161
Byte, 3

Case structure, 174-179
Central processing unit, 3
Character data, 135
CHR$, 137. *See also* Function
CHR$ (147), 15, 139
CHR$(4), 228
CLEAR, 142
CLOSE, 228-229
Closing files, 228-229
CLS, 15, 139
Coding
   definition, 39, 45
   mathematical functions, 101-102
   rules, 103
COLOR, 205-206
Comma, 28
Complements to relational operators, 58
Computer, 19
Concatenation of string, 141
Conditional transfer, 81
Control structure, 66

Control unit, 3
Counter, 59-60
CPU, 3
Crash, 244-248
Cross-reference table, 49
Cross-reference table generator, D1
Cursor, control, 9-10, 10-11

DATA, 23
Debugging, 161
   techniques, 179-185
Decimal point alignment, 149-150
Decision structure
   definition, 66
   double alternative, 69
   multiple alternative, 174
   single alternative, 66
Default value, 87
   for step size, 75
DEL, 31
DELETE, 32
Dependent statement, 57
DIM, 114
Divisibility test, 92
Documentation
   definition, 48
   external, 48
   internal, 48
DOS, 228
Dummy variable, 98

EBCDIC, 135
Editing, 31-34
Error codes (Apple), 231
Errors typology, 161

Field, 27-28
Files, 228
   definition, 225-226
   direct access, 234-239
   PET, 240-244, 248-249
   sequential access, 227-234
   TRS-80, 249-250
FIX, 91
FOR-NEXT loop
   definition, 75
   for summation, 78
   to calculate area, 82
   transfer from, 81
FRE (0), 11
Function
   ABS, 92
   argument of, 89
   as a processor, 89
   ASC, 138
   built-in, 89
   CHR$, 137
   definition, 89
   FIX, 91
   INT, 90
   LEFT$, 143-145
   LEN, 142
   MID$, 143-145
   modifying output, 90
   returned value, 89
   RIGHT$, 143-145
   RND, 93-97
   SEG$, 144
   SQR, 89
   STR$, 150
   user-defined, 97-100
   VAL, 151

GOSUB, 172
GOTO, 54
GR, 205-206
graphic image
   adding text, 289-292
   loading, 285
   printing, 286-288
   saving, 284

Hardware, 8
HCOLOR, 211-212
HGR, 211-212
HGR2, 215
Hierarchy of operations, 25
High resolution graphics, 211-215
Higher level language, 6, 19
HLIN, 207
HOME, 15, 139
HPLOT, 211-212
HTAB, 207
Human-computer interface, 5

IF-THEN, 55
Immediate mode, 8
Implied operations, 101
Indexed loop, 73-87
INPUT, 22, 230, 243,
   files, 230, 243
   validation, 155-156
Input-output, 3
INT, 90

Keyword, 20
Kilobyte, 3-4

LEFT$, 143-145
LEN, 142
LET, 22
Line feed, 28
Logical expression, 57
Loop index, 73
Loop
   definition, 53
   exit, 56
   nested, 120
   simple, 53, 56
Low resolution graphics, 204-210
Lower case, 157-159

Machine language, 7
Mapping
   computer, 273-276
   coordinate file, 276-278
   program, 279-284
Matrix
   addition, 127
   definition, 115
   identity, 129
   inversion, 129
   multiplication, 127-129
Median, 121-123
MEM, 11
Memory, 3
Microprocessor, 2
MID$, 143-145
Midrange, coordinates, 278-279
Model
   definition, 253
   Leontief, 254-257
   pasture ecosystem, 257-260
Monte Carlo method, 96-97, 108
Monte Carlo simulation, 268-271
MUBASIC, 138, 144

Nested loop, 120
NEW, 20
NOTRACE, 184
Null string, 141-142
Numeric input and output, 104-105

ON GOSUB, 175
ON GOTO, 175
ONERR GOTO, 230
OPEN (files), 228, 235, 240-241
Operators, arithmetic, 24
   relational, 57
Order exploding, 130-132

Parameter variable, 98
PEEK, 231
PLOT, 205
POKE, 158-159
Primitive operation, 40
PRINT, 26
PRINT @, 210, 223
Print image, 195-196
PRINT TAB, 192-195
Program, 5
   blocks, 167-170
   mode, 7
   structure, 162-166
Programming, 37
Prompt, 9-10
Pseudocode, 40
Punctuation, 27

RAM, 3
Random access memory, 3
Random integers, 95
Random words, 151-154
READ, 23
READ (files), 230
Read-only memory, 8
Real time displays, 220-221
Record
   logical, 225
   physical, 226
Relational operators, 57
REM, 34
Remark, 34
Reserved word, 21
RESET, 134, 210
RESTORE, 123-124
RETURN, 172
RIGHT$, 143-145
RND, 93-97
ROM, 8
Rounding, rules for, 91

Scientific notation, 104, 217-219
Screen
   characteristics, 13-15
   editing, 31-34
   grid, 8
Scrolling, 10
SEG$, 144
Semicolon, 28
SET, 209-210
Significant digits, 216, 219-220
Simulation
   definition, 253
   genetics, 266-268
   inventory, 268-271
   Okun's Law, 261-265
Soft switches, 286
Software, 8
Sorting
   numbers, 118-121
   strings, 154-155
SQR, 89
ST, 244
Statement, 20
Statement number, 20
STR$, 150
String
   assignment, 139
   comparison, 140-141
   concatenation, 141
   constant, 136
   functions, 137
   length determination, 141-142
   variable, 136
Structured programming, 166-167
Subroutine, 170-173
   library of, B1
Subscripts, 110
Substring, 143
   indexing, 145-147
   selection, 143-145
Summation notation, 78
Syntax, 7

TAB, 192-195
Teletype graphics, 197-204
Text, 206
TI, 220
TI$, 220
TRACE, 184
Trailer value, 56

User-defined functions, 97-100

VAL, 151
variable
  definition, 20-21
  dummy, 98
  list, 49
  parameter, 98
  string, 136
VLIN, 207
VTAB, 207

WRITE (files), 228

X-Y plots, 200-201

DATE DUE